Explorative Mediation at Work

Roger Seaman

Explorative Mediation at Work

The Importance of Dialogue for Mediation Practice

Roger Seaman
Swanage, Dorset, United Kingdom

ISBN 978-1-137-51672-5   ISBN 978-1-137-51674-9 (eBook)
DOI 10.1057/978-1-137-51674-9

Library of Congress Control Number: 2016938644

© The Editor(s) (if applicable) and The Author(s) 2016
The author(s) has/have asserted their right(s) to be identified as the author(s) of this work in accordance with the Copyright, Designs and Patents Act 1988.
This work is subject to copyright. All rights are solely and exclusively licensed by the Publisher, whether the whole or part of the material is concerned, specifically the rights of translation, reprinting, reuse of illustrations, recitation, broadcasting, reproduction on microfilms or in any other physical way, and transmission or information storage and retrieval, electronic adaptation, computer software, or by similar or dissimilar methodology now known or hereafter developed.
The use of general descriptive names, registered names, trademarks, service marks, etc. in this publication does not imply, even in the absence of a specific statement, that such names are exempt from the relevant protective laws and regulations and therefore free for general use.
The publisher, the authors and the editors are safe to assume that the advice and information in this book are believed to be true and accurate at the date of publication. Neither the publisher nor the authors or the editors give a warranty, express or implied, with respect to the material contained herein or for any errors or omissions that may have been made.

Printed on acid-free paper

This Palgrave Macmillan imprint is published by Springer Nature
The registered company is Macmillan Publishers Ltd. London

Acknowledgements

I would like to especially thank Prof. Hugh Willmott of Cardiff Business School, who has most generously and kindly given me support at various turns on my way to completing this book. I was also inspired by discourse theory seminars at Essex University and the related literature. My friend Ian Coates was punctilious in helping me with punctuation and other textual corrections. I am also grateful to Maddie Holder at Palgrave for her friendly support. My greatest debt is to my family and so this book is dedicated to Yasmin and Amelia.

Contents

1	**Introduction**	1
	Mediation: An Age-old Practice	1
	Definitions of Mediation	2
	The Myth of Mediator Neutrality	3
	The Parties Seek 'Settlement' Whilst the Mediator Imagines Dialogue	7
	Three Layers of Mediation Objective	9
	Book Structure	11
	References	13
2	**A Spectrum of Mediator Influence**	15
	Simplified, Generic Mediation Processes	16
	Theories and Models Encapsulating Mediation Behaviours and Practices	20
	An Overview of Styles and Varieties of Influence	28
	Evidence of Mediator Influence	30
	References	35
3	**Mediation in the Workplace**	37
	The Adoption of Mediation in the Workplace	37
	Government Policies	39

The Individualisation of the Employee	44
Human Resource Management Policies	46
How Mediation Practice Aligns with Organisational Needs	49
Contradictory Currents of Mediation Power	53
References	55

4 Political Awareness and Dialogue — 59
The Potential of Mediation	59
Broadening Responsibility for Conflict	61
Organisational Justice and Democracy	67
Emancipation in Workplace Mediation?	72
On Dialogue	74
References	85

5 Instrumental Mediation — 89
Levels of Awareness of Mediator Power	89
Investigating Facilitative, Problem-Solving Mediation Practice	93
Approach to Interpretation of the Role-Play Material	95
First Case Study: Commentary, Analysis and Interpretation of Facilitative Role-Play	99
Summary Interpretation of the Facilitative Mediation Role-Play	149
References	154

6 Relational Mediation — 157
Narrative Mediation	158
Transformative Mediation	165
Second Case Study: Commentary, Analysis and Interpretation of a Quasi-Transformative Role-Play	175
Summary Interpretation of the 'Transformative' Mediation Role-Play and Comparison with the Facilitative Mediation Role-Play	213
Closing Remarks	216
References	218

7	**Explorative Mediation: An Instrumental, Ethical and Political Approach**	223
	A Description of Explorative Mediation	224
	Constraints and Challenges for Explorative Mediation	229
	Barriers to Dialogue	237
	References	241
8	**Conclusion**	243
	A Final Characterisation to Contrast Mediation Styles	243
	The Myth of Neutrality	244
	A Democratic and Dialogic Intervention in the Workplace	245
	The Paradox of Selfless Engagement	246
	An Evolving Practice	247
	References	249
Index		251

1

Introduction

Mediation: An Age-old Practice

Cycles of conflict and reconciliation, as all recognise, have long been part of the fabric of life. Jared Diamond (2013) explains how small-scale traditional societies viewed other peoples (clans and tribes) in a threefold manner. These other groups were known as friends, as enemies or as strangers, and strangers were initially perceived as being potential enemies. When conflict arose between individuals from neighbouring friendly clans, reconciliation was highly valued, since relationships with neighbours were long-term; these individuals lived their lives mostly within the same small geographic area. Furthermore, if feelings of hurt could not be ameliorated and mutually resolved, disputes would likely persist and fester. Given the closely knitted relationships inside each clan, feelings of hurt would have been likely to spread within the clan. Hence, a serious argument between two individuals from neighbouring clans could easily escalate into a dangerous destabilisation of relationships between whole clans. Thus, the mediated resolution of conflict was important in traditional societies for these two reasons, because inter-clan relationships were often life-long and individuals within any clan were

© The Editor(s) (if applicable) and The Author(s) 2016
R. Seaman, *Explorative Mediation at Work*,
DOI 10.1057/978-1-137-51674-9_1

embedded in strong networks of intra-group relationships. In the modern workplace, people are also bound into extended-term relationships, both intra-group and inter-group, and so the resolution of conflict, in which good relationships are recovered, may be expected to be as valuable today as it ever was amongst traditional societies. In the past three decades there has been a spread of formal mediation practice from the community and court sectors to many other fields (Beer and Stief 1997, p. 3; Kressel 2006, p. 726), including the workplace. In the UK, contemporary workplace mediation practice seems to have transferred from community and family sectors.[1] Workplace mediation also seems to have roots in related forms of conciliation that arose, in the UK and the USA in the early to mid-twentieth century, out of governmental industrial relations policies.[2]

Definitions of Mediation

To give a sense of how present day workplace mediation (and much mediation more generally) is defined and to highlight significant words and themes that characterise these definitions, it will be helpful to lay out three typical definitions. The UK government's Advisory, Conciliation and Arbitration Service (Acas) and the Chartered Institute of Personnel and Development (CIPD) jointly published a report entitled, 'Mediation: An approach to resolving workplace issues'. It states that mediation 'involves a *neutral* third party bringing two sides together with the aim of reaching a mutual agreement' (Acas and CIPD 2013, p. 3, italics added). The UK Centre for Effective Dispute Resolution (CEDR), an organisation that has trained thousands of commercial and workplace mediators around the world, describes mediation as

> a flexible process conducted **confidentially** in which a **neutral person actively assists** parties in working towards a **negotiated agreement** of a

---

[1] See article by Katherine Graham http://www.mediate.com/articles/GrahamKbl20150321.cfm posted 21 march 2015.
[2] http://www.mediationmatterssd.com/mediationmatters/history.html

dispute or difference, with **the parties in ultimate control of the decision to settle** and the terms of resolution. (CEDR 2014, emboldening as on the CEDR website)

Lastly, the American mediator and author Christopher Moore describes mediation as an

> intervention in a negotiation or conflict of an acceptable third party who has limited or no authoritative decision-making power, who assists the involved parties to voluntarily reach a mutually acceptable settlement of the issues in dispute. (2003, p. 15)

Most significantly, in two of the above definitions, the mediator is said to be 'neutral'. As per these definitions, this *neutral* person actively assists, intervenes and conducts a *process* to help those in conflict *negotiate* to find their own form of *settlement* to their dispute. Diamond (2013) also describes how, in traditional societies, if one person was wronged by another, a go-between would arrange compensation negotiations between their respective family or clan groups to settle the conflict. In this 'traditional' context a settlement was necessary to avoid an eruption of physical, often life-threatening violence involving clan members. Although in the UK and the USA, present-day neighbour or workplace conflict that is not resolved rarely results in physical violence, we can see that this idea of mediation found in traditional societies, as a *neutrally facilitated, negotiation process* aimed at *settlement*, still persists in the field of contemporary mediation and in workplace mediation in particular.

The Myth of Mediator Neutrality

However, on an intuitive level it is quite hard to imagine how *neutrality* can be maintained when one *actively assists* in a *negotiation* that has a goal of *settlement*. Cloke comments that '[w]hen mediators "merely" listen, they may still have a profound, even *directive* impact upon the parties' (2001, p. 13). The idea of a neutral facilitator would appear to be an oxymoron. Riskin acknowledges that

[t]he idea that the mediator should be neutral or impartial—both in fact and in appearance—is deeply embedded in the ethos of mediation, even though observers disagree about the meaning and achievability of the notion. (1996, p. 47)

With a slight refinement to Moore's view (2003, p. 53) but in accord with Kressel (2006, p. 743), it is suggested that the concept of neutrality in mediation embraces two facets of the interaction between the mediator and the people seeking to resolve their conflict. Firstly, mediators endeavour not to favour the position of one party over the other. Thus, they remain impartial with respect to each party. Secondly, they try not to influence the outcome of the mediation meeting and avoid the potential trap of prompting or leading a resolution of their own devising (which may or may not favour one of the parties). Any complete or partial solutions to the dispute that are created are said to be the sole preserve of the parties. In summary, the mediators neither judge the parties nor influence the outcome of their discussion. Mediation can thus be differentiated from adjudication or arbitration.

In local UK community mediation organisations, mediators work in pairs and this enables new mediators to train as apprentices working in support of a more experienced mediator. The mainstream style of mediation, taught and practiced in such community organisations, is referred to as facilitative, problem-solving mediation.[3] Being mainstream, it is this broad style that has been imported into workplace practice, except in this case mediators operate as singletons. In the UK, Acas, as cited above, proffers a facilitative mediation style (and an optional, more directive and deliberately less than neutral style) (Acas 2005, p. 7). Under the facilitative style and more directive styles, the mediator manages a structured meeting process. Given this management of the process, it is improbable that mediators can lead an interaction with the people in dispute at the same time as maintaining a neutral disposition towards them. Concerning the first facet of neutrality, it would seem possible to recognise one's own prejudicial thoughts and feelings, which may lead

---

[3] Camden Mediation in London practices transformative mediation. There may be others that diverge from the facilitative model.

one to be less than impartial between two parties. Thus, on most occasions we may assume mediators are able to suspend otherwise innate and learned evaluative or judging tendencies and not intervene in an overtly biased manner.[4] Practitioners such as Cloke (2001, p. 13), who reject simple notions of neutrality and mediator objectivity, suggest the mediator should seek fairness through an omnipartiality, not siding with one party but supporting both simultaneously. However, concerning the second facet of neutrality, we may imagine that it is probable that mediators may succumb to a desire to ask subtly leading questions that contain an evaluation of the conflict and give a veiled pointer towards forms of solution. This desire to 'lead' parties towards solutions obviously runs counter to mediation training, which emphasises a neutral disposition. Those in conflict who come to mediation would possibly not do so if they thought the mediator was other than neutral. To offer to act other than neutrally would, at first glance, seem to compromise the very concept of facilitative mediation. Hence, the notion of mediator neutrality is understandable.

Nevertheless, the simple activity of posing questions to the parties or reflecting back statements made by them in the execution of the mediator role reveals the inherent power and agency of this role. That is, the mediator acts with intent, whether conscious or unconscious, and has influence, however minimal, due to both physical presence and any utterances made. Mediator neutrality must therefore be mythical. Kressel says of the facilitative style and its claim to neutrality that

> [i]t is ... the most popular philosophy of the mediator's role, albeit one that is frequently contradicted by empirical studies of mediator behaviour. (2006, p. 743)

---

[4] Touval (1975) describes how mediators known by the parties to be partial may be accepted in international/warfare disputes because of the hope that the mediator may have leverage to persuade parties to deliver on promised agreements. It is usual in commercial mediation for mediators to work with parties separately to bring their legal and contract knowledge to bear, assessing parties' positions, giving advice and engineering a mutual face-saving compromise (far less costly than going to court). Carnevale, referenced in Chap. 2 below, also examines mediators' motivations that may undermine impartiality. Of course mediators, like anyone else, are fallible, as explored in Chap. 7.

There are certainly subtle hints that this may be the case if we read between the lines in the above cited definitions referring to assistance in finding a mutually acceptable settlement under parties' ultimate control. Nevertheless, it would seem that both mediators and parties to mediation often do not overtly recognise the operation of mediator influence. This may be called the problem of mediator neutrality.

Acknowledging this problem raises the question of what the effects of mediator influence might be. Furthermore, any influence vested in the mediator's interventions will be conditioned by the property of language to carry the hidden, hegemonic power of the dominant cultural norms of organisational life. As noted by Fairclough,

> the exercise of power, in modern society, is increasingly achieved through ideology and more particularly through the ideological workings of language. (2001, p. 2)

Torfing further asserts that

> our cognitions and speech acts only become meaningful within certain pre-established discourses which have different structurations that change over time. (1999, p. 84)

That is, speech acts (our commonplace utterances) are historically situated and subject to variation over time due to political and social events. These understandings of the power of language and the constraints placed upon meaning—that is, what we 'mean' or are trying to 'say'—by the operation of language suggest a particular need for sensitivity by mediators to their own potential to influence mediation outcomes.

This book will argue that mediators should openly recognise the myth of neutrality and become sensitive to their position of effective authority vested in their quasi-professional status. By dispensing with the myth of neutrality, mediators may purposefully work to become self-aware of their inevitable influence upon outcomes in order to try to render their influence more transparent to the parties and also to contain and minimise it as appropriate. In summary, an *aspiration* of minimal mediator influence would seem sensible but its absolute achievement should be recognised as impossible. The major styles of mediation practice will be reviewed in order to construct an outline of a new explorative practice that attempts to make practical sense of this aspiration.

The ensuing critique of mediation practice is based upon an assumption that the workplace mediator's principal concern is to serve the needs of the organisational employees who find themselves in conflict, although the benefits of a successful resolution of a conflict will inevitably also accrue to other colleagues and the organisation itself. In the workplace, where the mediator serves both parties and the organisation's commissioning manager, it becomes significant to understand the possible influential tendencies of a mediation intervention that is so often promoted as being neutral. The practice of mediation has unsurprisingly been adopted as an additional human resource department tool, in part for the instrumental reason of seeking a *negotiated* resolution of conflict that would reduce the associated costs (CIPD 2011; Gibbons 2007). The use of mediation services to avoid costs related to grievance and disciplinary procedures or claims to employment tribunals is a logical and reasonable business practice. But in doing so it is important to maintain the integrity of mediation practice, which itself holds a primary, compassionate concern for the people in conflict. Because the workplace mediator has a pecuniary interest in 'succeeding' in the achievement of settlement, a perceived pressure to settle may subvert the primacy of the parties' interest in finding their own solutions. Under a cloak of mythical neutrality, mediators may, knowingly or unwittingly, engineer a resolution to meet a perceived organisational requirement. Hence, consideration of mediation practice in the workplace affords a sharp focus upon the investigation of the general problem of mediator neutrality. From the mediator's perspective, an instrumental requirement for settlement must be viewed as a by-product (fortuitously inevitable) of their principal concern to serve the parties.

The Parties Seek 'Settlement' Whilst the Mediator Imagines Dialogue

We might ask why workplace mediation is not simply a process that operates to benefit both the parties and the organisation equally. This demands a closer scrutiny of the purpose of mediation. It would appear obvious that the purpose is for parties to resolve their conflict—to achieve a *settlement* to end their conflict—with the help of a meeting process operated by the mediator. However, this statement, with its focus upon a settlement process, can conflate the ambition of the parties with that of the mediator. It will be argued that the mediator does not, even should not, desire a settlement of the dispute. As counter-intuitive as this may sound, it will be further argued that to do so would lead mediators to intervene in ways that tend to compromise their ability to recognise, control and reduce their potential influence. As noted, in facilitative mediation the mediator manages the mediation process (described more fully in Chap. 2). This process management often entails the construction of the mediation meeting as a form of negotiation, defined as such above. Folger (2001) argues convincingly that, by mere control of the process, a mediator's power and influence are increased. Mediation understood as managed or 'facilitated negotiation' (Riskin 1996, p. 13) becomes tantamount to a practice that leads parties towards solutions envisioned by the mediator.

In contrast, by containing the mediator's influence, more scope may be created for the parties to better consider and more deeply understand their conflict on their own terms. This being so, any resolution found will more certainly have been mostly generated by the parties themselves and therefore be more robust and likely to endure, whereas a resolution or compromise that had been in large part created by the mediator would most likely be fragile and short-lived. For parties to find a stable form of resolution they obviously need to re-establish respectful communication, but more than this, it will be argued, they need to attempt to hold a dialogue. Renee Weber has defined dialogue as

> open-ended, flowing, and tentative. It explores rather than settles questions, and allows for—demands—a participatory mode. (1990, p. 17)

Hence, we might reframe the overall purpose of mediation from the mediator's perspective as follows. It is for the mediator to assist in bringing people into conversation whilst exercising minimal influence over them so that they can create their own form of reconciliation. The role of the mediator is therefore to promote conditions to facilitate dialogue, helping the parties, as unintrusively as possible, to explore their conflict.

Any mediator influence that does occur should ideally be apparent to the parties. The pursuit of an 'ideal' of dialogue does demand an engagement in which the mediator collaborates with the parties and so necessarily intrudes and yet somehow, simultaneously, tries not to intrude.

A Just Process

Lasting reconciliation is of real immediate benefit to the organisation and moreover, in small but important ways, can contribute to a broader sense of organisational justice. Drawing on Greenberg (1987), employees may be expected to consider if policies for the use of workplace mediation appear to be fair and impartial and whether mediation's processes and outcomes, when implemented, are also recognised as fair or unfair. Any inadvertently or deliberately manipulated settlement, which would in any case be liable to break down, would also tend to undermine a sense of organisational justice and generally give mediation processes a bad name in the workplace.

Hence, we may conclude that 'settlement' clearly becomes the most probable objective of the parties but not directly of the mediator. As noted above, if the mediator actively views settlement as a mark of success, interventions are likely to move away from an ideal of minimal intrusion or influence. The mediator would still of course work to support a search for understanding and possible reconciliation but would be wary of the aim of 'settlement'. This distinction between the mediator's and the parties' objectives may become clearer if we look more closely at the various levels of mediation objective inherent in the *means* (being the procedures and methods of mediation practice) that lead to the *ends* (being the resolution of a conflict or some form of reconciliation).

Three Layers of Mediation Objective

It is debatable whether mediators follow a given style of mediation due to pre-stated philosophical understandings of conflict causation, or whether they more intuitively adopt a style and then seek to justify it on the grounds of an ideological premise. Zizek notes that ideology 'is a fantasy-construction which serves as a support for our "reality" itself' (2008, p. 45). He further suggests that we do not adopt a belief just from custom or through intellectual assessment but because we are already predisposed to identify with a particular belief (pp. 39–40). This suggests mediators may have a temperamental proclivity to practice in one way or another and then justify this preferred method by reference to a social and political worldview by way of explanation afterwards. After the event we may say that practices of actors appear to be 'embedded within philosophical positions' (Wight 2009, p. 8), but linking mediation style to an underlying philosophy of practice would seem to constrain mediators and prevent them from reacting to different situations. Perhaps we may adduce multiple philosophies to given forms of practice. This book will propose a hybrid style of practice and link it with particular poststructural theories of discourse (to be elaborated in the chapters that follow).

However, the mediator explicitly or implicitly chooses a style or conversational method of mediation and this method may be correlated to the objective or intent the mediator holds. Facilitative mediation focuses on issues. Narrative mediation addresses the parties' 'conflict stories' and the transformative mediation approach deals solely with the parties' 'crisis of interaction'. Notwithstanding these discrete schools, the choice of style and therefore the effective mediation objective may often remain unspoken and possibly may not be reflected upon by the mediator. Given the variety of all conflicts and conflict resolution work that have come to be discussed under the umbrella term of mediation, it is also likely that intended styles do not always fully correspond to styles applied. Also, there is a uniqueness to every single mediation event and therefore a fluidity and potential flexibility in any mediation case. Pruitt advocates a 'contingent' approach 'involving diagnosis followed by a choice among treatments [different mediation methods]' (2006, p. 860), although certain claims of stylistic eclecticism were not verified under observation (Kressel et al. 2012). Whilst there are many shades of mediation practice, this book will trace three categories of practice defined by a varying blend of overarching objectives. These differentiated layers of 'objectives' enable theorising that can be used to inform the reflective development of practice.

From the parties' perspectives, all types of mediation have an instrumental and practical imperative to find a workable solution, even if this amounts to an agreement to disagree. Parties also want to feel that any resolution is achieved independently of an external authority, in a fair manner on a relatively equitable basis. Thus, we can discern dimensions of the instrumental, the pragmatic, the moral, the democratic, the just and consequently the political, in very general terms, in all kinds of mediation. These dimensions may be summarised under the three broad categories: the instrumental, the moral and the political. Pruitt (2006, p. 861) interestingly refers to Dugan's analysis of conflict causation as lying in a hierarchy of three distinct levels, which accord very closely with the above three categories. These are the substantive issues of a dispute, matters of the parties' relationship beneath the 'issues', and, at the deepest level, the wider social system. Mainstream, facilitative problem-solving mediation practice, as the name suggests, addresses 'issues' and may be regarded as having a settlement-driven and mostly instrumental objective. Narrative and transformative approaches to mediation have been termed 'relational styles' (Kressel 2006, p. 744) and may be said to have an instrumental but also a more marked moral objective. This is especially so in the case of transformative practice, whose advocates regard conflict as an opportunity for a 'moral conversation' (Bush and Folger 2005, p. 255). Lastly, mediation practice that recognises underlying systemic causes of conflict may be said to bring a political objective that enfolds ethical and instrumental objectives. Such a practice, which will be called 'explorative', seeks to enable opportunities for a dialogic exchange in which the political and ideological context of conflict may be recognised.

Book Structure

To establish a context for a deeper consideration of facilitative, narrative, transformative and explorative mediation, Chap. 2 reviews many facets of various styles of mediation practice to delineate a spectrum of mediator influence, from the minimally intrusive to the very directive, and thus debunks the myth of mediator neutrality. As mediation is found to be a far less than neutral intervention, the possibility is raised that workplace mediation may be subject to an organisational colonisation that is used as a means of conflict containment or suppression. To further evaluate this possibility, Chap. 3 documents the adoption of facilitative mediation practice within the workplace and underscores how assumptions of neutrality and the individualisation of the employee may indeed allow an organisational colonisation of mediation. It looks at contradictory currents of mediation power that may on the one hand be used for the efficient containment of conflict and on the other hand hold potential for micro-emancipation and democracy in an otherwise hierarchical environment. Against the practical context of mediation usage inside the workplace set out in Chaps. 2 and 3, Chap. 4 develops the pivotal argument of this book, that mediation should pursue an ideal of dialogue (albeit one that is impossible to fully realise). This qualified notion of dialogue has potential to support learning and self-learning within the political context of conflict causation. As such, mediation can be a micro-emancipatory, democratic and just intervention that is less about instrumental containment and more about opening up an ethical exploration of conflict. To commence putting some practical flesh on the bones of the theoretical arguments of Chap. 4, Chap. 5 examines, by means of a role-play case study, the operation of workplace facilitative mediation to analyse how mediators often position themselves in a place of authority. From such a position, it is argued, they seem to bring a mostly instrumental objective to the assessment of the issues brought to the mediation. Chapter 6 reviews both narrative and transformative mediation styles, contrasting them with the mainstream facilitative problem-solving model. It is argued that the narrative style requires the mediator to subtly channel parties towards forms of resolution. Transformative mediation very differently presents a minimally intrusive form of intervention that supports and follows the parties' conversation. Chapter 6 presents a second role-play case study of a quasi-transformative mediation style that demonstrates the merit of relinquishing mediator control of process to the parties.[5] Based upon the critiques of the facilitative, narrative and transformative schools offered in Chaps. 5 and 6, Chap. 7 describes an alternative explorative style of mediation. This style aims to support the

---

[5] Note that Bush and Folger reject the idea that transformative mediation may be mixed with other approaches and argue that it can only be 'coherently practiced' (Bush and Folger 2005, p. 45) in a pure fashion.

parties to pursue a dialogue (as defined in Chap. 4). Chapter 7 goes on to provided a deeper consideration of the challenges and difficulties posed by this practice, some of which also pertain to other mediation styles. Despite the critiques offered below, all styles of mediation have the great merit of aiming at the reduction of conflict and the dissemination of techniques for avoiding conflict, and able practitioners from all schools of mediation carry out necessary, highly valuable work. This book presents an explanation of an explorative approach to mediation that has been built upon elements of other methods and continues through theory, practice and discussion to evolve heuristically. It is offered in a spirit of engagement with other practitioners.

References

Acas (Advisory, Conciliation and Arbitration Service). (2005). *The Acas small firms' mediation pilot: Research to explore parties' experiences and views on the value of mediation*. Acas Research Paper Ref: 04/05. London: Acas. Retrieved from http://www.acas.org.uk/index.aspx?articleid=4701&q=small+firms+pilot

Acas & CIPD (Advisory, Conciliation and Arbitration Service & the Chartered Institute of Personnel and Development). (2013). Mediation: An approach to resolving workplace issues. London: Acas. Retrieved from http://www.acas.org.uk/media/pdf/2/q/Mediation-an-approach-to-resolving-workplace-issues.pdf

Beer, J. E., & Stief, E. (1997). *The mediator's handbook* (3rd ed.). Gabriola Island, British Columbia, Canada: New Society Publishers.

Bush, R. A. B., & Folger, J. P. (2005). *The promise of mediation: The transformative approach to conflict*. San Francisco: Jossey-Bass Inc.

CEDR. (2014). The Centre for Effective Dispute Resolution. Retrieved from http://www.cedr.com/solve/mediation/

CIPD (Chartered Institute of Personnel and Development). (2011). *Conflict management: Survey report, March*. Retrieved from http://www.cipd.co.uk/hr-resources/survey-reports/

Cloke, K. (2001). *Mediating dangerously: The frontiers of conflict resolution*. San Francisco: Jossey Bass Inc.

Diamond, J. (2013). *The world until yesterday*. London: Penguin Books.

Fairclough, N. (2001). *Language and power* (2nd ed.). Harlow, England: Longman.
Folger, J. P. (2001). Who owns what in mediation?: Seeing the link between process and content. In J. P. Folger & R. A. B. Bush (Eds.), *Designing mediation: Approaches to training and practice within a transformative framework* (pp. 55–60). New York: Institute For the Study of Conflict Transformation, Inc.
Gibbons, M. (2007). *Better dispute resolution: A review of employment dispute resolution in Great Britain*. An independent Report commissioned by DTI (Department of Trade and Industry), published on March 21. London: DTI.
Greenberg, J. (1987). A taxonomy of organizational justice theories. *Academy of Management Review, 12*(1), 9–22.
Kressel, K. (2006). Mediation revisited. In M. Deutsch, P. T. Coleman, & E. C. Marcus (Eds.), *The handbook of conflict resolution: Theory and practice* (pp. 726–756). San Francisco: Jossey-Bass Inc.
Kressel, K., Henderson, T., Reich, W., & Cohen, C. (2012). Multidimensional analysis of conflict mediator style. *Conflict Resolution Quarterly, 30*(2), 135–171.
Moore, C. W. (2003). *The mediation process: Practical strategies for resolving conflict* (3rd ed.). San Francisco: Jossey-Bass Inc.
Pruitt, D. G. (2006). Some research frontiers in the study of conflict resolution. In M. Deutsch, P. T. Coleman, & E. C. Marcus (Eds.), *The handbook of conflict resolution: Theory and practice* (pp. 849–867). San Francisco: Jossey-Bass Inc.
Riskin, L. L. (1996). Understanding mediators' orientations, strategies, and techniques: A grid for the perplexed. *Harvard Negotiation Law Review, 1*(7), 7–50.
Torfing, J. (1999). *New theories of discourse: Laclau, Mouffe and Zizek*. Oxford: Blackwell Publications Ltd.
Touval, S. (1975). Biased intermediaries: Theoretical and historical considerations. *The Jerusalem Journal of International Relations, 1*(1), 51–69.
Weber, R. (1990). *Dialogues with scientists and sages: The search for unity*. London: Penguin Arkana.
Wight, C. (2009). *Science, discourse and materiality: What's material about an economy with no money?* Paper given at Political Economy, Financialization and Discourse Theory Conference held at Cardiff University, May 28–29. Retrieved from http://www.cardiff.ac.uk/carbs/conferences/pefdt09/index.html
Zizek, S. (2008[1989]). *The sublime object of ideology*. London: Verso.

2

A Spectrum of Mediator Influence

To borrow a word from the title of Bush and Folger's famous work (1994, 2005), many mediators and mediation organisations 'promise' that they will be neutral and will not interfere in the shaping of a dispute's resolution. Mediator neutrality is meant to ensure that the concept of party self-determination is realised. As already noted, to do otherwise, to imply that mediators do in effect interfere, would perhaps not attract people to request the services of a mediator. Nevertheless, by considering a variety of theories and models of mediation practice, we can see that many shades of mediator influence become apparent. Examining these theories in some detail will help to understand how mediators become entwined in the exercise of influence and power, even though this influence is often obscured behind professions of (professional) neutrality. Recounting evidence of mediator influence will lay ground for developing a new way of enacting mediation that overtly recognises mediator power. This will allow a more nuanced and engaging description of what mediation entails to be proffered to parties. However, before reviewing this literature, it will serve to first briefly sketch a simple outline of a generic mediation process as a reference frame for the analysis that follows. Some short comments will then be made about how this very basic outline may alter when mediation is brought into the workplace. This sketch will help to indicate how some practitioners might persist in believing that they do remain neutral and that the parties are in 'ultimate control' (as cited in the CEDR definition above). An indication will also be given of how mediation is sometimes used in a highly directive manner.

Simplified, Generic Mediation Processes

Outline of a Typical Facilitative, Community Mediation Process in the UK

At the start of any mediation, telephone calls are made to each party to set 'first visit' dates. Sometimes this entails listening to preliminary descriptions of the disputants' problems. Mediators also explain 'first visit' routines and purposes. First visits are then made to each party separately, typically lasting around an hour. At these 'first visits', the pair of mediators listen to the parties' accounts of their conflict. Mediators explain the mediation process and the mediators' role and offer guidelines to encourage courtesy and respect in any joint meetings. They seek to build the trust of the parties in the process and in themselves as mediators. They ask if each party thinks mediation will be useful for them and invite voluntary participation in the next stage of a joint meeting. They also explain the confidentiality of the mediation process.

A joint meeting is then set up some days later at a 'neutral' location (not on anybody's home ground) and this may be a 'one off' or one of a series. These meetings in principle follow a plan thus:

- Each party has 'uninterrupted time' to speak. Often, the disputant's speech is initially directed towards the mediators.
- The mediators may then ask 'how do you both feel?' before giving a short summary.
- The mediators then orchestrate an exploration of the situation by both parties.
- An agenda is formed of issues, interests and needs.

- Common ground is sought and some forms of solution are mapped out.
- Scope for some agreement or consensus is developed.
- Some form of agreement is made and sometimes written down.
- The meeting is closed.

During the joint meeting, whilst mediators seek to listen, fully attentive to the words spoken and the whole emotional and bodily presence of each party, they will also direct interactions by asking questions of each disputant, prompting them to open up issues or to drill down into specific events. The mediators seek to diffuse anger and blaming. They may call for 'time outs' to speak with each party separately. A number of listening and interlocutory techniques are used, prominent among them being summarising, reflecting back/mirroring, affirming and understanding, reframing, and prompting disputants to problem-solve. Reframing is used to mitigate blaming and aggression, and to find the 'need' or 'interest' behind the 'position'. Thus, parties are encouraged to move in the direction of common ground and to turn negative emotion into a positive search for resolution. In doing this, the mediators do not seek to rewrite the individual's narrative or deny the history of the argument. Throughout, the mediators make use of words that have been used by the parties whenever possible.

A Typical Workplace Mediation Process: Variations on the Above Facilitative Mediation Outline

There are many similarities and some significant differences from the basic structure of the above model. A 'neutral' location conferring privacy may be sought away from the usual place of work. Often there is a single mediator, not a pair, for reasons of cost. The entire mediation will often take place over one day. Holding the 'first visits' and the joint meeting on the same day creates a focus and urgency in the search for a solution. The resolution of what may be a long-running and highly emotionally charged conflict is sought in just a few hours. The morning is spent seeing each party separately, sometimes twice (initially for one hour and then for 15 to 20 minutes). In these initial, separate meetings, as in the generic community model, the mediator will seek to diffuse blame by reframing the conflict descriptions in more neutral language. She or he will seek to uncover the parties' 'needs' beneath the mutual blaming and also seek to understand the parties and their 'interests' as distinct from their conflicting 'positions'. The role of the mediator and the process of the joint meeting are explained to the parties. The parties are directed to think about how they want to address the other party and what they want from the joint meeting, and they are invited reflect upon what sort of communications and relationship they would like to develop in the future. There is often an implication that they should become responsible for engendering some sort of positive resolution to the problem. In this way, the mediator primes the parties for the afternoon joint session.

The mediator opens the joint meeting with a carefully prepared script that covers inter alia their roles and a description of how the meeting will be structured. Crawley and Graham emphasise that, '[i]n mediation, structure is the parties' and the mediators' friend. It is their road map towards progress' (2002, p. 95). They argue that having a preset sequence helps to prevent the meeting from starting with a resurrection of 'the conflict's existing dynamic' (p. 95). In the joint meeting, following the opening comments from each of the parties in their 'uninterrupted time', the mediator will carefully sum up their stances. Then parties may be invited to speak to the mediator in the subsequent phase of exchanging their accounts of the conflict. At this stage the mediator will help parties explore histories, narratives and emotion by, for example, reducing blaming and highlighting common ground. In a difficult joint meeting, 'time outs' are likely to be used more than in the community model, in part to impress upon parties that a negative conclusion may be undesirable for them. Following the exchange of conflict accounts and a review of how the parties are feeling, the mediator is likely to lead the development of an agenda of issues and concerns to address. The agenda is then used to guide the development of agreements for resolving the conflict. It is likely that there will be an underlying impetus away from past hurtful events and towards the future and practical actions aimed at improving the parties' workplace relationship. During the joint meeting the mediator is again more likely than in a community setting to work actively to help prompt problem-solving thinking by the parties and to structure an action plan with contingencies based around the solutions that are generated. If a joint meeting is unsuccessful, the mediator will invite the parties to think about any necessary next steps and consider how they will work together in future.

As noted, these techniques tend to follow typical facilitative community mediation practice, although there may be more of a sense of the parties being coached to succeed in working through the joint meeting to secure a 'workable' resolution. They are at work and thus their position as contracted employees may also have a conditioning effect upon their overall disposition.

Directive Mediation

There is a style of mediation that exceeds the subtle directiveness found in facilitative styles of mediation that is tellingly referred to variously as 'bargaining' (Silbey and Merry 1986), 'evaluative' (Noll 2001) and 'settlement driven' (Boserup 2004). An example of this would be in a commercial setting, where quasi-legal officers manage a mediation session by mostly holding separate meetings with the parties with very limited joint sessions. They move 'to and fro' between parties with messages, and in the separate meetings they give advice and guidance, drawing upon their legal and contractual expertise. Parties are thus heavily directed toward agreeing to a form of solution that, whilst tying in to their interests, will have been crafted almost independently by the mediator. This style of mediation is most emphatically a 'managed negotiation' and, as noted, is commonly applied in commercial disputes. The mediator's skill involves prevention of loss of face by the parties so that a win/win settlement can be achieved thus pre-empting expensive win/lose legal proceedings.

These simplified mediation-process outlines form a reference structure for the following consideration of the ways in which mediator influence and power may be brought to bear upon the mediation encounter within many contemporary approaches to mediation practice. They also serve to introduce a pivotal difference between mediators' interventions that are termed 'facilitative' from those considered 'evaluative', the latter being more overtly judgemental. This distinction will be further delineated in the next section.

Theories and Models Encapsulating Mediation Behaviours and Practices

There are many theories of mediation practice, but the following selection gives a good overview. These theories provide insightful descriptions of the complexities of mediation practice, in which the scope for the mediator to exert influence may be discerned.

Kressel's Typology

Kressel, whilst explaining that mediation is a multifaceted and structured activity, presents a simplifying typology, dividing the behaviour of interventions into three mediator strategies: 'reflexive', 'contextual' and 'substantive' (2006, p. 738). By 'reflexive intervention' he means that mediators orient themselves to the dispute by 'establishing rapport and diagnosis' (p. 738). 'Contextual interventions' are about setting up a climate that is conducive for dialogue by, for example,

> establishing norms for respectful listening and language, managing anger constructively, maintaining the privacy of negotiations. (p. 740)

Finally Kressel asserts that

> [s]ubstantive interventions refer to tactics by which the mediator deals directly with the issues in dispute. (p. 741)

As explained above, at first sight mediation proffers an attractive 'promise' by the mediator not to take over the disputants' conflict or its solution, and thereby to remain 'neutral', 'impartial' and 'non-judging'. Instead, the disputants trust the mediators and hence assign them authority to manage a structured encounter. But it is in this 'management', 'structuring', 'diagnosis', 'norm' setting and deployment of 'tactics', as observed by Kressel, that the significant, obscured or even hidden power of the mediator resides.

The many opportunities for exercising mediator influence would seem to be further confused by the many different documented sub-varieties of mediation. To attempt a rationalisation of this variety, the work of Noll (2001) will be reviewed next, as he has surveyed mediation writing to resolve it into a general theory of mediation. Then another categorisation of differing styles of mediation by Boserup (2004) will be examined. This will afford a clearer view of the problem of obscured, hidden or unknowing mediator influence and importantly and firmly establish the concept of the spectrum of influence that is inherent in contemporary mediation practice.

Noll's Theory of Mediation

Noll has surveyed 'a vast literature' to find a

> theory ... to reconcile ... all the diverging views of practice and outcome into a unified view of mediation. (2001, p. 78)

He argues that such a theory of mediation has hitherto been lacking because the debates have not embraced an understanding of conflict dynamics. His theory contains four strands: conflict goals, levels of conflict escalation, the mediation style or process, and mediation outcomes.

(a) Conflict Goals

He explains by reference to other analyses how the interwoven and varying 'goals' of a conflict will influence its dynamic, listing these goals as relating to 'content' (I want something from you), 'relationship' (people not getting along), 'identity' (someone's sense of identity has been destabilised), and 'process' (the way someone wants to seek a resolution).

(b) Levels of Conflict Escalation

He then adopts a psychological, five-stage model of conflict escalation, ranging from not very serious to out of control. For example, stage four finds one or both parties regressing to the cognitive functioning level of six-year-olds, and at stage five to a 'hallucinatory narcissistic sphere' (pp. 79–81).

(c) Models of Style and Process

He lays out three complementary models of mediation style and process. The first is known as Riskin's Grid after its originator, the academic and mediator Leonard Riskin. This model looks at two dimensions of mediator orientation. The horizontal axis concerns problem definition, asking questions such as, '[D]oes the mediator tend to define problems narrowly or broadly?' The vertical axis concerns the role of the mediator, asking questions such as '[D]oes the mediator think he or she should evaluate … or facilitate the parties negotiation?' (p. 81). Drawing directly from Riskin (1996), the grid formed by the two axes results in four quadrants labelled clockwise, from the top left: evaluative narrow, evaluative broad, facilitative broad and facilitative narrow. Riskin attributes techniques to mediator behaviour, from urging or pushing parties and 'proposing' in the evaluative quadrants through to helping parties in the facilitative quadrants. Noll observes that Riskin's model has clarified mediation practice but 'has been criticised as tending to legitimise evaluative mediation' (Noll 2001, p. 82).

He then presents Kovach and Love's model that highlights a 'Great Divide' separating 'processes that require evaluation from processes that require facilitation' (p. 82). This seems to reinforce the criticism of Riskin's model, which would place evaluative processes beyond a definition of mediation.

In the third model he delineates another two-dimensional, four-quadrant grid conceived by Carnevale. According to Noll (2001), Carnevale argued that depending upon what value (from high to low) the mediator places on the disputants getting what they want, and also on whether the mediator thinks a mutual resolution is probable or not, the mediator will adopt one of four strategies. These are termed: 'compensation', 'pressure', 'integration' and 'inaction'. Noll explains Carnevale's logic as follows. Mediators 'compensate' if there is little common ground but the mediators want the parties to achieve their aspirations. They 'pressure' if they don't care and there is little common ground. They 'integrate' when they want parties to achieve their aspirations and there is common ground, and lastly they are 'inactive' if they do not care if the parties achieve their aspirations and there is common ground. Carnevale's assessment implicitly assumes mediators mostly want to succeed in their task but their psychological frailty manifests in these four ways. 'Compensating' can be understood as trying somehow to make up for the wide disparity of opinion between parties. 'Pressuring' implies a kind of 'let's go for it' attempt in the face of insurmountable differences between unsympathetic parties. The 'integrating' strategy is self-evident but a strategy of 'inactivity' is harder to understand, begging the question of why you should mediate if you are not committed to the process. It suggests an attitude of, 'I don't like them much but they seem to be able to resolve this so let them get on with it.' Carnevale's assessment would seem a little cynical and distant from mediation's origins in a compassionate desire to re-empower people trapped in conflict. It is based upon the idea that mediators can potentially control the outcome or somewhat petulantly don't care if they can't. However, this analysis is plausible, especially at a subconscious level. Mediators lacking any philosophical underpinning to their praxis may succumb to the behaviours he has detected. Mediators may certainly become frustrated with intransigent parties, but when a mediator is 'working well', perhaps guided by a supporting philosophical premise, selflessness may occasionally be achieved and Carnevale's 'strategies' become increasingly meaningless.

(d) Outcomes

Lastly, Noll categorises three types of outcomes. One is measured by tangible agreements, and the second by whether or not 'empowerment and recognition' has been achieved. This is a fleeting reference to Bush and

Folger's (1994, 2005) transformative model. (Noll surprisingly does not embrace this model as an example of style and process.) The third is similar to the second in that the degree of reconciliation is measured.

(e) Noll's Conclusion

He then states his theory as follows:

> The nature of the conflict dictates the mediation process to be used and the conflict's likely outcome. (2001, p. 83)

Noll's own theory and his discussion about other mediation theories presents a picture of mediators who judge and weigh up conflict situations and then deploy strategies to influence the outcomes they deem optimal. All these models implicitly acknowledge the wide extent of influence available to the mediator. Noll's theory is finally supported by formal theorems that effectively tabulate types of conflict and levels of conflict, which he argues lend themselves naturally to different types of mediation. If applied, these result in one of the above three outcomes. This is fairly commonsensical but he does, like Riskin, uncritically legitimate evaluative mediation. His theorems name five types of mediation:

- Facilitated—distributive bargaining
- Interest based negotiation
- Evaluative mediation
- Transformative mediation and
- Narrative mediation.

These blur and conflate the Riskin model, add in the transformative model, and further add the so far unmentioned narrative model. These latter two are discussed in detail in Chap. 6.

In his concluding discussion all these styles are reduced to either an 'evaluative' or a 'facilitative' approach. This would seem to be a sound summation, categorising two distinct and polarised approaches. However, if mediators, whilst never neutral, set out to act in ways that make any influence transparent and otherwise try to keep influence to a minimum, then it may be argued that only the 'facilitative' approach can be normatively regarded as a form of mediation. Given this opinion (which is perhaps a minority one), Noll's theory could usefully pertain to the broader activity of general dispute resolution but not to mediation. Notwithstanding this criticism, the so-called 'Great Divide' between the 'evaluative' and the 'facilitative' may prove an exaggerated metaphor since the area where facilitation slips over into evaluation is necessarily complex and grey, and furthermore there is much scope for mediators to wield power within the facilitative category itself.

Boserup's Categorisation

The work of Boserup (2004), who categorises and dates six basic mediation styles, will serve to penetrate this greyness a little further and reveal more facets of mediator influence that may arise from the diversity of mediation practice. These six styles are termed:

- Generic (1970)
- Settlement driven (1980)
- Cognitive, systemic (1980)
- Transformative (1990)
- Humanistic (1990) and
- Narrative (1990).

The simplified descriptions of community and workplace mediation processes given above arise from the 'Generic' and 'Settlement driven' models. In the 'Generic model,' mediators invite parties to express their feelings and to explore their interests and needs (moving away from entrenched positions). This is achieved by means of a structured process that is common to many types of mediation practice. Boserup summarises this structure in five stages:

1. Storytelling
2. Defining issues

3. Generating options
4. Negotiation and
5. Agreement.

He explains that, in this approach, it is important to allow feelings and emotions to be explored through active listening and free storytelling. Also, joint sessions are not usually interrupted by 'time outs' for separate meetings with each party. Beer and Stief (1997, p. 79), leading proponents of this style, exhort mediators to '[k]eep yourself in their present, out of their future'. However, there is also an inherent aim to help parties surface their interests and underlying needs and to find some form of practical solution.

To move away from this 'Generic model' to a style where a mediator feels obliged to always yield a productive, efficient outcome, measured in the form of an agreement made by the parties, will surely tend to compromise the 'key objective of consensual joint decision making [by the parties alone]' (Roberts 1992, p. 385). This style of mediation, as noted above, has been variously labelled 'bargaining' (Silbey and Merry 1986) and 'evaluative' (Riskin 1996) and is called 'settlement driven' by Boserup. Here the importance of defining issues and interests takes more prominence than exploration of related feelings and emotions. Information is gathered more than stories are told, and 'time outs' are used as an integral part of a strategy for getting to an agreement. There is a very heavy emphasis on getting the conflict practically resolved and a written agreement made. Mediators necessarily adopt a more overtly directive approach.

He describes the third style, called 'Cognitive, systemic', as a cyclical approach. Each problem surfaced is treated to a cognitive exploration in which information is privileged over emotion. Then the cycle is repeated with another problem. Each cycle seems similar in structure to the stages of the generic model. This style was developed by Haynes (1981, 1994) in the context of family and divorce mediation. Thus, concerns are of a highly practical nature to do with finance and custody of children. In general, Haynes believed that

> [t]he process of mediation is the management of other people's negotiations, and the mediator is the manager... The more coherent and orga-

nized the process, the easier it is for participants to arrive at solutions. (Haynes 1994, p. 1)

The fourth style is called 'Transformative' (Bush and Folger 1994, 2005), in which mediators seek to eschew 'problem-solving' in favour of encouraging 'empowerment and recognition' to support recovery of a respectful interaction. This is an innately facilitative style.

The fifth, 'Humanistic' style is applied to 'victim-offender' meetings. This is a specialist form of mediation for a specific situation. Interestingly, because it requires high levels of mediator modesty and respect in the joint sessions, it may also appear an innately facilitative style. Much preliminary work that is not necessarily 'facilitative' is carried out in private preparatory meetings before parties will agree to sit down together. When they do, the mediator tries to be 'as invisible as possible' (Boserup 2004, p. 6).

The last of the six styles identified by Boserup is the 'Narrative' style developed by Winslade and Monk (2001). Its process has three aspects: 'engagement', which involves listening, rapport-building and storytelling, 'deconstruction' of the conflict story through externalising language (to separate the 'problem' from the party[1]) and locating alternative stories, and lastly, 'construction' of an alternative mutual story. It appears to commence in a relational mode (with an emphasis on the relational interactions between the parties) but then moves; towards a more problem-solving style. Thus, it operates to free parties from their conflict-saturated story and to build a new conflict-free story led by the mediator, and it is perhaps tantamount to a mediator-guided solution. This style will also be further examined in Chap. 6.

Boserup identifies these six styles, asserting that the adoption of any one will 'change the whole concept of mediation as a practice' (2004, p. 1), but he notes this in order to suggest that mediators should learn all styles in order to be able to select the one most appropriate for a given situation. Pruitt (2006, p. 860), as already noted, similarly advocates selecting an approach to suit the particular circumstances of a given con

---

[1] 'As mediators externalize a problem, they speak about it as if it were an external object or person exerting influence on the parties' (Winslade and Monk 2001, p. 6). Thus, a mediator might ask, 'how did the "problem" make you feel', rather than 'how did you feel about the "problem?"'

flict. This echoes Noll in suggesting any style is as good as another as long as it is appropriate for a given conflict situation. For example, Boserup advocates a settlement-driven style if the mediator senses that the parties are impatient for an agreement. Alternatively, he suggests a cognitive style is best when one or both parties are not willing to reveal 'emotional aspects of the conflict' (Boserup 2004, p. 2).

An Overview of Styles and Varieties of Influence

It may be concluded that contemporary mediation is a very diverse discipline. But for those practices that purport to be forms of a 'neutral' third party intervention that have transferred from the community sector into the workplace, it is possible to arrive at a summary categorisation brought into focus by Kressel. Kressel effectively condenses Boserup's and Noll's surveys into two styles of mediation, being "either a *problem-solving* or *relational style*" (2006, p. 742). Kressel lists relational styles as transformative mediation, narrative mediation and victim offender mediation. He notes that these styles 'focus less on agreement-making and more on opening lines of communication' (p. 744). He states that '[t]he problem-solving style has long been the dominant mediation approach' (p. 743). Under 'problem-solving', like Noll, Kressel differentiates subtypes of 'facilitative' and 'evaluative' styles but also adds a 'strategic' style. Strategic mediation sets out to reveal 'powerful latent causes of which the parties are unaware' (p. 743).

The work of Kressel, Noll and Boserup confirms a wide range of practice in which power is exercised by mediators to achieve agreements across a spectrum of influence from the very intrusive to the more minimally intrusive. However, Boserup, unlike Kressel and Noll, fundamentally warns against 'pushing and social control' (Boserup 2004, p. 8). He notes that those mediators who choose a least-directive style try to surface information by listening closely and reflectively, and by asking the minimum number of open-ended questions. This is because 'questions reflect our own intentions' (Boserup 2004, p. 2). Boserup warns that it is very easy for mediators to become manipulative, and that manipulation by mediators can only be avoided through mutual and open discussions and demonstrated facilitation between mediators in order to identify styles of manipulation, and the creation of values preventing their occurrence. (2004, p. 2)

This exhortation against knowing or unknowing use of mediator influence becomes all the more resonant in light of research undertaken by Kressel. He found that

mediator style appeared to operate below the level of consciousness; style was something mediators "did" without fully recognising the underlying coherence or "logic" behind their style. (Kressel cited by Riskin 1996, p. 24)

Hence there may be a danger inherent in the supposedly less intrusive style of facilitative, problem-solving mediation, specifically that sub-conscious influence may become manipulative. Chapter 5 will study manipulative tendencies that seem to be inherent in facilitative workplace mediation. This study will form a backdrop for the delineation of an alternative stylistic approach rooted in values of dialogue and compassionate curiosity, with the potential to avoid some of mediation's manipulative tendencies.

The overview of mediation literature, thus far, shows that in the evolution of mediation styles there was a branching between 'problem-solving' and 'relational' styles in the 1990s. Transformative mediation in particular arose from a critique of problem-solving mediation, whether at the evaluative/directive or facilitative ends of the scale. Workplace mediation that grew from the community model seems to sit astride the 'generic' and 'settlement driven' types. In the discourse of these practices, mediators are impartial neutrals and the parties are self-determining agents. However, facilitative mediation is structured around mediator control of the meeting process, and the theoretical literature reviewed above would seem to indicate many facets of mediator influence arising from such control. Retaining control of process whilst holding to a drive for settlement would, on the surface, seem to lead the mediator into a trap of 'evaluating' the conflict situation. From such evaluation we may surmise that mediators' conceptions of possible solutions can and do develop.

The following two empirical studies re-enforce the view that mediators who facilitate 'problem-solving' necessarily exercise considerable influence upon the outcome of a mediation session.

Evidence of Mediator Influence

Dingwall's Evidence and a Counter Claim

Dingwall (1988) studied a charitable, independent English divorce mediation service and observed mediation interactions in 45 interviews across 15 cases. He concluded that

> mediators can play a very active role in orchestrating these encounters in ways which seem inconsistent with the aspiration to party control. (1988, p. 165)

He also noted that this conclusion may be arrived at theoretically, quoting Simmel, who was writing at the beginning of the last century:

> A gesture, a way of listening, the mood that radiates from a particular [third] person are enough to change the difference between two individuals. (Simmel cited by Dingwall, p. 165)

This idea is reinforced if the mediation encounter is compared with therapy in which 'transference and counter-transference between therapist and patient is unavoidable' (Cohen et al. 1999, p. 342). In addition to these observations, Dingwall further noted that because the mediator creates the frame of the encounter,

> [t]he dispute is no longer a private matter but one which involves their [the parties'] standing in the eyes of an outsider, who is defining what will count as an acceptable, in-character behaviour. Given this, the element of enforcement seems ineradicable from mediation. (1988, p. 166)

Roberts (1992), also writing about divorce mediation in the UK, cites Gulliver to endorse the view that 'mediation serves a negotiation process' and 'the role of the mediator is understandable only within an understanding of that process' (p. 375). Despite Dingwall's earlier findings, Roberts attempts to reconcile this service to 'negotiation' with the principle of self-determination or party control, asserting that

> the explicit adoption by the mediator of a "modest profile" is essential if the authority of the parties to create their own agreement is to be safeguarded. (p. 383)

Thus, Roberts distils the mediator's conundrum. It is to support the management of a negotiated agreement on the one hand and to ensure the agreement is wholly owned and created by the parties themselves on the other. Yet Irvine, (2009) a lawyer, academic and practising mediator, speaking from his own experience, supports the findings of Dingwall contrary to Roberts' trust in a 'modest profile'. Irvine explains that within family mediation it is well recognised that some mediators set out norms of behaviour to influence parties towards particular choices. He argues for honesty with clients about what mediators do and a reflective practice (citing Schon 1983) from which mediators may understand and make transparent the values that affect the moment-by-moment choices they make. Irvine seems prepared to give up the claim of party self-determination with an acknowledgement of mediator influence. He describes Waldman's (1997) typology of mediation practice, which sets out three forms of practice according to their treatment of social norms. These are the norm-generating model (in which neutrality is assumed to be maintained), the norm-educating model and the norm-advocating model. In the first it is believed that the parties generate their own norms within which solutions may be defined. In the second the mediator will indicate appropriate norms for the parties to work within. In the third the mediator ensures compliance with certain norms. Oberman (2009), commenting on Irvine's article, states that she is open about being a norm-educating practitioner. She says:

> [h]ow can mediators call themselves "neutral" (regarding the outcome) and at the same time have a bias for joint custody [of the divorcing parties' child or children]? (Oberman 2009)

In family mediation, in which disparities of party power may be significant and outcomes may have a profound impact upon children, who are also often not included in mediation sessions, mediators would seem to be forced to confront the values and beliefs that influence their management of the mediation process. Non-neutrality can thus be more transparent and acceptable to parties and commissioners. It takes the form of a partiality in favour of the children in front of both parents. In the workplace, the overt acknowledgement of 'power' is often taboo. Again, note that the stance of neutrality is also seen as a foundation for acceptance of the mediation intervention (both as an organisational policy and on an individual party basis). Hence, the specific reasons why neutrality in the family domain has come to be questioned do not prevail in the context of workplace mediation. This comparison with family mediation may illuminate, to a degree, the persistence of the myth of neutrality amongst workplace mediators. There are reasons to retain it in the workplace and, unlike family mediation, no pressing circumstances, as of yet, that point towards exposure.

Silbey and Merry's Identification of the Settlement Problem

Silbey and Merry (1986) also identified mediation's inherent tension or conundrum, explaining that mediators face 'a dilemma: to settle a case without imposing a decision' (1986, p. 7). They researched over 40 mediators in 175 mediations from three mediation programs in the USA over a period of three years. One program was court-affiliated, the second was community-based and the third dealt with conflicts between teenage children and parents. They also discerned a spectrum of influence in describing how 'mediation styles fall along a continuum between two types: bargaining and therapy' (p. 8). Thus their study affords examples of a more facilitative style of practice labelled 'therapeutic'. The therapeutic mediator's mandate is 'to facilitate conversation, not to bargain' (p. 22). They describe therapeutic mediation as a

> communication process which resembles therapy in its focus on exploring and enunciating feelings. (p. 8)

In order to resolve the tension between the need to settle and the inability to impose a solution, mediators are seen 'employing a variety of sources of power' (p. 12). They identified power operating within four strategies:

- How mediators present themselves and the process
- How they control the process
- How they control issues—broadening, selecting, eliminating, narrowing, concretising or postponing and
- Application of assumed norms about conflict causation and how and why to settle

The different mixes of usage of the above four strategies determine where a mediation style is placed on a continuum between the poles of 'bargaining' at one end and 'therapy' at the opposite end—that is, from the more 'directive' to the more 'facilitative'. But in both cases, perhaps prefiguring transformative mediation, they see

> the aim of mediators is to convert [the parties] accounts into a language of relationships, (p. 26)

and again in both cases it is argued that

> they share an orientation toward relationship and interdependence as the basis for settlement. (p. 26)

In conclusion they suggest that because

> therapeutic mediators are forced by exigencies of some institutional umbrella to produce results competitive with some other yardstick of efficiency, ... therapists will become bargainers. (p. 30)

Dingwall's and Silbey & Merry's critiques would seem irrefutable and yet they appear to be either unknown or unaccepted by many practising mediators in both the community and in workplace arenas. This is evident from the quoted definitions of practising mediation organisations given above. These evidenced-based critiques of neutrality predate but mirror the analyses of Noll and Boserup. Unlike Noll, but in harmony with Boserup, they also find the manipulative behaviours of mediators problematic. Silbey and Merry's most powerful critique is that facilitative, 'modest' mediators ('therapists' in their terminology) necessarily become directive 'bargainers' to achieve settlement in institutional settings. What emerges from a consideration of mainstream mediators' language of 'neutrality' and 'impartiality' is a picture of a practice rooted in an individualistic humanism, being a view of the parties as self-determining, rational, autonomous persons enjoying the exercise of free-will. But due to a mostly benign desire to problem-solve, mediation practice tends to contradict its own values, so that the mediator may play a significant role in determining outcomes and may even direct the outcome.[2] 'Neutrality' becomes an illusion behind which the actual engagement between parties and mediators becomes one of containment. That is to say the parties, without noticing during the session, come to align themselves with the needs of the mediator to achieve settlement of the dispute, probably within the terms of the dominant norms and values of the organisation.

Reflecting on the above descriptions of mediator behaviours and strategies, the notion of mediation as a managed negotiation aimed at settlement can be seen to embrace many aspects, including the meeting's purpose, process and staging, the mediator's 'authority' and role (including strategic and tactical control of the conversation interactions), the mediator's disposition and body language, the location (being removed from the usual workplace), the encounter's voluntary nature (in so far as this is possible in the workplace), and guidelines/ground rules. Of key significance are the spoken, unspoken and possibly unrecognised values and aims a mediator brings to a session and how these play out through both the control of the process (e.g., how many meetings, when they occur, whether parties meet together or separately, whether there will be structured uninterrupted time, and the management of turn-taking to speak) and the micro-management of each conversation interaction (e.g., whether questions are posed at all, how they are posed, and whether questions probe for issues and not feelings, or vice versa, or both). Thus, it becomes apparent that there are many dimensions and planes upon

---

[2] In some situations this may result in the enactment of a social 'good', in that violence may be curtailed or prevented in situations of war or the interests of children may be protected in family disputes.

which the mediator may hold powerful influence over the mediation session. Such influence may be obscured through the use of technical skills to both orchestrate communication and to present an appearance of minimal intervention in the substance of any solution to a dispute. But as documented above, mediators and mediator course providers lay claim to a common principle that the disputants should make their own decisions, separately or together, to achieve some consensus or arrive at some form of understanding. Parties are said to possess self-determination over the outcomes.

In the workplace, this discourse of self-determination may well align with an atomising organisational focus upon each individual employee that justifies the intervention on grounds of cost-effectiveness and the hoped-for restoration of productivity. (The term atomisation here refers to the assumption that each employee is an independent entity wholly responsible for their behaviour and hence their conflict.) The concept of mediator neutrality reinforces this belief in party autonomy. Mediation therefore becomes problematic if obscured mediator influence operates to effect settlement to primarily serve an overriding institutional purpose. Thus the purported 'neutral' mediation intervention may be colonised by the organisation. To ground an assessment of this problem of influence beneath a veil of neutrality, the background of the adoption of mediation in the workplace as a tool of the Human Resource Management (HRM) department for the management of conflict will now be reviewed.

References

Beer, J. E., & Stief, E. (1997). *The mediator's handbook* (3rd ed.). Gabriola Island, British Columbia, Canada: New Society Publishers.

Boserup, H. (2004). *Advanced techniques and dilemmas in mediation: The issue of autonomy and social control in particular.* Paper presented to the Third Conference of the European Forum for Victim Offender Mediation and Restorative Justice, Budapest, Hungary, October 14–16. Retrieved from http://www.euforumrj.org/readingroom/Budapest/workshop19.pdf

Bush, R. A. B., & Folger, J. P. (1994). *The promise of mediation: Responding to conflict through empowerment and recognition.* San Francisco: Jossey-Bass Inc.

Bush, R. A. B., & Folger, J. P. (2005). *The promise of mediation: The transformative approach to conflict.* San Francisco: Jossey-Bass Inc.

Cohen, O., Dattner, N., & Luxenberg, A. (1999). The limits of the mediator's neutrality. *Mediation Quarterly, 16*(4), 341–348.
Crawley, J., & Graham, K. (2002). *Mediation for managers: Resolving conflict and rebuilding relationships at work.* London: Nicholas Brealey Publishing.
Dingwall, R. (1988). Empowerment or enforcement? Some questions about power and control. In R. Dingwall & J. Eekelaar (Eds.), *Divorce mediation and the legal process.* Oxford: Clarendon Press.
Haynes, J. M. (1981). *Divorce mediation: A practical guide for therapists and counsellors.* Oxford: Blackwell Science Ltd.
Haynes, J. M. (1994). *The fundamentals of family mediation.* Albany, NY: SUNY Press.
Irvine, C. (2009). Mediation and social norms: A response to Dame Hazel Genn. *Family Law, 39,* 352–356.
Kressel, K. (2006). Mediation revisited. In M. Deutsch, P. T. Coleman, & E. C. Marcus (Eds.), *The handbook of conflict resolution: Theory and practice* (pp. 726–756). San Francisco: Jossey-Bass Inc.
Noll, D. E. (2001). A theory of mediation. *Dispute Resolution Journal, 56*(2), 78–84.
Oberman, S. (2009). Retrieved from www.mediate.com/articles/irvineC1.cfm?nl=218 then click on 'more comments.'
Pruitt, D. G. (2006). Some research frontiers in the study of conflict resolution. In M. Deutsch, P. T. Coleman, & E. C. Marcus (Eds.), *The handbook of conflict resolution: Theory and practice* (pp. 849–867). San Francisco: Jossey-Bass Inc.
Riskin, L. L. (1996). Understanding mediators' orientations, strategies, and techniques: A grid for the perplexed. *Harvard Negotiation Law Review, 1*(7), 7–50.
Roberts, M. (1992). Who is in charge? Reflections on recent research on the role of the mediator. *Journal of Social Welfare and Family Law, 15,* 372–387.
Schon, D. (1983). *The reflective practitioner: How professionals think in action.* New York: Basic Books.
Silbey, S. S., & Merry, S. E. (1986). Mediator settlement strategies. *Law and Policy, 8*(1), 7–32.
Waldman, E. (1997). Identifying the role of social norms in mediation: A multiple model approach. *Hastings Law Journal, 48,* 703–759.
Winslade, J., & Monk, G. (2001). *Narrative mediation: A new approach to conflict resolution.* San Francisco: Jossey-Bass Inc.

3

Mediation in the Workplace

The Adoption of Mediation in the Workplace

There has been a growth of the use of mediation in the workplace in recent years, and it is the facilitative style used in the family and community sectors that has been adopted (Bennett 2012, p. 2). Mediation has been taken up more in the public and voluntary sectors than in the private. This is borne out anecdotally through meetings with mediators and at mediation conferences, where public sector personnel managers seem to predominate. This is not to say that some very large private corporations have not embraced mediation, as can be seen by viewing the websites of larger mediation service providers. This anecdotal evidence is supported by surveys conducted by the UK Chartered Institute of Personnel and Development (CIPD 2011, p. 12), which find a slow growth in workplace mediation with a skewing towards adoption in the public sector. However, whilst there is a visible and active workplace mediation industry that is, in particular, supported by public sector bodies, it operates at very modest levels in the general economy in percentage terms. As *The Workplace Employment Relations Study: First Findings 2011* (a sampling exercise) found:

Provision for mediation is included in 62% of grievance procedures and 62% of disciplinary and dismissal procedures ... However, this has not translated into a high level of use. Of all workplaces, 7% had used mediation to resolve an individual dispute in the 12 months prior to the survey: 4% with an internal mediator and 3% with an external mediator. (WERS[1] 2011, p. 27)

These WERS findings led the authors to conjecture that this low take-up is due in part to 'the fact that mediation may not be embedded in the culture of conflict handling' (WERS 2011, p. 27).

Where it is embraced, workplace mediation brings (usually) two employees of an organisation, voluntarily and confidentially (as their conversation is private) together, to look for a resolution of a dispute. From this apparently simple description it seems obvious that workplace mediation potentially helps to resolve conflict to the material benefit of both the organisation and the parties. Thus, the mediator serves two constituents: the parties and the organisation. However, several questions arise over the balance and nature of the benefits that may accrue to the organisation and the parties and, despite the assertion that mediation is a voluntary engagement, there are necessarily elements of organisational power in the 'bringing' together of parties in conflict.

Mediation, at one extreme, could be regarded as a method for containing and suppressing conflict, potentially separating individuals from the pursuance of grievances via the formal processes of employment tribunals (Dolder 2004). As such it would fall into alignment with the dictates of 'organisational cost-effectiveness'. From a very different perspective, mediation may hold potential to empower individuals within an organisation to democratically resolve their issues 'in the sense of having a greater say in the process and outcome' (Bennett 2012, p. 3).

Whether mediation is empowering, just and even 'democratic', and whether it is containing or inherently tending to suppress conflict, will

---

[1] 'WERS is a multi-sponsored project and the input of the various sponsors is one of the reasons why the study has maintained its rigour over a sustained period of time. The 2011 WERS is co-sponsored by the Department for Business, Innovation and Skills (BIS), the Advisory, Conciliation and Arbitration Service (Acas), the Economic and Social Research Council (ESRC), the UK Commission for Employment and Skills (UKCES) and the National Institute of Economic and Social Research (NIESR)' (WERS 2011, Acknowledgements page).

therefore significantly depend upon how the mediation is carried out. That is, the adopted style or method of mediation and the behaviour of the mediators will materially affect whether parties are treated fairly or otherwise. The choice and application of mediation style, which dresses itself in a language of 'neutrality' but obscures practices that are far from neutral, as noted above, may become problematic, especially if it serves organisational needs above those of the parties. That is, a mediator may, inadvertently or otherwise, manipulate parties towards a resolution, thus reducing costs associated with the disruption caused by conflict, but the parties may be left dissatisfied, having felt coaxed or directed to agree to a form of resolution. As also noted above, mediation could find itself being colonised by the 'organisation' and applied for instrumental reasons that devalue the worth of mediation. Intrinsically mediation affords a means of supporting people so they can emerge from conflict and in so doing learn about themselves, each other and their organisation.

Upon adoption in the workplace, the mainstream facilitative style of contemporary mediation may be expected to be further conditioned by the values, norms, practices and above all the meanings and understandings of the social and economic world that dominate organisational life. This conditioning and the social relations of power that prevail will be, to a significant degree, framed and influenced by three factors: government policies about mediation, the contemporary individualised position of the employee, and the overarching rationale of the Human Resource Management (HRM) function. It is towards a consideration of these three contextualising aspects of modern workplace mediation that we shall now turn.

Government Policies

The UK Government, which notably funds Acas, a major provider of workplace mediation and mediation training, has long been an advocate for increasing mediation usage. *Inside the Workplace: First Findings from the 2004 Workplace Employment Relations Survey*, published by the then Department of Trade and Industry (DTI), found that workplace conflict has been subject to dynamic change during the period [1998–2004], most notably in the gradual decline in collective conflict, measured through industrial action, and in the concurrent rise in individualised conflict, measured most overtly in the number of employment tribunal claims. (WERS 2004, pp. 22–23)

Employment legislation enacted in October 2004 was designed to reduce the level of employment tribunal work by mandating the introduction of set grievance and dismissal procedures in all organisations. That a reduction did not occur led the DTI to commission a study by Michael Gibbons called *Better Dispute Resolution: A review of employment dispute resolution in Great Britain*. Gibbons reported in March 2007. He expressed a 'vision of a greatly increased role for mediation', recommending that the Government should 'offer a free early dispute resolution service, including where appropriate mediation' (Gibbons 2007, p. 5). He further recommended that

> The Government should challenge all employer and employee organisations to commit to implementing and promoting early dispute resolution, e.g. through greater use of in-house mediation, early neutral evaluation, and provisions in contracts of employment. (Gibbons, p. 10)

Despite the Gibbons Report's robust set of recommendations, the Employment Act 2008, which came into force in the UK on 6th April 2009, only mandated a voluntary Code of Practice for Disciplinary and Grievance Procedures. This CoP, written by Acas, contained the following paragraph in the foreword.

> Employers and employees should seek to resolve disciplinary and grievance issues in the workplace. Where this is not possible employers and employees should consider using an independent third party to help resolve the problem. The third party need not come from outside the organisation but could be an internal mediator, so long as they are not involved in the disciplinary and grievance issue. In some cases an external mediator might be appropriate. (Acas 2009)

This foreword also states that

[Employment] Tribunals will also be able to adjust any awards made in relevant cases by up to 25% for unreasonable failure to comply with any provisions of the Code. (Acas 2009)

Thus, elements of 'carrot and stick' were evident in Government thinking about the use of mediation. Although the focus of this thinking was to ameliorate the high levels of employment tribunal claims arising out of discipline, and of grievance procedures initiated in troubled workplaces, there was no specific legislation directly supportive of an increased use of mediation.

However, following the introduction of the CoP, the increase in employment tribunal cases showed no signs of slowing, and the provision of workplace mediation services did not significantly increase. Therefore in 2010, with the arrival of a new UK Government, these issues were taken up again, this time by the Department for Business, Innovation and Skills (BIS). Businesses were complaining that fear of the tribunal system was preventing them from taking on staff and thereby inhibiting economic growth (BIS 2011b). BIS noted in a report that the Government is 'even more convinced about the role that mediation can play, as one of the forms of early dispute resolution' (BIS 2011b, p. 8). This report, *Resolving Workplace Disputes: Government Responses to the Consultation*, also recognised that mediation is appropriate for issues such as relationship and communication breakdowns, bullying allegations, discrimination and diversity issues, issues of fairness or perceived injustice, and anything related to 'nipping' disputes 'in the bud' (BIS 2011b, p. 12). But overall, mediation was regarded as an effective method 'of resolving disputes without recourse to an employment tribunal' (BIS 2011b, p. 14). As in 2009, Government policy in 2011 did not seem to value mediation as a meritorious practice, in and of itself, for working with conflict inside organisations. This is despite the views of personnel managers responding to a CIPD Survey (2011) who ranked the benefit of mediation '[t]o improve relationships between employees' highest above all other more instrumental concerns, such as the 'costs involved in defending ET claims' (p. 14). This management survey thus demonstrated that reparative concerns are interwoven with matters of organisational efficiency in the minds of personnel managers, if not in those of Government policy makers.

By reviewing Government policy surrounding the employment tribunal process that impacts levels of mediation usage, it is also possible to discern an instrumental stance. The Government's intention to charge fees for tribunals was announced in January 2011 in a paper published by BIS and the Tribunals Service entitled *Resolving Workplace Disputes: A Consultation* (BIS 2011a). Despite an acute Government awareness of issues of access to justice, on page 50 it is stated that

> [p]roviding access to justice is not the same as providing other "goods" or "services". But charging fees for tribunal cases and appeals has the potential to play a central role in our strategy to modernise and streamline the employment dispute resolution system, helping to safeguard the provision of services, at an acceptable level, that are so important to the maintenance of access to justice.

An underlying ideology is present in this statement that could be transposed to read as 'rather than allow free access as in the past we are going to charge a fee to improve access'. One may wonder if this policy was believed or whether there was an element of wishful thinking or even cynical pretence. Here we are reminded of the definition of ideology as 'a system which makes a claim to the truth' and promulgates 'a lie experienced as truth, a lie which pretends to be taken seriously' (Zizek 2008, p. 27). Fees were introduced in July 2013 with total charges for claimants subsequently set at £1200 per party for discrimination and dismissal claims.[2] A Ministry of Justice press release on 13th July 2013 was headed 'Employment tribunal fees set to encourage mediation and arbitration'. By this logic it is implied that employers and employees, frightened of incurring fees, will pre-empt tribunal claims via an increased use of mediation. However, it is not unreasonable to assume that many employees will regard these costs as unaffordable and will simply not pursue their claims. It is also possible that employers will ride out conflict or settle it by other means and not see a clear reason for spending money on mediation. The Government has argued that fees will stop claims that are

---

[2] This fee covers an 'issue fee' to start the claim and a 'hearing fee' for the tribunal hearing. There is a possibility of fee remission for people on certain state benefits or on low monthly incomes (Source: www.citizensadvice.org.uk).

termed weak and fictitious, made in the hope of gaining quick out-of-court settlements. However, many lawyers and unions regard the fees as a barrier to access to justice for many employees with genuine claims. The Government's own research seems to support this view (BIS 2014, p. 5), finding that claimants were likely to be influenced by the need to pay a fee, and that those on lower salaries would be most affected. Saundry and Wibberley's (2014) interview research found that 'restricting access to the employment tribunal system will do little to encourage organisations to manage conflict ... *within the workplace*' (2014, p. 3). Certainly, in 2014, the Government reported very large percentage falls in tribunal 'receipts', including for employment tribunals.[3] Hence, policies aimed at reducing the incidence of employment tribunals have likely also suppressed the uptake of mediation services.

In the USA, organisations are reported to be taking a more strategic view of conflict and are embedding a variety of conflict management systems rather than just occasionally resorting to the use of mediation (Acas 2014, p. 10). But the incentive for these initiatives is said to be 'the extremely high cost of litigation' (Acas 2014, p. 10) that prevails in the USA. Once again a transactional factor underpins policy rather than a more in-depth analysis of causation. Causation is ignored on the probable assumption that conflict is somehow just a natural phenomenon.

It may be concluded that UK Government policy on mediation is mainly derived from instrumental concerns such as the multifarious business costs of disputes that culminate in employment tribunals. Gibbons' recommendations for making dispute resolution a feature of employment contracts were not implemented and the formally structured grievance and disciplinary procedures were abolished in 2009. As noted above, they were replaced by a new code of practice issued by Acas that was intended to allow employers more flexibility to handle disputes at work. These factors—an objectifying concern with costs of employment, a suggestion (although not implemented) for making mediation a legal element in individual employment contracts, and the removal of formal frameworks for employees to turn to when in dispute—all reinforce the identification by WERS (2004) of the growing trend in the individualisation of work-

---

[3] See www.gov.uk/government/statistics/tribunal-quarterly-tribunal-april-to-june-2014

place conflict. Despite the above-mentioned recognition by personnel managers of the use of mediation at a human level for the amelioration of conflicted relationships, against a background of complex organisational dynamics, mediation itself, as a private, confidential encounter, would appear to also contribute towards the trend in the individualisation of the employee.

The Individualisation of the Employee

WERS (2004), as noted above, documents a move away from collective representation and the concurrent rise in the individualisation of conflict. Acas (2014, p. 1) has also more recently confirmed this continuing phenomenon. This 'individualisation' is part of a larger trend in the overall employment relationship. Gratton and Ghoshal argue that

> in a competitive knowledge based-economy … Each individual must now accept the responsibility for managing his or her personal human capital. (2003, p. 4)

They laud this as a democratisation of the employment relationship, placing 'a premium on individuation … the opportunity each individual has to reach his or her fullest possible development' (p. 4). There is an inadvertent hint that this new world of work may be more elitist than egalitarian in the acknowledgement that it applies 'at least for managerial and professional careers' (p. 2). Whether or not a commercialised notion of Jungian individuation is at all feasible for the elite, a process of 'individualising' the workforce follows from the logic of Gratton and Ghoshal.

Until recently, statutory guidance for dismissal and grievance procedures operated by Human Resource (HR) departments afforded some protection for both individual employees and the employer within this individualising trend. Gibbons' recommendations (cited above) pressed for the greater use of mediation within this overall pattern of individualising employee relations. The subsequent legislation watered down these recommendations but still gave some impetus for an increased introduction of the option of mediation, if only as a box-ticking exercise ahead of the threat of a potentially adverse tribunal judgement.

Carroll (1996, p. 21) cites a critique of workplace counselling that is homologous to the mediation setting in that problems are individualised by being decontextualised, and made apolitical and the responsibility of the parties. Thus, a process of 'individualisation' operates to detach people from other significant relationships and wider causes of conflict. This tendency is exacerbated by mediation's private, confidential and hence isolating nature, which itself has been criticised as potentially oppressive for the weaker party. (Menkel-Meadow 1995; Bush and Folger 2005). Barratt similarly warns of a Foucaultian subjectification that may be channelled via HRM practises:

> It is in the role of practices analogous to the confessional … mentoring, self development activities, employee counselling and most obviously the confessional appraisal … —activities in which the subject is required in the presence of an authority figure to reflect on his or her own conduct, feelings and aspirations with the aim of inducing corrective effects or self transformation which have provided the most obvious analogies for the functioning of this modality of power. (Barratt 2003, p. 1073)

This dynamic is recognisable to anyone involved in contemporary work organisations and has strong echoes with a type of directive or evaluative mediation that may be sponsored, wittingly or unwittingly, by HRM. However, on the contrary, it may be argued that mediation holds an as yet unrealised potential to de-individualise and re-contextualise conflict. Furthermore, it may be claimed that mediation has potential to be deployed in a fashion that is reparative and better accords with the responses of the personnel managers surveyed by CIPD, who believed that mediation's primary use is for the 'improvement of relationships'. For now it can be accepted that the facilitative style of workplace mediation is likely to become a lasting feature of HR work (even though small in scale) and that this may contribute to an existing trend in the individualisation of the employee. Whether it does will in part rest upon the wider discourse of HRM policy that shapes how and why mediation may be adopted. After all it is HRM that commissions mediation, seeing it as a useful tool in the fulfilment of their general remit.

Human Resource Management Policies

The key aspect of HRM discourse that frames mediation policy may be simply represented as a tension between the 'personal' (as in *Personnel* Management) and the 'economic' (as in Human *Resource* Management). Turning to more sophisticated academic assessments of this dynamic discursive tension, Legge (2005, p. 39) explains that 'the personnel function is centrally concerned with achieving the control and consent of employees'. Some see this as 'an essentially and continuing bureaucratic' function (Watson 2007, p. 1). Others may view HRM's role as such: 'to assist in the extraction of surplus value through obscuring the commodity status of labour' (Legge 2005, p. 39). Keenoy (1999) notes that

> HRM as an operational facticity has been routinely associated with attempts to effect a significant change in the organisational ideo-culture. (1999, p. 2)

'Ideo-culture' refers to management-driven notions and concepts of 'appropriate behaviour' and 'the way we do things around here'. Keenoy further suggests that HRM entails the 'management of meaning' against a socio-economic context increasingly concerned with the '"effective" utilisation of human resources' (p. 3). This more strategic assessment is at once discursive but also has a flavour of the utilitarian and bureaucratic, albeit with overtones of the false consciousness of a Marxist interpretation. Such a multi-faceted description accords with the metaphor of HRM as hologram that Keenoy develops, although Keenoy does echo Legge and Watson, by offering a reduced definition of HRMism as

> no more than a collective noun for the multitude of concepts and methods devised to manage and control the employment relationship. (p. 17)

Within this array of methods, Legge (2005) notes the replacement of earlier conceptual models of HR strategy, labelled 'soft' and 'hard', with new models of high commitment management (HCM) and high performance work systems. HCM, she says, 'focuses on job security, job design and employee development as the route to high productivity/profits' (2005, p. 19). HCM also seeks to secure the consent and commitment of employees to organisational values and demands by treating them as valuable assets and with respect. (p. 39)

Legge (p. 15) observes that HCM work practices tend to be more prevalent in larger workplaces and in the public sector. As recognised above, these same places are more likely to deploy mediation in the management of workplace conflict. Workplace mediation services seem consistent with an HCM strategy that values staff in order to maximise productivity. Incidents of conflict clearly detract from productivity. Thus, mediation is one way of mitigating the 'bottom line' effects of conflict at work.

Legge (2005, p. 39) suggests traces of Aristotelianism are discernable in the 'unitary, inclusive and supportive culture' of HCM. This assertion would seem to be based upon a metaphor of the organisation as a mini-state, given the Aristotelian belief in the state and citizenship as the root of the good life, wherein humans are viewed as political rather than social creatures (Miller et al. 1991). Aristotle attributed the underlying cause of political strife to inequality:

> [R]evolutions generally occur when the poor rise against the rich. The statesman, ... is offered advice on how to produce equality or its appearance and on how to restrain or divert the passions of the unequal.[4] (Miller et al. 1991, p. 22)

If the modern organisation is like a mini-state, then HR managers act as 'statesmen' within it. To move from antiquity to contemporary life and extend the metaphor, we might view HR directors as government secretaries of state and HR managers as junior ministers, with a small element of their portfolio extending to the management of mediation services. Junior ministers must of course tow the party line to stay in office. Perhaps these 'statesmen' from HR simply need to restrain and divert the

---

[4] From Magna Carta to the French and American revolutions, history tends to suggest it is often those just below the rulers who have the capacity and intention to resist inequalities. In this context it might be middle/senior management who have power to become the usurpers. But there is a difference between states and organisations; some of them today are much larger than nation states, in that Boards and their shareholders seem all-powerful. Employees may often hold no more power than peasants did in a feudal society.

passions of the unequal, and they have co-opted the mediator to assist in this task. However, this overly simple view unnecessarily disparages those personnel managers who combine the instrumental aspect of their work with a more benign and sometimes compassionate disposition towards their employees. It is also undermined by the fact that mediation is used to resolve interpersonal disputes between managers at the top levels of the organisational hierarchy. Nevertheless, this tension between the employee as person and as contracted work resource cannot be resolved inside a hierarchical organisation (in the sense of an undemocratic system designed for the uneven distribution of employment benefits). Drawing upon another philosopher, Legge reinforces this point:

> HCM may appear Kantian in its respect for the person, [but] the likely instrumentality of that respect rules out a truly Kantian ethical position. (2005, p. 39)

Again Miller et al. (1991) help to decode Legge's philosophical allusions. Kant's categorical imperative states that people must always have 'good will'[5] so that persons are treated as ends in themselves and never merely as means to arbitrary ends. The HR manager may view the employee as a human deserving of respect and good will but may simultaneously treat them as an objective factor of production in the service of profit that sustains all their employments. (In the public sector, the metric of 'profit' is replaced by some measure of an efficient and effective tax-funded service provision). Mediators may bring an ethical code of compassion and humanism to their dealings with those in conflict, and yet they may become instrumental in delivering the wider objectives of the HR function. The mediators are themselves used by HR and in turn may inevitably treat the parties in dispute as mere means to arbitrary ends. Kallinikos underscores

---

[5] Russell (1962) explains more fully that Kant held the principle that every man (or woman) is to be regarded as an end in himself (or herself), and more generally the categorical imperative may be represented as an admonition to '[a]ct as if the maxim of your action were to become through your will a general natural law'. (Russell 1962, p. 683). Although Zizek describes such moral compulsion as 'irrational' (Zizek 2008 [1989], p. 88).

the distinctive mark of the modern workplace [as being] the fact that humans are involved in it qua roles not qua persons. (Kallinikos 2003, p. 597, cited in Watson 2007, p. 4)

And yet mediation is emphatically concerned with how people feel and how they respond to each other as persons. This of course embraces their own and others' understanding of their role in the workplace. Thus, there is a tension between a facet of HRM, in its alignment with the ethos of mediation with a reflective and human developmentalism at its heart, and practical aspects of the HR role, in a modern, mixed market economy that is basically capitalistic and 'driven by short-termism and management accountancy values rather than developmental humanism' (Keenoy 1999, p. 5).

How Mediation Practice Aligns with Organisational Needs

The way this tension is negotiated is likely to depend upon how the mediator carries out her/his work, whether the style used is facilitative or directive. A directive style may be prone to deliver an institutional objective of efficient conflict containment. That is to say, a style of mediation whose objective is to solve problems through the hidden use of mediator power, whilst pretending the parties are self-determining, may well become absorbed by and aligned with organisational discourses of efficiency, productivity and employee atomisation. The handling of this tension will also be affected by how the mediator engages with the HR manager referring the conflict to the mediation service. For example, inequalities and deeper, structural causes of conflict may be up for discussion or they may be taboo (assuming obligations of confidentiality admit such discussion). Given this ongoing informal negotiation of power, when mediators intervene in workplace conflict, it may be argued that they need to be self-aware of how they do so, for at least two reasons. Firstly, in the Kantian sense, they need to be attuned to their influence as a means to HR's strategic ends. Secondly, they need to have sight of the wider organisational inequalities that potentially foment an Aristotelian political strife or, in this case, workplace conflict.

At worst the mediator may become enmeshed in an organisational schizophrenia (Bateson 2000) potentially implicit in the adoption by organisations of in-house or routine external mediation and conflict management services. Bateson explains how an individual may be caught in a 'double bind' when, in a vitally important relationship, she/he is asked to respond to a directive containing 'two orders of message and one of these denies the other' (Bateson 2000, p. 208). An honest answer to one message gives a 'wrong' answer to the other. Some form of pretended, dissembling response may be given. If this situation is repeated systematically it may literally drive the person crazy. For example, there is one message that says the organisation wishes to work with conflict and not suppress it, that people should surface their issues for dialogue in a safe environment and that people are the valued, most important asset of the organisation. Conflict transformation requires that the root causes of conflict in relationships, structures and cultures be addressed; otherwise interpersonal conflict will continue to erupt (see review of Lederach, (2003), below). But it is these wider relational and structural sources of conflict that the organisation may often be unable or unwilling to address without destabilising its own preferred power structures. Thus, the other message the organisation issues says the following to its employees: 'Whilst we want you to engage with conflict in a healthy, open way, there are on the contrary some lessons within conflict that must not be spoken about for fear of recriminations.' Thus, madness may arise from mixed messages of 'damned if you do, damned if you don't' as issued from an 'inhuman' HR department (Schneider 1999, p. 280). Schneider argues that such '"irrationality" is not in the person but in the system' (Schneider 1999, p. 278). She suggests it is important for HR academics and managers to attain a 'better understanding of how systems (here organisations) create conditions that challenge healthy human functioning' (Schneider 1999, p. 283). However this view seems to overlook our own place as irrational members of the 'system'. It would appear insufficient (and unlikely to succeed) to simply attempt to manufacture good 'systems' from within unchanged or unchallenged wider social and political parameters.

A central purpose of this book is to consider how the well-meaning mediator may unconsciously become party to the perpetuation of such 'schizophrenic' practices, and also whether there is any possible escape from entrapment in such practices that does not result in a jettisoning of the mediation project and the consequent loss of its positive potential. As noted above, such an escape would seem to depend upon mediators' awareness of all aspects of their role and power inside the culture of contemporary organisations, as well as an attunement to the wider conflictual backdrop surrounding the parties in conflict.

Reference has been made above to the importance of the 'wider discourse of HRM policy'. Concepts of 'discourse' and 'ideology' are pertinent to an understanding of how mediation may become aligned with organisational needs, and they will become increasingly valuable for the theoretical and practical analysis used to clarify optional approaches to mediation practice in the chapters that follow. At this juncture it is timely to give short explanations of the usage of these terms and the related concept of hegemony.

A Brief Note on Discourse, Ideology and Hegemony

A broad brush definition of 'discourse' suggests that the term refers to the way language is used to create meaning in social life (Wetherall et al. 2006). Howarth (2000) provides an excellent overview of various strands of discourse analysis and theory. Two of these are especially helpful for understanding practices of workplace mediation. The first is Norman Fairclough's school of critical discourse analysis (Fairclough 2001). Here 'discourse' and 'orders of discourse' infer that language shapes our ideas about the social world and the ways we act in it. The term 'orders of discourse' refers to sets of institutionally based conventions for interpretation, explanation and (habitual) action. Thus, 'discourse' is a name for the way we speak about these ideas and about how we think about our own agency in this linguistically negotiated world. Hence, language is not some sort of free-floating system of objective signs referencing an equally objective world of social objects. Instead it is always structured as discourse, affording a framework of reference and understanding. But this framework is imbued with systems of ideas, ideologies by which relations of power within society are set up and maintained or altered. Where ideologies become dominant, they, by definition, are taken for granted and naturalised, and they become commonsensical and hidden beneath the surface of practical activity. Ideology, operating through discourse, effects a totalising vision of social reality that obscures an inherent contingency of social and political relationships (Torfing 1999). For example, consider the ideological belief that a 'free market' will optimise economic wellbeing for every member of society. This book is a consideration of the ideological belief that mediators are 'neutrals' and that parties independently determine their own outcomes.

Fairclough (2005) draws a distinction between the complex and differing social structures that have causal powers and the social processes and events that are contingent upon these powers. Social practices, including discourses, are subject to human, creative agency, so that structures and social practices interact to either reproduce themselves or generate change in the 'practices' or in both 'structures' and 'practices'. Howarth (2000), following Laclau and Mouffe (1985), disagrees with Fairclough that there is any (partially) detached and distinct level of structural reality (with causal powers) and instead argues that discourse theory includes 'all social practices such that discourses and discursive practices are synonymous with systems of social relations' (2000, p. 8). There is no quasi-independent level of social or institutional structuring. Thus, the concept of discourse embraces all social practices in any given historical, cultural setting. Hence, we make meaning and engage with systems of meaning through 'a socially constructed system of rules and significant differences' (Howarth 2000, p. 8).

Whilst Fairclough and Howarth share some philosophical premises (such as the work of Foucault), their models of society are supported by different ontologies. This results in differing, although in some respects overlapping, conceptions of the subject (of agency, identity and subjectivity). These conceptions will be elucidated further in subsequent chapters for use in critiquing mediator practice. However, these similar but ultimately different conceptions of social and political life would nevertheless both admit a definition of hegemony as 'a moral, intellectual and political leadership' achieved by the persuasive 'expansion of a particular discourse of norms, values, views and perceptions … of the world' (Torfing 1999, p. 302). The important point is that contemporary organisations are sites of hegemonisation. After Critchley, organisations engage in 'actions that attempt to fix the meaning of social relations'

(2004, p. 113), as has been alluded to by Keenoy above. They do this through the use of discourse that assumes the truth of various ideologies.

Interpersonal or group conflict inside organisations often arises because views, values, norms and ideologies clash. Just when the mediator may be called upon, dominant ideologies and assertions of what is considered fair or just may be exposed to challenge. The style of mediation enacted will serve as a conduit for discursive practice and holds the potential to align and affiliate with a prevailing ideology or, alternatively, allow space for questioning and uncertainty. Perhaps the authority of the mediator may paradoxically enable usual relationships of power to be momentarily suspended. However, any such suspension would always seem precarious in an environment so enmeshed in webs of power, which will now be sketched out.

Contradictory Currents of Mediation Power

This book will focus upon the relationship of the mediator to the parties, recognising that this is necessarily conditioned by the presence, behind the scenes, of the commissioning referrer, the personnel manager who pays the mediator's fee. Thus, a story of certain relationships of power within a context of organisational power will be charted. Because prevailing discourses of efficiency are largely seen as natural within the workplace, they become beyond question (Fairclough 2001). In this way, the ideology of the marketplace may smother attempts at an ethical questioning of the mediator's role and power. If this is so, the instrumental needs of the workplace and HRM might be expected to colonise mediation beneath its guise as a neutral intervention. Hence, the role of the mediator may be interpreted as less of a laudable supporter of the sovereign, self-resolution of conflict and more of an instrument of social control over a fragmented, individualised workforce. The above review of the take-up of mediation services by the HRM function would seem to suggest that, despite mediation's foundational claim to be a neutral intervention, this is at least a real danger and at worst already the case. But what also emerges from this review of the application of mediation, as a tool of HRM, is a more complex picture. There is a symmetry of internal contradiction found in both HRM and mediation. The former is divided over its attitude towards employees, viewing them as both an object of 'resource' and as autonomous 'people'. The latter espouses mediator neutrality and the humanistic, independent capacity of the parties to find resolution but also practices non-neutrality, directiveness and persuasion (as demonstrated in Chap. 5), all of which may infantalise the parties. It is this symmetry of internal contradiction (parties are people/resources to be facilitated/directed) that would seem to have enabled a smooth adoption and colonisation (bending mediation to primarily instrumental concerns) of mediation by organisations.

Ironically, in the hard-edged school of HR that eschews the concept of high-commitment management practice, mediation may be suspected of being too humanistic and even democratic and therefore may not be taken up at all. Saundry and Wibberley identified resistance from line managers 'who felt that the ability of employees to ask for mediation threatened their authority' (2014, p. 33) and that their management of performance could be challenged. Mediation represents a (potential) momentary relinquishing of control, thereby freeing employees to decide for themselves what to do about their conflict. Indeed workplace mediation does also hold potential to represent a possibly radical, albeit mildly radical, departure from the standard practices of control within organisational hierarchies of power. This term 'mildly radical' may appear a little strange. Mediation could have a limited and yet also a far-reaching and progressive effect on relationship dynamics within the workplace and as such could represent a micro-emancipatory intervention (Alvesson and Willmott 1992). Those in conflict are invited to talk about their clash or communication breakdown in a private space that is partially removed from the workplace. (The extent of any radicalism inherent in the differing approaches to workplace mediation will be assessed in the following chapters.) Yet there is a shadow of authority cast over the 'neutral' venue of the mediation meeting. Zizek cautions us not to assume organisational authority is easily eluded since

> [w]e all know very well that bureaucracy is not all-powerful, but our "effective" conduct in the presence of bureaucratic machinery is already regulated by a belief in its almightiness. (Zizek 2008, p. 34)

Nevertheless, people entering a mediation process metaphorically and momentarily step to one side of the hierarchy and enter into conversation with the mediator and each other in an at least confidential bubble of space and time. As indicated, from the employers' standpoint, it is this seemingly radical aspect that has perhaps limited a more widespread adoption than is otherwise evident.

However, this momentary relinquishing of hierarchical control may be both desired and simultaneously feared by the employee. From the employees' perspective this process, conferring confidentiality within a temporary private space, may also feel isolating. That is, they may come to feel further isolated in an already isolating world. The employees in conflict, being offered the opportunity of a mediation process, may feel as if they are being singled out as wholly responsible for the conflict they are embroiled in, and in some way guilty of an error in behaviour. Furthermore, because conflict 'violates their [the parties] very identity' it will be felt as 'a profoundly disturbing experience' (Bush and Folger 2005, p. 61). Workplace mediation can induce additional anxiety in the prospective parties on top of the anxiety induced by conflict itself.

Thus, the phenomenon of mediation serving the purportedly individualised employee generates reasons why both employees and employers and may embrace the offer of mediation and at the same time shy away from it. Employees may be doubly anxious in the face of conflict but may also desire the relatively democratic opportunity proffered by mediation. Personnel managers genuinely concerned for their employees' wellbeing may welcome mediation. It also confers value upon employees whilst simultaneously efficiently managing and containing conflict. Alternatively, mediation as an HR tool may be rejected due to the apparent radicalism of such a process, which could undermine the usual operation of hierarchical power. The next chapter considers further how an intervention and process that is so easily understood as a means to control staff might be redeemed and, in contradiction, cast as holding the scope to be just and democratic and supportive of employees at a time of high stress.

References

Acas (Advisory, Conciliation and Arbitration Service). (2014). *Reframing resolution—Managing conflict and resolving individual disputes in the contemporary workplace*. Acas Policy Discussion Papers March. London: Acas. Retrieved

from http://www.acas.org.uk/index.aspx?articleid=4701&q=reframing+resolution+policy+paper
Acas & CIPD, (Advisory, Conciliation and Arbitration Service & the Chartered Institute of Personnel and Development). (2009). *Mediation: An employer's guide*. London: Acas. Retrieved from http://www.acas.org.uk/index.aspx?articleid=4701&q=mediation+an+employers+guide
Alvesson, M., & Willmott, H. (1992). On the idea of emancipation in management and organization studies. *Academy of Management Review, 17*(3), 432–464.
Barratt, E. (2003). Foucault, HRM and the ethos of the critical management scholar. *Journal of Management Studies, 40*(5), 1070–1087.
Bateson, G. (2000). *Steps to an ecology of mind*. London: University of Chicago Press.
Bennett, A. (2012). *Mediation: A critical analysis of the changing nature of dispute resolution in the workplace*. Paper to BUIRA Conference June 28–30, 2012 held at Bradford Universtiy.
BIS (Department of Business, Innovation and Skills). (2011a). *Resolving workplace disputes: A consultation*. London: BIS.
BIS (Department of Business, Innovation and Skills). (2011b). *Resolving workplace disputes: Government responses to the consultation*. London: BIS.
BIS (Department of Business, Innovation and Skills). (2014). *Findings from the survey of employment tribunal applications 2013*. Research Series No. 177. Retrieved from https://www.gov.uk/government/publications/survey-of-employment-tribunal-applications-2013.
Bush, R. A. B., & Folger, J. P. (2005). *The promise of mediation: The transformative approach to conflict*. San Francisco: Jossey-Bass Inc.
Carroll, M. (1996). *Workplace counselling: A systematic approach to employee care*. London: Sage Publications.
CIPD (Chartered Institute of Personnel and Development). (2011). *Conflict management: Survey report, March*. Retrieved from http://www.cipd.co.uk/hr-resources/survey-reports/
Critchley, S. (2004). Is there a normative deficit in the theory of hegemony? In S. Critchley & O. Marchart (Eds.), *Laclau: A critical reader* (pp. 113–122). London: Routledge.
Dolder, C. (2004). The contribution of mediation to workplace justice. *International Law Journal, 33*(4), 320–342.
Fairclough, N. (2001). *Language and power* (2nd ed.). Harlow, England: Longman.

Fairclough, N. (2005). Discourse analysis in organisation studies: The case for critical realism. *Organization Studies, 26*(6), 915–939.
Gibbons, M. (2007). *Better dispute resolution: A review of employment dispute resolution in Great Britain*. An independent Report commissioned by DTI (Department of Trade and Industry), published on March 21. London: DTI.
Gratton, L., & Ghoshal, S. (2003). Managing personal human capital: New ethos for the 'volunteer' employee. *European Management Journal, 21*(1), 1–10.
Howarth, D. (2000). *Discourse*. Buckingham: Open University Press.
Kallinikos, J. (2003). Work, human agency and organizational forms: An anatomy of fragmentation. *Organization Studies, 24*(4), 595–618.
Keenoy, T. (1999). HRM as hologram: A polemic. *Journal of Management Studies, 36*(1), 1–23.
Laclau, E., & Mouffe, C. (1985). *Hegemony and socialist strategy: Towards a radical democratic politics*. London: Verso.
Lederach, J. P. (2003). *The little book of conflict transformation*. Intercourse, PA: Good Books.
Legge, K. (2005). *Human resource management: Rhetoric and realities*. Basingstoke: Palgrave Macmillan.
Menkel-Meadow, C. (1995). The many ways of mediation: The transformation of traditions, ideologies, paradigms and practices. *Negotiation Journal, 11*(3), 217–242.
Miller, D., Coleman, J., Connolly, W., & Ryan, A. (Eds.). (1991). *The Blackwell encyclopaedia of political thought*. Oxford: Blackwell Publications Ltd.
Mouffe, C. (2000). *Deliberative democracy or agonistic pluralism*. Political Science Series No. 72. Vienna: Institute for Advanced Studies.
Russell, B. (1962[1946]). *History of western philosophy*. London: George Allen and Unwin.
Saundry, R., & Wibberley, G. (2014). *Workplace dispute resolution and the management of individual conflict A thematic analysis of 5 case studies*. Acas Research Paper Reference No. 06/14. Retrieved from www.acas.org.uk/researchpapers
Schneider, S. C. (1999). Human and inhuman resource management: Sense and nonsense. *Organization, 6*(2), 277–284.
Torfing, J. (1999). *New theories of discourse: Laclau, Mouffe and Zizek*. Oxford: Blackwell Publications Ltd.
Watson, T. (2007). *HRM, critique, pragmatism and the sociological imagination*. Critical Management Studies Conference Proceedings 2007, Stream: Where

is Critical HRM? Retrieved from http://www.mngt.waikato.ac.nz/ejrot/cmsconference/2007/default.asp

WERS (Workplace Employment Relations Survey). (2004). *Inside the workplace: First findings from the 2004 workplace employment relations survey.* London: DTI (Department of Trade and Industry).

WERS (2011). *The 2011 Workplace Employment Relations Study: First Findings.* London: Government Department for Business Information and Skills. Ref: BIS/14/1008.

Wetherall, M., Taylor, S., & Yates, S. J. (Eds.). (2006). *Discourse theory and practice: A reader.* London: Sage Publications.

Zizek, S. (2008[1989]). *The sublime object of ideology.* London: Verso.

4

Political Awareness and Dialogue

The Potential of Mediation

This chapter develops the argument that the potential of mediation should not be limited to a method for negotiating the instrumental settlement of conflicts viewed as isolated personal events. It makes a case for a mediation practice that opens up the parties' understandings of conflict to the 'politics' and the 'political' of the everyday. Mouffe describes politics as the

> ensemble of practices, discourses and institutions which seek to establish a certain order and organize human coexistence in conditions that are always potentially conflictual because they are affected by the dimension of "the political". (2000, p. 15)

The political she defines as 'the dimension of antagonism that is inherent in human relations' (p. 15). Unless mediation practice is knowingly aware of the political it will be unable to create space for the emergence of more just and democratic outcomes, and its attractiveness to employees will ultimately become tarnished. If mediators' interventions are informed by a sense of the political, there is scope for enemies to be transformed into adversaries whose opinions can be heard, and sometimes, through dialogue, adversaries may be able to alter their worldviews and discover new identities together.

In Chap. 2 it was made clear that there are many shades of mediation intervention across a spectrum from the very directive to the less intrusive, and whatever style is adopted, it is not possible for the mediator be neutral. This points to the need for mediators to be aware of their influence upon the parties. This need for awareness of our own influence as mediators becomes more acute in the workplace because we enter a domain intersected by governmental, organisational and human-resource departmental policies. Whilst surveyed personnel managers valued mediation as a means to improve relationships, in Chap. 3 we saw a tendency for government policy-making to focus upon the use of mediation for instrumental ends, the primary motivation being one of minimising the costs that are incurred by conflict and employment tribunals. The mediation space within the organisation is thus a site criss-crossed by dimensions of power, and the mediator brings an additional dynamic of power to an already complex situation. Chapters 2 and 3 thereby highlight the inherently political nature of workplace mediation interventions. On recognising mediation as a political act, it becomes unsurprising that claims have been made that workplace mediation has potential to enhance both justice and democracy within organisations (Acas 2014; Bennett 2012; Van Gramberg and Teicher 2005; Nabatchi et al. 2007; Ridley-Duff and Bennett 2010). Drawing upon these claims, this chapter will distil some pertinent aspects of justice and democracy as they relate to the role of the mediator and the deployment of mediation services inside organisations.

At initial mediation meetings, parties' presentations of their perceptions of the 'facts' of conflict are informed by emotion, hurt feelings, anger and often a sense that their very self-identity is besieged. The parties are bound to be concerned with how a relatively uncommon process like mediation can help them achieve redress for unfair criticism, injury or offences they feel they have suffered. Therefore, they may be expected to critically question the overall fairness of the mediation process and the extent to which it affords them an opportunity to express themselves. How the mediator intervenes is likely to contribute to or detract from the parties' sense that a mediation intervention has treated them justly and provided them with a 'voice' in how their conflict is resolved. If mediators are cognisant of their inevitable influence within a social and political setting, they will necessarily seek to manage their influence, contain it, or at least make it transparent. Given the impossibility of complete neutrality, they may come to understand their role as one of supporting parties in a co determination of any resolution in which their influence is reduced to a minimum. The challenge for the mediator is to contain their influence whilst also helping parties to become aware of the context of their conflict.

It will be argued that the mediator may meet this challenge by means of an intense and compassionate concern to understand the conflict, to understand each parties' perspective (which may be fraught with emotion) and to understand the contextual setting of the conflict. If the parties are similarly able to find their own understandings (which are not necessarily the same as the mediator's or each other's) they may be able to chart a path to resolution and even to a just and democratic transformation of the conflict and their part in it. Herein lies the full potential of mediation.

Broadening Responsibility for Conflict

In the UK, the government-financed Advisory, Conciliation and Arbitration Service (Acas 2006) delineates the following types of workplace disputes that mediation services can help with: bullying and harassment, communication issues, personality clashes, unresolved or ongoing grievances, and facilitating a return to work following an absence. One could add disciplinary and discrimination issues to this list. These are the labels attached to the typical conflicts that line managers and human resource managers will at times refer to mediators. At such times the focus of attention, conjured by this list of workplace conflict types, is less upon understanding any deeper sources of the conflict and very much upon the individuals (usually two) so embroiled. There is an implicit assumption and acceptance that conflict will occasionally, inevitably and naturally occur between people. These people are regarded as sovereign agents who are deemed responsible for the conflict they have created, and there will always be a need to find ways of dealing with it. Mediation is just one such option. This perspective upon workplace conflict has been described as a transactional approach to the 'problem' of conflict, but in this approach there is a lack of realisation by (some) organisations that 'conflict management is a strategic … issue' (Saundry and Wibberley 2014, p. 3). It can be argued that, if conflict were in part to be traced to wider systemic causes and not wholly attributed to interpersonal antagonisms, it could be used for both organisational and wider personal learning. The (possibly untapped) potential of the 'mediation response', were it part of a larger, as yet mostly unrealised strategic embrace of organisational conflict, will be made more visible by briefly examining some theories of conflict and conflict transformation.

Deutsch (2006) notes that as the discipline of social psychology emerged in the early twentieth century, a view of conflict as instinctual and as a naturally occurring symptom of competitive struggles began to wane. That this view had previously predominated he attributes to the influence of 'three intellectual giants—Darwin, Marx, and Freud' (p. 13), who respectively charted the struggles of species, classes and the psyche. Deutsch states that this instinctual view of conflict was replaced by two others, 'the psychological and the social-political-economic' (p. 14). He comments that these two modes of understanding the origins of conflict are not mutually exclusive and that weight may be given to one or the other, subject to the educational background and preferences of the assessor. The psychological mode explains conflict

> in terms of the perceptions, beliefs, values, ideology, motivations, and other psychological states and characteristics that individual men and women have acquired as a result of their experiences and as these characteristics are activated by the particular situation and role in which people are situated. (Deutsch 2006, p. 14)

In contrast he observes that the social-political-economic mode considers 'objective conflicts between economic and political interests and the like' (p. 14). The distinction he draws appears very weak in consideration of the latter mode's relationship with aspects of beliefs, values, ideology and motivations. Deutsch's expression of a psychological view of conflict has a strong social constructionist flavour in that our beliefs arise from our experience and situation. However, this 'situation' is not more or less than our personal engagement in social-political-economic relationships. His distinction is more sustainable if we assume actors in the social-political-economic sphere are autonomous individuals with a unique core and inner essence of identity rather than identities formed from the outside by our interactions with the world we perceive around us. It seems that how we view conflict and how the mediator intervenes will be conditioned by our philosophy of agency, being either a humanist one (in that the agent is sovereign and autonomous) or a more social-constructionist one (in that the agent both forms and is formed by her or his environment and by language).

However, Deutsch's dual (although overlapping) representation of conflict causality is reflected in Kressel's (2006) observation on mediation noted in Chap. 2 above, specifically that '[m]ost stylistic accounts portray the mediator acting in either a *problem-solving* or a *relational* style' (p. 742). 'Problem-solving' mediation could arise from a largely social-political-economic mode of understanding conflict in which sovereign, autonomous individuals clash over substantial issues of self interest while 'relational' mediation may seem to have its base mostly in the psychological view of conflict, which privileges concern with communication breakdown above the substance of a dispute. That these internal and external perspectives of conflict causation obviously intertwine suggests that the pursuit of either a purely 'problem-solving' or a purely 'relational' mediator orientation would prove problematic. It would seem necessary to find a balance in the mediator's approach to the issues and the substance of conflict, on the one hand, and the emotionally driven, communicative interactivity within conflict on the other.

Deutsch argues that the view of conflict as something innate and instinctual is no longer supported and yet in the subsequent analytic frameworks of the 'psychological', the 'socio-political', or his own 'competitive-cooperative' axis for conflict resolution, there appears to be an underlying assumption that conflict is a part of the human condition, that it is somehow eternal and universal and in our species-wide psychology or in our genes. These traditional readings of conflict, like Deutsch's social-political-economic account, seem to be founded upon the above-mentioned humanist view of social individuals as sovereign agents, whose very beings and identities reside in a unique essence and continuity of self-hood. This view derives from an Enlightenment humanism in which progress (towards universal wellbeing) through reason and science is believed attainable. A clash of personalities due to unmet needs or interests or conflicting value systems is understood to occur between autonomous individuals momentarily distracted or diverted from a more positive, rational and objective interaction. In Howarth's words these individuals are believed to have 'fully constituted identities and interests' (2000, p. 105).

Somewhat differently, Howarth (2000), documenting the political and social theory of Laclau and Mouffe, offers another reading of social antagonism and conflict. Here antagonism arises not between agents with fully formed identities but 'because social agents are *unable* to attain their identities (and therefore their interests)' (Howarth 2000, p. 105). The 'enemy' is construed as someone blocking the agents' ability to realise their desired identities.[1] This political theory has a strong resonance with the felt experience of individual conflict in which one's sense of 'who one is' feels threatened and destabilised. This view of social antagonism rests upon the concept that the identities (who we think we are) and subjectivities (how we apperceive the world) of agents are indeed socially constructed through discursive ideological practices. By this it is meant that we are affected and shaped by apparently natural, consistent, coherent and exclusive ways of talking and writing (and hence imagining and thinking) about the social and political world. As Billig (2001) notes, 'each act of utterance, although in itself novel, carries an ideological history' because speakers 'use terms which are culturally, historically and ideologically available' (p. 217). But this process of the ideological construction of meanings of the 'social' and of 'identity' is ultimately open, dynamic, incomplete and uncertain. The poststructuralist model of the

---

[1] Zizek (2006) radically develops this thought, suggesting that 'it is not the external enemy who is preventing me from achieving identity with myself, but every identity is already in itself blocked, marked by an impossibility, and the external enemy is simply a small piece, the rest of reality upon which we 'project' or 'externalize' this intrinsic immanent impossibility' (p. 252). This might explain the depth of anger that is aroused when attachment to 'identity' is disturbed, as it yields a glimpse of an underlying existential 'lack.'

social world propounded by Howarth (2000) and Torfing (1999) rests upon an anti-humanist concept of identity and agency in which there is no internal essence of identity and the subject is viewed as always incomplete and 'lacking' rather than potentially whole (but fragile). It points to a certain fluidity of identity as well as the possibility for identity to become 'sedimented', that is, fixed and resistant to change.

This glimpse of a post-Marxist discourse theory is offered because it locates the subject within conflict in ways significant for the interpretation of how mediators act and how they might develop new practices that will be expanded upon in subsequent chapters. Central to this interpretation is the extent to which mediation practice affords opportunities for parties to engage in a far-reaching exploration of their conflictual situation. Therefore, it will be necessary to return to these understandings of identity and subjectivity to inform a critical development of mediation practice.

Returning to a more positivistic view of the social, Lederach (2003) sees conflict (at group, national and international levels) not entirely dissimilarly from the views sketched above, as a 'normal and continuous dynamic within human relationships' (p. 15), but he argues for an understanding of conflict *transformation* rather than mere transitory and isolated resolution. Thus, he implies there is potential for progress towards a lasting and absolute reduction in the levels and extent of conflict in societies. 'Transformation' connotes an achievement of *change* that surpasses resolution of specific problems. Lederach defines conflict transformation thus:

> Conflict transformation is to envision and respond to the ebb and flow of social conflict as life-giving opportunities for creating constructive change processes that reduce violence, increase justice in direct interaction and social structures, and respond to real life problems in human relationships. (2003, p. 22)

He emphasises that the changes required to transform conflict, rather than merely resolve it, need to occur at personal, relational, structural and cultural levels, and that structural change processes must enable increases in justice. To address 'justice issues' Lederach suggests that

> [p]eople must have access and voice in the decisions that affect their lives … the patterns that create injustice must be addressed and changed at both

relational and structural levels. ... Dialogue is essential to justice and peace on both an interpersonal and a structural level. (2003, p. 21)

Conflict is still regarded as 'natural' but his analysis of the causes and responses to conflict is also explicitly political. Lederach stresses a dialogic, dynamic and systemic view much wider than the typical mediation focus upon individuals, their relationship and their narrow conflict situation. This begs the question of whether mediation, operating on an interpersonal level as an aspirationally neutral intervention, can ever amount to more than a short-term cure for the episodic flaring of conflict inside the workplace. McAllister (2002)) asks how can we get 'beyond mere interpersonal conflict to address the extent to which conflict is shaped by organisations' (p. 5). Cloke (2001) also counsels that, by viewing conflict in personal, psychological ways, the systemic causes of organisational conflict will be overlooked. He suggests that mediators 'invite parties to recognise the context of their conflicts' (p. 197) if they are to find ways to change dysfunctional systems. Hence, we might more positively ask what type of workplace mediation service could be accepted and used in the workplace to harness the transformative potential that is implied by Lederach's, McAllister's and Cloke's understanding of the causes of conflict? Cloke's systemic view of conflict is political in its advocacy of systemic change yet seemingly limited to the immediate contextual system, whereas Lederach looks beyond the immediate structures to wider social and cultural concerns. (This reflects his subject matter of national and international conflict situations.) Like Lederach, Cloke views conflict as a natural part of the human condition, wherein systems are either autocratic and hierarchical, and hence prone to conflict, or heterarchical and democratic, and therefore 'less deeply conflicted' (2001, p. 204). He argues that mediators can help by 'normalizing honest communication... [and integrating] conflict resolution principles' (p. 217) within the organisation. Unlike Lederach's more radical analysis, Cloke's appeal, although it may be read as very radical (as it implicitly appeals for heterarchy and democracy within our organisations), seems to limit itself to a demand for better management within the present economic system. This critique of supposed bad management implies a need for incremental change that is internal to work organisations. A more far-reaching critique of the wider supporting economic system, the corollary of Lederach's understanding of transformation, is absent, being probably beyond the scope of any mediation practice. Notwithstanding this likelihood, the works of Lederach and Cloke together powerfully imply the potential of workplace mediation to enhance organisational justice and democracy and to support notions of 'voice' and 'dialogue' for employees.

Organisational Justice and Democracy

The notion of organisational justice tends to refer to how members of an organisation feel about the fairness of their interrelationships with colleagues, managers and the organisation at large and how these feelings affect behaviours and attitudes at work. This constitutes a sense of being treated fairly and equitably in an environment where the employee has, in most organisations, unequal status. Greenberg (1987) offers a helpful classification of organisational justice. He arranges ideas of justice into two dimensions, a 'reactive-proactive' dimension and a 'process-content' one. The former covers behaviours or actions that either seek to redress injustice or strive to attain justice. The latter describes the organisational procedural means to attain just outcomes and the justice or fairness of the outcomes or ends in themselves.

Immediately we can view mediation processes as a channel or path within the workplace for dealing with feelings of being treated unfairly. If employees are to seek some redress, perhaps in reaction to unfair remuneration (a breach of distributive justice) or a harsh performance review (a breach of procedural or interactional justice), it is necessary that they trust processes available for so doing. Thus, proactively setting up an in-house mediation service or making a policy commitment to the offer of a mediation process must be done in such a way that it is trustworthy. Furthermore, when the process is subsequently utilised it must be experienced as fair and equitable both during (in an interactional sense) and at the end (i.e. the outcome or 'content' must be perceived as just).

However, mediation has only limited potential to meet the needs of parties who have been frustrated or have simply not had their needs met in the course of usual workplace activity. Mediation is but one form of intervention within the complex operation of the organisation (including plays of power and politics) and of course the organisation itself is set within a wider economic, social and political context. This is made clearer when considering the following model of organisational justice.

Nabatchi et al. (2007) have extended earlier models of organisational justice to develop a model more applicable to the study of workplace mediation, one in which 'justice relationships' include several lines of interaction between the mediator and disputants and the disputants themselves. This model includes six factors for the measurement of justice:

- distributive justice, that is satisfaction with the outcome of a mediation
- procedural justice type 1, that is perceptions of the fairness of the procedural aspects of the mediation process
- procedural justice type 2, that is perceptions of the work (the 'procedural enactment') of the mediator
- informational justice, that is covering explanations of decision making procedures
- interpersonal justice (disputant to disputant), that is whether one has listened to the other person and whether they have listened to you (in other words, the parties have listened to and understood each other and a dialogue has been attempted)
- interpersonal justice (disputant to mediator), that is whether the mediator helped the parties to understand each others' viewpoints

This model has been developed and tested in the context of the United States Postal Service (USPS) REDRESS transformative mediation scheme.[2] It is possible to simplify and summarise this 'six factor model' as follows: is the mediation process and outcome fair, is the mediator impartial and non-judgemental, and has the mediator facilitated an exploratory dialogue between the parties? From the perspective of the mediator's role, this all may be further condensed into a concern about how the mediator has worked with the parties throughout the mediation process (in the

---

[2] REDRESS stands for Resolve Employment Disputes, Reach Equitable Solutions Swiftly and is the United States Postal Service's employment mediation program.

joint meeting(s) in particular), and how the mediator's influence may have materially affected the final outcome of the mediation. In conclusion, a fair and just process may be measured by whether the parties have enjoyed an opportunity for dialogue and arrived at a resolution, or otherwise, without undue interference from the mediator. But note that the term 'undue' represents a grey area open to a multitude of interpretations that will be considered in the chapters below.

To illustrate what may or may not be a fair and just mediation intervention, two polarised extremes will be sketched. If the mediator had led or directed the parties to agree to a quick resolution of their conflict to expedite a speedy return to productive work activity and, in so doing, had glossed over the parties' hopes for a deeper exploration of the conflict, then justice, on behalf of the parties, would not have been served. The parties would most likely not trust such a process in future. We might categorise this type of mediation as 'controlling'. Conversely, perhaps at the opposite extreme, a sensitive, humble and supportive intervention by the mediator, with him or her open to all contingent outcomes, may help parties enter into dialogue, consider the wider context surrounding their conflict, find a lasting resolution and rebuild a strong and respectful working relationship. If so, the parties would probably find that, measured against the above six-factor model, justice had been done. We might categorise this type of mediation as 'emancipatory'.

However, disturbing this ideal 'emancipatory' type is a Foucaultian notion of the microphysics of power which views 'power as exercised in a context of a complicated network of power relations and struggles' (Alvesson and Willmott 1992, p. 442). The primary concern of this book is with the ways the mediator becomes a conduit of power within any existing complex network. This idealised representation of a very successful mediation conjures the image of the mediation space as a place where organisational politics and power imbalances are, to a degree, shut out, so that parties may engage in conversation and dialogue without being distracted by the mediator. Away from the direct gaze of 'authority' we might argue that the parties are momentarily emancipated from any oppressive aspects of a hierarchical organisational structure. This representation may potentially approximate a truth where the parties are peers in the organisation. For example, two members of an organisation who have fallen out, in part due to unreasonably high working pressures, may find a common cause in mounting a critique of their managers and their organisation. It is less easy to imagine any such emancipation when parties are from different hierarchic levels, such as a manager and a member of staff. Zizek's almighty bureaucracy (see Chap. 3) looms behind the walls of the mediation room. This is why workplace mediations sometimes take place off-site in a 'neutral' venue, or at least away from the immediate place of occupation. Paradoxically, we might say that this act of physical detachment is a silent or unspoken and unacknowledged recognition of the potential for mediation to become more a medium of control than one of emancipation. It is as if we know that the parties cannot escape the demands of the organisation but we pretend that they can. This very pretence, buoyed by meeting 'in confidence' and off-site, whilst a necessary part of the mediation proposition, could assist mediation to function as an obscured or completely hidden process chiefly for the containment of conflict.

Furthermore, the concept of organisational justice delineated by Greenberg would appear to place matters of fair treatment within an acceptance of prevailing organisational norms. There is no mention of the absent presence of organisational power in the form of discursive norms of behaviour. Indeed most of us go to work, accept an employment contract and by and large abide by the rules of the organisation. Our concerns for being treated justly do not usually extend to any fundamental critique of these rules and norms. However, when conflict arises, norms are often destabilised and rendered open to question. Questions of justice within the process and outcome of a mediation intervention may be brought into focus and become sensitised. The way the mediator behaves may open up or close down understandings of what may amount to a just outcome. Hence, within the confines of the above seemingly straightforward concepts of organisational justice, workplace mediation may be able to carve out a social space conceived in an emancipatory or even democratic light, one that could broaden the notion of organisational justice and connect it with wider societal questions of justice.

As already noted, Bennett (2012) points out that mediation, just by giving the parties to a dispute a say in the process and outcome of conflict resolution, is a 'more "democratic" approach' (p. 3) than alternative

4 Political Awareness and Dialogue

methods such as litigation, arbitration or conciliation. Ridley-Duff and Bennett (2011) assert that it is also one with potential to question the 'legitimacy of hierarchical power' (p. 115, cited by Bennett 2012, p. 5). Ridley-Duff and Bennett (2010) have further argued that when mediation seeks to help disputing parties recover a workable relationship it 'errs … towards a Marxian perspective on emancipation and transformation' (p. 9). They identify mediation as a force for direct democracy in the workplace, one that

> provides a framework within which the appropriateness of social norms, and the underlying interests that support them, can be more freely questioned and discussed (p. 10).

In order to arrive at this view, Ridley-Duff and Bennett draw upon Gramscian and Lukesian concepts of hegemonic control whereby the values and beliefs of the ruling elite shape the thoughts and feelings of the wider population. They argue that facilitative and transformative mediation can disrupt this hegemony if, out of conflict, alternative agendas may be put forward. They suggest that

> [c]onflicts are not simply focussed on negotiations to re-stabilise the status quo, but are treated as *transformative* with the potential to redistribute power (p. 4).

This view of workplace mediation as a potentially radical intervention is plausible and strongly echoes Lederach (2003), and it invites an extended consideration. Bennett is an academic/practitioner but many of those who mediate are likely to be unaware of or even opposed to mediation's propensity for radicalism. One practitioner in a research seminar was reported to have 'observed light-heartedly that employers … might be surprised to find they [mediators] had Marxist tendencies' (Branney 2013, p. 9). This apparent contradiction of opinion may be unpicked in two ways. First, the claims of emancipation and transformation, which are in any case modest, can be further contextualised and brought into perspective. Second, in Chaps. 5, 6 and 7, specific styles of mediation intervention will be examined and interpreted to assess any present influence that either tends to support containment of conflict and hence the status-quo or may, alternatively, open up the possibility for a deeper assessment of the context in which conflict arises. This has some potential to lead ultimately to recognition by the parties of the need for a redistribution of power. This would imply an emancipatory transformation, as Cloke notes, from hierarchy towards heterarchy.

Emancipation in Workplace Mediation?

When an individual signs an employment contract, it is assumed that this is done freely, of their own will. There is a purported equality between the employer and employee, although this depends upon whether the market happens to be skewed in favour of the 'buyer' or the 'seller'.[3] Also, as Graeber (2014) points out, this is 'an agreement between equals in which both agree that once one of them punches a clock, they won't be equals anymore' (p. 120). To imagine one possible situation, if the employee subsequently argues with the manager and comes into conflict, mediation may afford a situation in which they both may talk together on more equal terms. The manager may choose to leave his/her cloak of positional authority at the door to the mediation room. Thereby he/she may listen to the member of staff and reflect deeply upon the staff member's criticism of his/her behaviour. As such, mediation may represent a temporary emancipation from an ordinarily unequal relationship. On finding a resolution (or otherwise) and returning to work the unequal status of the staff member is re-established.

In order to understand more broadly what, if any, emancipatory effects are latent in mediation it is necessary to further define some of the significant surrounding concepts. Emancipation loosely refers to the securing of equality by those suffering inequality. The 'Marxian perspective' referenced above may be traced through the Critical Theory of the Frankfurt School (Farganis 2004). Emancipation is a

---

[3] This observation glosses over arguments about the commodification of labour and the extraction of surplus value. See Harvey (2015), *Seventeen contradictions and the end of capitalism*, (London: Profile Books).

process through which individuals and groups become freed from repressive social and ideological conditions. (Alvesson and Willmott 1992, p. 432)

Thus, by means of a critical understanding of oneself and one's social conditions it may be possible to liberate the self from a system of ideas (i.e. an ideology) viewed as repressive and promulgated by a leadership or ruling elite that holds dominance over the society (i.e. a hegemony). These concepts from sociology and politics may at first seem far removed from the activity of the workplace mediator and the 'light-hearted' rebuttal of one practitioner comes to mind again. However, organisations and people in them are influenced, shaped and formed by, and in turn are formative of, ideological systems. Organisations are cultural entities, where 'culture' is understood as all the things that we learn from each other that are sustained and become tradition. Of course organisations are permeable. Ideologies criss-cross the social sphere and the institutions within it. The parties and the mediator are actors within these systems. Their language, their social practices and norms of behaviour form a *discourse* of what is 'natural' and perceived as 'normal' in the day-by day activities and relationships of a given organisation.

If we begin from a presumption that contemporary workplaces are sites of various forms and varying degrees of oppression and that this 'reality' is glossed over by ideological conditions, then emancipation would be the escape from such oppression. These ideological conditions are said to convince most people much of the time that even where feelings of repression occur this is nevertheless the normal and natural way of things. Or at least there is nothing that can be done about them. One contemporary example might be that the current disparities in pay levels, with senior executives commanding salaries hundreds of times higher than workers at the bottom of the hierarchy, tend to go unchallenged even in so called 'progressive' organisations, such as large scale consumer cooperatives.

Against such a backcloth alluded to by this example, it is hard to imagine a mediation intervention holding emancipatory potential. However, the observations made by Bennett and Ridley-Duff surely hold true. Mediation processes do give people a say in the resolution of workplace disputes and mediation does afford a framework within which social norms and their supporting interests may be debated and questioned. Lederach and Cloke also highlighted the links between 'voice' and justice. But it is probable that mediation processes, which have limited penetration within workplace culture, will only potentially result in very small, transient shifts in hierarchical relationships. As mentioned above, any potential shift that is realised may be deemed less an emancipation and more what Alvesson and Willmott (1992) have termed a micro-emancipation. This term refers to the possible formation of temporary spaces of resistance to dominant ideologies, spaces where people may collectively engage in more reflective political and emotional consideration of histories, differences and the wider contexts in which action is taken. A mediation process does create a temporary space, and because it is established for people to discuss their conflict, it is a politically-charged space replete with unanswered questions. Whether it becomes a site open to the possibility of micro-emancipation for its participants hinges upon the discursive, interlocutory action that occurs within the space. Thus, the recurring question posed by this book is this: does the style of mediating re-enact and mirror the prevailing discourses within an organisation or, alternatively, leave the space open for parties to question and thereby potentially disturb the ideologies and hegemony established by an organisation's discursive formation? For the mediation space to be one of a critically reflective questioning of differences within the wider context of the conflict, a form of dialogic engagement must be presupposed. In the next section it will be argued that it is relevant to reactivate 'dialogue' as a primary aspiration of any mediation process.

On Dialogue

The Place of Dialogue Within Mediation Practice

> Our mediation model grew out of Quaker processes for finding the "sense of the meeting," where the group as a whole tries to discern the right action to take.

Thus Beer and Stief (1997, p. 8) trace their Philadelphia Quaker roots in the 'Mediator's Handbook' first published in 1982. Collins (2002) explains that 'in the Quaker meeting … there is no one meaning being striven for', and that '[d]ialogue depends on difference and difference depends on the other' (p. 295). However, whilst Beer and Stief refer to their roots in a practice of dialogue, they still conceive of the purpose of mediation, when resolving workplace and community disputes, as a negotiation aimed at settlement. The literature on mediation practice, as demonstrated by the definitions of mainstream, facilitative mediation cited in Chap. 1, all similarly emphasise problem-solving and settlement and thereby seem to relegate the possibility of dialogue to the status of a by-product (albeit a fortuitous one) of the mediation encounter. Cloke (2001) does recognise that 'dialogue forms part of most mediation processes' (p. 176) but differentiates between the two. Drawing on David Bohm, he describes dialogue as 'thinking *together*, a kind of "participatory consciousness"' (p. 175). In Cloke's view, mediation 'focuses on finding solutions' whereas dialogue is about 'clarification, de-escalation, and improved understanding' (p. 176). He seems to imply that mediation is a job to be done, whilst dialogue is about 'adjusting rather than resolving differences' (p. 176). Nevertheless, he does seek to bring an ambition for dialogue into his mediation practice. Bush and Folger (2005), who reject 'problem-solving' or finding solutions, implicitly link their 'transformative' practice to a form of dialogue that rests upon the human desire and 'capacity for agency and empathy' (p. 253). The transformative method, supporting shifts in 'empowerment' and 'recognition', would appear to create an atmosphere conducive for the emergence of dialogue. Narrative mediation, somewhat differently, seeks to encourage what is termed dialogue through astute questioning by the mediator, as the meanings of conflict narratives are picked apart and defused (Winslade and Monk 2001). But the concept of dialogue as a 'participatory consciousness' does present a challenge to the more instrumental approach of facilitative, problem-solving mediation, on the one hand, and to the relational models of transformative and narrative mediation on the other. (Chapter 6 will examine these relational models in more detail.)

Cloke's logic of a formula of mediation (as solution-finding) with the possible addition of dialogue may be usefully reversed. It can start with the aspiration of dialogue and then later, as necessary, resort to 'problem-solving' in varying degrees, subject to the wishes of the parties. By supporting parties to work towards dialogue, as a primary rather than a secondary objective, the parties will themselves often engage in unprompted solution-finding, and the mediator is less likely to inadvertently press his/her own solutions (consciously or otherwise) upon the parties. Mediation, from the mediator's perspective, can be viewed in two parts, with the mediator working to open space for dialogue and the parties choosing how and when to search out resolutions. Of course this requires that the mediator must respect the parties' capacity for constructive engagement rather than treat them as if they were immature or recalcitrant. Moreover, directive styles of mediation intervention are likely to smother, as opposed to enhance, scope for dialogue, although this will depend, to some degree, upon what our beliefs are about the very meaning of the term 'dialogue', which will now be investigated further.

Meanings of 'Dialogue'

Socrates, according to Plato, was challenging in his interlocution with others and comfortable with a proactive disposition toward debate and dialogue. In the preface to his translation of 'The Great Dialogues of Plato', W.H.D. Rouse noted that

> Socrates himself described his object as that of a midwife, to bring other men's (sic) thoughts to birth, to stimulate them to think and to criticise themselves, not to instruct them. (Warmington and Rouse 1956, preface)

It is believed that Socrates ultimately alienated himself from many members of his community, albeit they were perhaps those deserving of criticism but least able to harness it. To help others criticise themselves implies a stance of at least subtle judgement, which may be more the role of the mediator as 'detective' or as 'counsellor', and perhaps not the role of the non-directive mediator. Thus, the role of a more non-directive mediator might be described as a humble "midwife" of dialogue, in that the mediator defers to the parties and seeks to understand the conflict through their eyes. It is this curiosity that helps the mediator to model dialogical behaviour. However, the concept of 'dialogue' is caught up in obscured assumptions about the agency of the interlocutors and about the influence of power relations upon them. It is questionable whether we really are free spirits who can easily choose to participate in dialogic interaction, even if we set to one side our conflict-heightened, emotional states, which would tend to militate against this. From the following consideration of various meanings of dialogue, which will take account of issues of power and agency, a qualified confirmation of the value of an aspiration of dialogue for mediation practice will now be offered.

A fascination with mediation may begin with an awareness of how difficult and yet possible it is, in *limited* ways, to enter into 'dialogue' with others. Bohm (1999) described a 'dialogue' as a stream of shared meaning. He sketched out a 'vision of dialogue' in the following manner:

> I'm looking at your assumptions and my assumptions. They're all suspended. I'm not deciding they are right or wrong. Or, if I think I prefer mine, well, that's OK. But I'm still looking at the meaning of what you say. And therefore we share a common meaning. (Bohm 1994, p. 205)

This concept of dialogue is about exploration rather than agreement and demands a sense of selfless participation in which persuasion is foregone. As such, this definition captures the mediator's hopes for parties to emerge from conflict and dispute by means of hearing themselves and listening to others in a profound, dialogic way. Is this too much to ask? It would be ideal if parties could desist from defending their own position. Because of its attractiveness, the idealism of 'dialogue' is found quite commonly. Although, as indicated, conceptions of dialogue, at times, overlook the disruptive influence of power.

Gergen et al. (2004) survey several definitions of dialogue. They agree that 'most contemporary analyses of dialogue [are] derived from an ideal form of relationship' (p. 41). For example, they cite Putnam and Fairhurst (2001), who define dialogue as 'a mode of communication that builds mutuality through awareness of others' by use 'of genuine and authentic discourse, and reliance on the unfolding interaction' (p. 116 cited in Gergen et al., p. 41). This notion of authenticity in discourse suggests a belief in the sovereign agency of individuals. Gergen et al. also quote Eisenberg and Goodall (1993), who see dialogue as 'providing parties with a chance to speak and be heard and to challenge the traditional positioning of authority' (p. 9 cited by Gergen et al., p. 41). Such a challenging stance would not accommodate a non-directive mediation style but it does introduce an aspect of power. Thirdly, and of interest, they note the view of Hawes (1999) that dialogue is a 'praxis for mediating competing and contradictory discourses' (p. 229). Hawes recognises 'discourse' as the stuff of power and struggle '[I]nsofar as it is possible for dialogue to break apart and dissolve into violence', (p. 230). Again this view recognises how power may subvert dialogue and it also begs the question of how non-directive mediation might work with and reveal competing discourses.

Gergen et al. (2004) observe that these definitions are normatively imbued with values and therefore they prefer to offer 'an elemental descriptive definition' of dialogue as 'discursive co-ordination' (pp. 41–42). This phrase, born of their social constructionist philosophy, distinguishes itself from what might be termed an everyday conception of conversation in which individuals create thoughts and opinion and engage in debate. Thus, for Gergen et al., dialogue is a form of co-ordinated action, embedded in context, culture and history, and dependent upon interactional influences of momentary 'movements of the speakers bodies, tone of voice and physical proximity' (p. 43). Above all they see dialogue as publicly co-ordinated and not as an emanation of language originating from within the minds of individuals to form intersubjective connections.

Despite this descriptive, constructionist spin on dialogue, it would seem that Gergen et al. themselves return to a more normative, value-based concept they call 'transformative dialogue [which] is essentially aimed at facilitating the collaborative construction of new realities' (p. 56). The term 'collaborative' used here seems to hold both a moral connotation as well as an instrumental one. Such an idea of 'transformative dialogue' again moves in the direction of an ideal, finding echoes with the view of Bohm (1994) in which the shared, communicative relationship partially dissolves the sense of self. This form of communication requires the speakers to yield up a desire to assert their own view as more correct than an 'other's' view. However, Gergen et al. (p. 56) note that organisational relations of power may prevent forms of dialogue that could otherwise lead to change in organisations. Mediators may hold up this ideal of dialogic behaviour as a beacon and yet they should not pretend that power, as a conditioning factor of any mediation setting, is absent.

The Impossibility, yet Necessity, of a Pursuit of Dialogue

To be able to attempt to hold a dialogue that speaks to power would seem to be a precondition for working through a conflict. But much mediation practice, which sets out a primary goal of achieving settlement, is often carried out as if a relative equality of power between parties is assumed. This is because the question of hierarchical power is often silent.[4] When the mediator does not support the expression of competing discourses and disparities of power it is possible that the mediation process is more likely to result in the coercion or disciplining of the weaker party. This problem may be addressed by a mediation approach that both models dialogue and speaks to issues of power. Here it must be noted that speaking to power does not amount to a direct attempt to equalise an uneven power relationship.

However, there is a danger in privileging the aim of dialogue above that of settlement if dialogue is conceived simply as a benign conversation in which once again issues of power go unrecognised. Therefore, a pursuit of *an aspiration* of dialogue is favoured but with the following warning. A blind and uncritical pursuit of 'dialogue' may presuppose existent, idealised symmetrical power relations of a Habermasian ideal speech situation coupled with the 'counterfactual (humanist) ideal of the

---

[4] Anecdotally there is a belief, arising out of community mediation, that even when an imbalance is obviously apparent, the mediator should not in any case interfere. To do so risks undermining impartiality. Bush and Folger (2005) do not endorse use of the mediation process to rebalance power in an asymmetrical relationship, whereas Moore (2003) most emphatically does. Of course in practice a mediator cannot affect contextual structures of power that exist around a given conflict situation, although a practicing workplace mediator once explained how she would take the powerful party (the boss) to one side and challenge them to behave better in order to open a possibility of finding a resolution. If there is a disparity in the parties' abilities to express themselves, the mediator can choose to assist one party to better articulate their interests without compromising their impartiality.

autonomous agent' (Willmott 1994, p. 116). If neither of these assumptions—an equality of power between each party, and the sovereign agency of each party—is valid, but their invalidity is somehow hidden, the concept of 'dialogue' must become fantastical. Thus, the mediator may think, 'I know very well that communication is broken and perverted, but still … (I believe and act as if the ideal speech situation is already realised)' (Zizek 2006, p. 260). Zizek (2006) calls this a 'fetishist logic of the ideal' in which fantasy obscures an 'ethics of the real' (pp. 259–260). If, in workplace mediation, this fantasy remains unacknowledged, 'dialogue' may become employed as an ideological norm. A mediator who assumes both he and the parties possess a fully responsible, self-governing agency may be vulnerable to an acceptance of this ideological fantasy of 'dialogue'. Should such a blinkered concept of 'dialogue' be held to be the primary scheme of value, workplace mediation may simply become a mechanism for the institutional reintegration of supposedly autonomous but recalcitrant spirits. Mediation may thus be reduced to a therapy of containment in which parties are exhorted to discuss their differences but ultimately obliged to bury them and get on with the job.

Dialogue, in which one's own opinion is suspended so that we may listen without persuasion and find an understanding of the other, requires a humble, concerned and selfless engagement. Thus, the mediator may listen and reflect the parties' concerns and feelings but, in contradiction to a wholly selfless stance, there is also a need for the mediator to consider the substance of each parties' perception of the conflict. This requires the mediator to evaluate and judge the conflict stories (not the parties) in order to, at times, re-articulate their views of each other. The mediator thus finds an understanding of the parties' stories from within his or her own experience.

The mediator as subject, therefore, attempts to move around a self-identity that is open and fluid, escaping an everyday illusion of self, in order to fully embrace an understanding of each party. Yet the mediator is also paradoxically grounded in a sense of agency that apperceives their stories from within in a learned, cultural context. (This tension is further examined in Chap. 7.) This model of mediation necessarily functions from within an ontological worldview in which the mediator as 'subject' is, to a significant extent, socially constructed rather than viewed as a person centred around an essentially unique identity, freely interacting with an objective external reality. An insightful critique of the illusion of 'free' agency as very often one's 'normal' mode of awareness, made by Willmott, leads to a more nuanced understanding of the dialogic mediator style being advocated here.

Willmott (1994) describes how the assumed free agent of modernity anxiously searches for a sense of some anchoring identity, which opens up this agent to subjectification by prevailing discursive power. Subjection, Foucault writes:

> categorises the individual, marks him by his (sic) own individuality, attaches him to his own identity, imposes a law of truth upon him which he must recognise and which others must recognise in him. (Foucault 1982, p. 781, cited by Willmott, p. 105)

Foucault's project is to resist this subjectification and yet, as Willmott explains, Foucault traps us in a deconstructive process of perpetually undermining power relations despite the fact that we remain subjected to them. Willmott acknowledges Foucault's suggestion that escape from the subjection of power and knowledge relations might come by means of a new form of subjectivity that denies the individuality of humanism. But Foucault, it seems, does not pursue what this 'new paradigm of human freedom' (Fraser 1989, p. 50 cited by Willmott p. 115) might look like. Willmott finds an answer in a post-dualistic analysis of agency that does not separate mind and body, but rather than simply denying human agency, regards it as 'a complex, contradictory and shifting process that is open to many possible modes of being' (p. 117). In addition Willmott argues that Habermassian communicative action requires 'the development of a selfless ... mode of being' (p. 116) in which thought, mind and body merge and in which we do not strive and scheme for benefits for the self misconceived as an autonomous being. This thought is also well captured by Rahnema (1990), who advocates an ideal of an intransitive disposition to the other. '[A]ny transitive form of participation—that is interested participation—becomes destructive of the intrinsic act of relating' (pp. 221-223). From a religious perspective, Buber (2002, p. 6) describes dialogue as a form of embodiment in which 'a genuine change from communication to communion' occurs.[5] Referring again to a Quaker mode of dialogue, Burson (2002) describes 'striving to listen carefully to the verbal and non-verbal questions that others are posing from their own depths (p. 28). In practices entailing the 'self-knowledge of no self' (Willmott, p. 121), a paradoxically agentless agency may at times momentarily shrug off a Foucaultian, perpetual subjection to discourses of power/knowledge and also realise a state of being in which dialogue and communicative action become possible.

By decentring our sense of identity we may also recognise 'thoughts' that play through the body rather than originate from within it. This brings to mind Bohm's concept of dialogue (Bohm 1994, 1999), in which people in relation become that relation rather than two or more distinct points in conversation, tied together in shared thought. According to Bohm (1994) it is "[t]hought as a system" (pp. 163–169) that fools us into believing, in our own autonomous agency, to believe that 'I' am an identity. (Some would argue that 'memory' also significantly contributes to this belief.) Such a belief can only serve to obstruct a selfless engagement in dialogue. The mediator who becomes selfless, who casts off an illusion of autonomy and resists the fixing of identity through processes of subjectification, is best able to afford support for dialogue to emerge between conflicted parties. But of course this represents an idealised and rarified conception of behaviour distant from daily 'realities' of antagonism and conflict, 'realities' that the mediator also needs to be cognisant of. Moreover, whatever is achievable by the mediator, dialogue by definition can only be initiated by two or more corporeal individuals as a voluntary, collective social activity. It is however imaginable, in rare and fleeting moments, that something that feels like dialogue may sometimes be experienced. For this reason the aspiration of dialogue is centrally important for the mediation project and it would appear perverse to act in ways that could obstruct potential for its emergence.

So far an ideal of dialogue that is important for mediation but often based upon unspoken assumptions of humanism and symmetrical power

---

[5] Whilst Buber (2002) speaks of dialogue in terms of a mutual connection that is unreserved and open-hearted, his essentialist view does not seem to encompass selflessness so much as a stripping of the self of artifice.

relations has been critiqued. By means of this critique another ideal of selfless engagement has re-emerged that is not very different from the one we started with. What has been stressed, however, is the danger of an imagined dialogue that does not address issues of power and ontology. Yet still, multiple discourses of Western culture regenerate our sovereign identities and our dualisms between mind/body, subject/object, observer/observed, problem/solution and mediator/party and draw us back to the paradoxical security and anxiety of our egoistic selves. This condition is often a starting point for any mediation encounter since when we are in conflict we have usually withdrawn inwards to a defence of the viewpoints and narratives invested in our senses of identity.

These different yet related notions of dialogue, the Socratic, that of Bohm and those recounted by Gergen et al., nevertheless encapsulate aspects of the intent and the behaviour of the idealised, non-directive mediator. Such mediators, by striving for dialogue, hope to help create a meeting space in which forms of dialogue between parties may have a chance of occurring. In this definition of mediation, the mediator seeks to help conflicted parties to meet and talk with each other, hopefully dialogically, in order to largely enact their own chosen changes to their existing relationship and/or their feelings about it and themselves. Hence the mediators, that is, third parties, may seek to enact for themselves a resolution of two contradictory impulses, in which they both strive, in dialogical exchange, for a self-knowledge of no-self and also actively reflect upon contrasting and competing discourses (i.e., recursive representations of power) and contextual causes of conflict that are surfaced by the parties. Thereby, the mediator may engage in meaningful communication with the parties yet maintain a humble position in order not to interfere with the more significant inter-party communication. To be directive or not to be directive, that is the question. It would seem a paradox that the mediator could do both. However, the mediator is never wholly non-directive and can seek to limit and make transparent the interventions that are relatively more directive.

In any case, the striving for a perfect 'dialogue', for communicative action, would seem beyond reach. There can never be an equality of power or the complete absence of antagonism between parties. This thought conjures the idea of 'dialogue' being an 'empty signifier', an attractive mirage that dissolves as we approach it. An 'empty signifier' is defined by Torfing (1999) as '[a] signifier without a signified' (p. 301). He explains this as a word that is over-coded and means everything and nothing, 'as the signifieds slide under the signifier' (p. 301). The notion of an 'empty signifier' is further described by Reyes (2005) as something that promotes

> a particular and ideologically loaded notion as a universal panacea to the fundamental lack that prevents society from achieving its full realization (p. 242).

Thus, the practice of 'dialogue' may in and of itself represent an impossible mode of being in which it is believed that its widespread realisation would significantly reduce much of the conflict experienced in the world. The ability for humans to selflessly and harmoniously coexist is the desired goal, but harmony is fundamentally 'lacking' and the practice of dialogic communication therefore promises to fulfil this desire and make good this 'lack'. As Glynos and Howarth (2007) explain,

> [i]t is because the master [or empty] signifier simultaneously promises a meaning, and yet withholds it, that subjects can be politically engaged (p. 131).

Hence, it is valuable to engage with an ideal of dialogue and to be guided in mediation practice by a kind of beacon of dialogue whilst in the same moment realising its full achievement to be impossible. In identifying with an 'enigma that promises meaning' (Glynos and Howarth 2007, p. 130) the mediator may recognise mediation as a political act dealing with antagonisms inherent in social relations from which outcomes are always uncertain. In this recognition of impossibility and uncertainty, the act of mediating might become an inherently ethical act. It is ethical because the mediator becomes selflessly absorbed in listening, suspending judgment of the parties, but necessarily works with them to assess and understand different perspectives. In this unbiased assessment the mediator holds to an enjoyment of the uncertain and the contestable until the parties decide upon a new (temporary) certainty. Pursuit of 'dialogue' may then become less fantastical as it mobilises parties and mediators in a collaborative search for understanding with recognition that, at the root, uncertainty will abound until a new provisional objectivity is constructed. To follow Critchley (2004), the parties and the mediators may, through discussion, render the interaction of hidden hegemonic power explicit, transforming that which appears 'natural' into something contestable and open to interpretation. It is by this intrinsic and explorative openness to uncertainty, which brings an inquiring and concerned humility to the mediation meeting, that workplace mediation might democratically operate in the service of fairness and justice. Parties in conflict would welcome the support of a mediator so disposed. In the next chapter this vision of an explorative style of mediation will be contrasted with a detailed study of the more mainstream, facilitative approach, in which options seem to be closed down, rather than opened up, in the struggle for settlement.

References

Acas (Advisory, Conciliation and Arbitration Service). (2006). *Acas London newsletter*. Issue 6. London: Acas.
Acas (Advisory, Conciliation and Arbitration Service). (2014). *Reframing resolution—Managing conflict and resolving individual disputes in the contemporary workplace*. Acas Policy Discussion Papers March. London: Acas. Retrieved from http://www.acas.org.uk/index.aspx?articleid=4701&q=reframing+resolution+policy+paper
Alvesson, M., & Willmott, H. (1992). On the idea of emancipation in management and organization studies. *Academy of Management Review, 17*(3), 432–464.
Beer, J. E., & Stief, E. (1997). *The mediator's handbook* (3rd ed.). Gabriola Island, British Columbia, Canada: New Society Publishers.
Bennett, A. (2012). *Mediation: A critical analysis of the changing nature of dispute resolution in the workplace*. Paper to BUIRA Conference June 28–30, 2012 held at Bradford Universtiy.
Billig, M. (2001). Discursive, rhetorical and ideological Messages. In M. Wetherall, S. Taylor, & S. J. Yates (Eds.), *Discourse theory and practice: A reader* (pp. 210–221). London: Sage Publications.
Bohm, D. (1994). *Thought as a system*. London: Routledge.

Bohm, D. (1999). *On dialogue*. London: Routledge.
Branney, V. (2013). Grievance procedures and workplace mediation: The case for peaceful coexistence. Retrieved from www.uclan.ac.uk/research/explore/.../virginia_review_of_series.pdf
Buber, M. (2002[1947]). *Between man and man*. London: Routledge.
Burson, M. C. (2002). Finding clarity in the midst of conflict: Facilitating dialogue and skillful discussion using a model from the Quaker tradition. *Group Facilitation: A Research and Applications Journal, 4*, 23–29.
Bush, R. A. B., & Folger, J. P. (2005). *The promise of mediation: The transformative approach to conflict*. San Francisco: Jossey-Bass Inc.
Cloke, K. (2001). *Mediating dangerously: The frontiers of conflict resolution*. San Francisco: Jossey Bass Inc.
Collins, P. (2002). Both independent and interconnected voices: Bhaktin among the Quakers. In N. Rapport (Ed.), *British subjects: An anthropology of Britain*. Oxford: Berg.
Critchley, S. (2004). Is there a normative deficit in the theory of hegemony? In S. Critchley & O. Marchart (Eds.), *Laclau: A critical reader* (pp. 113–122). London: Routledge.
Deutsch, M. (2006). Introduction. In M. Deutsch, P. T. Coleman, & E. C. Marcus (Eds.), *The handbook of conflict resolution: Theory and practice* (2nd ed., pp. 1–20). San Francisco: Jossey-Bass Inc.
Eisenberg, E. M., & Goodall, H. L., Jr. (1993). *Organizational communication: Balancing creativity and constraint*. New York: St Martin's Press.
Farganis, J. (2004). *Readings in social theory: The classic tradition to post-modernism* (4th ed.). New York: McGraw-Hill.
Foucault, M. (1982). The subject and power. In H. L. Dreyfus & P. Rainbow (Eds.), *Foucault: Beyond structuralism and hermeneutics*. Brighton, England: Harvester.
Fraser, N. (1989). *Unruly practices: Power, discourse and gender in contemporary social theory*. Cambridge: Polity.
Gergen, K. J., Gergen, M. M., & Barrett, F. J. (2004). Dialogue: Life and death of the organization. In D. Grant, C. Hardy, C. Oswick, & L. L. Putnam (Eds.), *The SAGE handbook of organizational discourse*. London: Sage Publications.
Glynos, J., & Howarth, D. (2007). *Logics of critical explanation in social and political theory*. Abingdon, England: Routledge.
Graeber, D. (2014). *Debt: The first 5000 years*. London: Melville House Publishing.

Greenberg, J. (1987). A taxonomy of organizational justice theories. *Academy of Management Review, 12*(1), 9–22.

Harvey, D. (2015). *Seventeen contradictions and the end of capitalism*. London: Profile Books Ltd.

Hawes, L. C. (1999). The dialogics of conversation: Power, control and vulnerability. *Communication Theory, 9*(3), 229–264.

Howarth, D. (2000). *Discourse*. Buckingham: Open University Press.

Kressel, K. (2006). Mediation revisited. In M. Deutsch, P. T. Coleman, & E. C. Marcus (Eds.), *The handbook of conflict resolution: Theory and practice* (pp. 726–756). San Francisco: Jossey-Bass Inc.

Lederach, J. P. (2003). *The little book of conflict transformation*. Intercourse, PA: Good Books.

McAllister, B. (2002). Quoted in interview in *Mediation Matters*, Issue 70, June 2002. Published by Mediation UK: Bristol (now disbanded).

Moore, C. W. (2003). *The mediation process: Practical strategies for resolving conflict* (3rd ed.). San Francisco: Jossey-Bass Inc.

Mouffe, C. (2000). *Deliberative democracy or agonistic pluralism*. Political Science Series No. 72. Vienna: Institute for Advanced Studies.

Nabatchi, T., Bingham, L. B., & Good, D. H. (2007). Organizational justice and workplace mediation: A six-factor model. *International Journal of Conflict Management, 18*(2), 148–174.

Putnam, L. L., & Fairhurst, G. T. (2001). Discourse analysis in organizations. In F. M. Jablin & L. L. Putnam (Eds.), *The new handbook of organizational communication: Advances in theory, research and methods*. Thousand Oaks, CA: Sage Publications.

Rahnema, M. (1990). Participatory action research: The last temptation of saint development. *Alternatives, 15*, 199–226.

Reyes, O. (2005). New labour's politics of the hard-working family. In D. Howarth & J. Torfing (Eds.), *Discourse theory in European politics: Identity, policy and governance* (pp. 231–254). Basingstoke: Palgrave Macmillan.

Ridley-Duff, R. J., & Bennett, A. J. (2010). *Mediation: Developing a theoretical framework to understand alternative dispute resolution*. Paper to British Academy of Management Conference, University of Sheffield, September 14–16.

Ridley-Duff, R. J., & Bennett, A. J. (2011). Towards mediation: Developing a theoretical framework to understand alternative dispute resolution. *Industrial Relations Journal, 42*(2), 106–123.

Saundry, R., & Wibberley, G. (2014). *Workplace dispute resolution and the management of individual conflict—A thematic analysis of 5 case studies*. Acas Research Paper Reference No. 06/14. Retrieved from www.acas.org.uk/researchpapers

Torfing, J. (1999). *New theories of discourse: Laclau, Mouffe and Zizek*. Oxford: Blackwell Publications Ltd.

Van Gramberg, B., & Teicher, J. (2005). *Managing neutrality and impartiality in workplace conflict resolution: The dilemma of the HR manager*. Retrieved from www.buseco.monash.edu.au/mgt/research/working-papers/.../wp57-05.pdf

Warmington, E. H., & Rouse, P. G. (Eds.). (1956). *The great dialogues of Plato* (W.H.D Rouse, Trans.). London: Mentor Books, The New English library, Routledge.

Willmott, H. (1994). Bringing agency (back) into organizational analysis: Responding to the crisis of (post) modernity. In J. Hassard & M. Parker (Eds.), *Towards a new theory of organization*. London: Routledge.

Winslade, J., & Monk, G. (2001). *Narrative mediation: A new approach to conflict resolution*. San Francisco: Jossey-Bass Inc.

Zizek, S. (2006). *Interrogating the real*. London: Continuum.

ID # 5

Instrumental Mediation

Levels of Awareness of Mediator Power

In the workplace, employees are under contract to obey the rules of the organisation. Eruptions of conflict are often regarded as inconvenient aberrations in normal working relationships. Senior management may not deem conflict management a priority or they may have little time to spare for it and instead maintain a focus on performance indicators that do not embrace dealing with conflict (Acas 2014). As a fallback, in compensation for a shortage of conflict management skills within management, mediation at worst may transfer responsibility for conflict from organisational causes, such as working pressures, to the individual, thus 'reinterpreting unfair treatment as an interpersonal issue' (Acas 2014, p. 9). Dolder warns of the risk that mediators who drive through compromises between parties may become 'dealmakers protected by a cloak of confidentiality' (Dolder 2004, p. 329). This pattern of the misapplication of mediation in the workplace could lead to a colonisation of mediation by the organisation that translates a benign project into a merely instrumental one. Whilst it can bring some benefits to participants, it may be primarily deployed in pursuit of organisational efficiency. The lasting effect could be to cover over deeper-rooted organisational problems of poor management practice in the widest sense. The mediation role-play material below will lend practical evidence to this theoretical analysis of the organisational colonisation of mediation. It will show how the facilitative model of mediation is highly susceptible to becoming an instrumental function, in no small part because mediators may lack a clear awareness of the power they have to influence parties in the determination of outcomes.

That the parties should *largely* determine their own outcomes is a necessary and defining aspiration of both community and workplace mediation. Such outcomes are bound to be more robust than settlements that are imposed in some way. In mainstream, facilitative mediation, which sets itself a primary goal of settlement, party self-determination and mediator neutrality are two sides of the same coin. But, if the myths of neutrality and full self-determination persist, by definition mediators will perform their task unaware of their actual influence and, at worst, they may inhibit and even obstruct the parties in their determination of outcomes. Alternatively, if these myths are dispelled but the notion of maximising self-determination is still valued, mediation may become an act of co-determination in which the mediators, aware of their influence, work to limit and even minimise it, with any persuasive affects that may arise from the mediator's own conscious or subconscious preferences being held in check. It is contended that this latter approach would help parties feel greater ownership of any resolutions achieved. However, this chapter will look at the implications for the parties of the mainstream, facilitative approach to mediation, implications that are premised upon mediator neutrality, party self-determination and a goal of settlement.

Workplace mediations can occur at all levels in an organisation's hierarchy and may involve disputes between peers or between managers and those managed. At a mediation conference, a representative of a long-established workplace mediation organisation was heard to state that, in his experience, over half of workplace mediations take place between a manager and a member of staff. This also corresponds with my own experience. Thus, anecdotally, mediator influence is very often positioned at a fulcrum of unequal power between the manager and the managed. There will of course be a dynamic of power in relations between peers in conflict, but perhaps this will be less marked than between manager and

5 Instrumental Mediation   91

line staff. The presence of the mediator makes this dynamic more complex. From the review of 'neutrality' in Chap. 2, it can be discerned that mediators hold different attitudes towards their own sense of their power as it is brought to bear upon this fulcrum or this play of power between parties. At a simple level we may broadly categorise at least four types of mediator subjectivity regarding their own awareness of their power. (Table 5.1)

Referring to the following table:

1. Some mediators may not recognise their own power and lay claim to a certain neutrality.
2. Others may be aware of the scope to influence parties and deliberately deploy their power to secure agreements. This might be said to be accepted practice in a commercial mediation setting, often referred to by the generic title 'alternative dispute resolution'. Perhaps this also applies, albeit to a lesser extent, in family mediation.
3. Some mediators appear to be both knowingly directive, at least of the mediation process, and yet paradoxically in denial of their influence,

Table 5.1 Mediator power and subjectivity

Mediator awareness of their power	Mediator belief about neutrality/ non-directiveness	Implicit approach to conflict	Aim of mediator
1 Unaware	Neutral & non-directive	Conflict should be resolved	Settlement
2 Aware	Not neutral & actively directive	Conflict should be resolved	Settlement
3 Apparent professed unawareness	Neutral and not neutral as they direct a defined process, (directiveness is opaque or hidden)	Conflict should be resolved	Settlement
4 Aware and knowingly unaware	Not neutral (aim for minimal or at times a transparent directiveness)	An opportunity in which 'interaction' may be considered and conflict can be 'explored'	'Dialogue' or improvement in 'interaction' and relationship. Settlement may follow

or somewhat blind to it. They assert that the parties find their own solution within structures and processes imposed by mediation practice, which are necessary to prevent parties regressing to destructive confrontation. Thus, for example, they may lay down hard ground rules such as 'no verbal abuse' and then apply this rule judgementally to squash expression of emotion, in order to divert parties from working through their conflict interaction themselves. On occasions when mediators have admitted that absolute neutrality is an unrealistic ideal, they have described themselves as 'multi-partial', meaning that they simultaneously advocate the divergent needs of both parties. Cloke (2001) similarly refers to omni-partiality as being on both sides. This suggests a possible confusion about the mediator role, one perhaps born of an attempt to finesse the problem of mediator influence and possibly breach the objective of impartiality. But taking a 'multi-party' stance could lead the mediator to entrench himself or herself with arguments on both sides and in so doing block as yet unthought-of interpretations of the conflict in the minds of the parties. Rather than attempt to *take* both sides, impartiality may be upheld by seeking out the fullest understanding of each conflicted perspective so that it is possible to re-present these perspectives without playing the advocate. Thus, the mediator models dialogue by suspending his/her own opinions and striving to understand the viewpoints of each antagonist. The mediator may thereby align with each party by listening attentively, acknowledging their perspectives and reflecting back an appreciation of their view, without necessarily affiliating with either of them.

4. This mode of dual alignment brings us to the fourth type of critically reflective mediator, someone who is sensitive to their own influence and seeks to maintain an awareness of the exercise of their power. By definition, the ideal of striving for critical self-awareness is an incomplete activity. Unwitting directiveness, however minimal, is always likely to arise. By striving to be self-aware, mediators may at times reduce their influence to a minimum, or on other occasions, elect to more overtly use their power by directing the attention of the parties, hopefully in a transparent way. Beyond this notion of mediator reflectiveness, such a communicative transparency may be realised by a selflessness that detaches one from any role as 'fixer' of conflict and yet immerses the de-subjected 'self' (see Willmott above) in a non-judgmental concern for the parties.

As already documented there are two main approaches within contemporary mediating, either the problem-solving or the relational type. This book deals with differences between these two as characterised in categories 3 and 4 in the above table. This chapter will examine the third formulation of mediator awareness (Chaps. 6 and 7 will look at the fourth category from the above table). This third category describes a type of mediation that holds to a belief in 'neutrality' and self-determination, whilst applying a limiting and directive process, aiming at settlement, in an assumed situation of relatively equal power relations between two autonomous individuals. When this approach is aligned with a culture of an individualised workforce, caught up in the value system of the employer, in which conflict represents a cost overhead that must be managed, a kind of teleology of problem-solving or settlement arises. All types of mediation practice have an instrumental aim of conflict resolution, but the overbearing 'end' of settlement (and even control) in facilitative, problem-solving mediation, when applied for reasons of organisational efficiency, further enhances this instrumentality. The conflict relationship is complex, political, rational and emotional and embedded in a social context, so it may remain under-explored, resulting in missed opportunities for dialogue. The question arises as to whether problem-solving mediation in the workplace serves more to contain conflict than to work with the parties to help *them* find a deeper and lasting resolution. As has been already suggested, much will depend upon what role the mediator takes and how their agency and subjectivity, conditioned by their chosen role, influences the course of a given mediation.

Investigating Facilitative, Problem-Solving Mediation Practice

An experiment (with the author as researcher) was carried out with three experienced, professional workplace mediators (two from the facilitative school and one from the transformative school) in order to look more closely at the spoken interventions that are typical. The aim was to assess whether facilitative workplace mediators may influence parties in ways possibly hidden from both the parties and the mediator and conditioned by the organisational setting. In the absence of material from live mediations, three mediators and two actors playing the parties were invited to carry out role-play mediations that were recorded on video. The conflict scenario was written so that those acting out the conflict situation could do so from a basis of their own work experience. To a large extent they were able to play themselves in their working roles.[1] Greenberg and Eskew (1993) found that role-play affords realistic material for understanding behaviour in organisations when there is a high level of subject involvement, when they play themselves and when the subjects are free to improvise and act with spontaneity within a broad set of behaviours. In the following two case studies these conditions were met so that the mediators and parties demonstrated behaviours that would have been recorded in a real mediation had it been possible to make such a recording. Following an analysis and interpretation of the video material, the participating mediators discussed the findings with the researcher. They were asked whether they thought the role-play was a realistic exercise. The facilitative mediator known anonymously as Mediator Two in the first case study responded by saying that after quite a short time into the role-play she felt that 'this does feel real'. The first facilitative mediator then said

> 'yeah I think that's right you start off feeling this is a bit artificial but once you get going you sort of almost forget that the parties aren't real and they get into role as well and they begin to feel themselves you know the emotions start to come out I think that's when it starts to feel real.'

The transformative mediator, in the second case study, then said 'in any role-play whatever reactions or behaviours the parties show could happen in real life' (Seaman 2010).

The first role-play discussed below involved the two mediators practising in the facilitative mode. The next chapter draws upon material from a second role-play with a mediator from the transformative school. Before documenting and commenting upon some extracts from

---

[1] For a defence of the research method see Seaman (2010, pp. 127–144) at http://eprints.bournemouth.ac.uk/17117/

the 'facilitative mediation' role-play, it is necessary to explain the interpretive approach used for analysis of the interventions the mediators' made.

Approach to Interpretation of the Role-Play Material

The following interpretation of the role-play concentrates upon what the mediators were 'doing' to the parties when they spoke and what could be discerned about the mediator's enacted role, compared with the espoused role, on the basis of the power displayed in their interventions. As noted above, our speech carries an ideological history because speakers 'use terms which are culturally, historically and ideologically available' (Billig 2001, p. 217). In keeping with this insight, the theoretical concept of the 'subject position' developed by both political discourse analysis (Glynos and Howarth 2007; Howarth 2005; 2000; and Torfing 1999) and by critical discourse analysis (Fairclough 2006; 2005; 2001) has been chosen to render apparent the ideological and political nature of the practice of workplace mediation displayed in the video extracts shown below.

Subject Positions

The work of Glynos and Howarth (2007), Howarth, (2000) Torfing (1999) and their former mentor Ernesto Laclau draws upon poststructural and continental philosophy. These writers' understanding of the individual as 'subject' in part makes use of the work of Jacques Lacan, which is famously obscure, many-faceted and complex. Interpreters of Lacan understand the Lacanian 'subject' as a person/place of loss or lack. Sarup explains that

> Lacan suggests that all our fantasies are symbolic representations of the desire for wholeness … for a perfect union with the Other. … desire is ontological, a struggle for wholeness rather than a sexual force. 'Desire is the metonymy of the desire to want to be.' (Sarup 1993, p. 16)

Sarup sums up Lacan's ontology thus:

> we all have a need for wholeness, a longing for a state of unity, but the achievement of plenitude is a logical impossibility. (Sarup 1993, p. 14)

This desire for wholeness impels us to acquire identity to complete ourselves. Howarth describes how Pecheux refined Althusser's Lacanian-inspired idea of interpellation whereby 'an individual brings itself into existence by *identifying* with an external object' (Howarth 2000, p. 95). Through a plurality of identifications a 'subject position' is constructed by the social actor. The actor then takes pleasure and enjoyment from the performance of a presumed, fully achieved identity, positioning (fixing) themselves as a 'subject' in relation to others and within an imagined, often stable (but innately precarious) 'social totality' (Torfing 1999, p. 14). Actors being positioned within discursive structures are at times forced to act—that is, to enact a political subjectivity. This occurs when the same discursive structures in which identity has been formed, subject to contingency, undergo dislocation and change. Hence, the subject may strive for a totality (of the self within the social) but by definition can never fully and lastingly achieve it. There is thus an ontological undecidability and a 'radical contingency'[2] (Glynos and Howarth 2007) that conditions our being in the world.

This description of the social world differs ontologically from that of Fairclough, as already noted in Chap. 3, but Fairclough presents, on the surface, a similar picture of the subject. Fairclough (2005, p. 916) argues for a 'moderately social constructivist' position in which organisations are deemed discursive and non-discursive pre-structured entities with causal powers. Persons with identities are understood as pre-constructed 'permanences' (2005, p. 923), but being socially produced, they are

---

[2] The radical contingency of social relations is described by Glynos and Howarth (2007) in the following way: 'Radical contingency opposes empirical contingency's sense of possibility with a sense of *im*possibility: the *constitutive* failure of any objectivity to attain a full identity.' (2007, p. 110.) This negative social ontology, drawn from Lacanian theory, is 'conceptualised as the disruptive presence of 'the real' in any symbolic order, that is, a presence that marks the impossibility of any putative fullness of being, whether at the level of subjects, structures or discourses.' (2007, p. 11.)

contingent and subject to change and thereby have capacity for creative agency.

The mediators, if holding to such views of subjectivity and identity, must be aware that their interventions constitute a political engagement with the parties and not simply a humanistic encounter aimed at the amelioration of conflict. Furthermore, if the mediator is sensitive to their own and the parties' formation of identity they are more likely to hold back from intervening on the basis of unnecessary and misplaced evaluations of the conflict or of the characters of the parties. Mediator 'humility' in the face of an existential uncertainty might displace an overbearing mediator expertise. A mantel of expertise is more likely to be donned when the mediator chooses to view her/himself and the parties as 'whole' autonomous individuals with 'empowered' identities rightly deserving of 'recognition' and who are temporarily disturbed by the aberration of conflict. However, if a Lacanian-inspired ontology is accepted, the purpose and ethics of mediation are transformed and political implications unfold.

Discourse theory suggests the inevitable play of power in an interactive situation such as a workplace mediation and Fairclough (2001, 2006), in particular, highlights how ideology becomes obscured in everyday interactions. Again, as noted above, he underscores how

> the exercise of power, in modern society, is increasingly achieved through ideology and more particularly through the ideological workings of language. (Fairclough 2001, p. 2)

Thus, we as subjects, positioned within our various social groupings, to a very significant degree[3] are shaped through language and discourse.

---

[3] Many philosophers, from the Buddha to Lacan, view the idea of an essential, indivisible, autonomous 'self' as illusory and yet we live our lives as though our selfhood is formed of a unique individual essence. For a discussion on identity see Glover (1991) *I: The Philosophy and Psychology of Personal Identity*. (London: Penguin). Many argue that the individuality of the subject is conditioned by our biological make-up and by our genes (Gilbert 2010). Our emotions and our corporeality may both be traced to evolutionary factors as well as 'the social'. It might be said that we are comprised of a kaleidoscope of characteristics, if not essences. There is not space within this work to discuss this. However, the power of language and discourse to significantly form the social and subjects within it will hopefully become clear in the rest of this chapter.

Aspects of Fairclough's theory have been drawn upon in order to interpret apparent behaviour depicted by mediators' spoken interventions. At a level above linguistic, grammatical detail, aspects of the naturalisation of language may be detected that afford leverage directly to ideologies and power. It is these aspects of 'naturalisation' that will be used to help interpret mediator subject positions, namely 'meaning systems', 'situation types', 'interactional routines and turn taking' (Fairclough 2001).

Hence, we may approach the mediation meeting as a 'situation type' that may reveal naturalised, ideological 'meaning systems' of the mediator (Fairclough 2001). It is argued that the 'subject position' of the paid workplace mediator is a quasi-professional role, one vested with considerable power that is obscured by the naturalisation of language and shut off from scrutiny by its private and confidential character. The mediation meeting will always represent a 'situation type' (Fairclough 2001) but this leaves the questions of what 'type' it is and what 'type' could it be. Our purpose is to reveal and explore the different aspects of mediator power that constrain the mediation setting, so that alternative styles of mediation intervention may be considered and theorised. To be able to develop a picture of the 'subject position' of the mediators in the role-play, video recordings have been examined for moments of enacted power and influence and their presenting effects. Hence, in viewing the videos, the following types of question have underpinned the identification of such moments.

How have the mediators engaged with and addressed the parties? Is it with an overt sense of expertise or with humility? Is it with respect for them as people or are they viewed primarily as employees? How are their interventions likely to affect the parties? Are their interventions 'directive'? Does it seem that their interventions tend to suppress conflict or open it up to exploration and are the circumstances of the conflict held to be contingent? Did their interventions afford any opportunities to consider aspects of identity and subjectivity played out in the conflict? Did their interventions yield any scope for the emergence of dialogue and 'learning'? Do their interventions seem imbued with a workplace/management discourse? Do they display a concern for matters organisational? Do their interventions accord with espoused principles of mediation? The following interpretation of the role-play seeks to critically and plausibly illustrate what the mediators are 'doing in saying' in contrast with both what they purport to do and what another counterfactual mediator might alternatively have done.

Note on the Mediation Context

In approaching the role-play material, it is important to recognise the innately constraining nature of all mediation settings. To state the obvious, placing one or two mediators in a room with two or more parties who are in the midst of conflict will set a conditionality of time, space and expected activity. The prominent purpose of a mediation meeting is simply to meet to talk. It is suggested that the workplace mediator's primary role should be to provide support for the ambition to hold a conversation that leads toward some mutual understanding, of each other and of the wider context of the conflict and hence, in a relative sense, away from conflict. However, as already noted, there are other motivations underlying the impetus to mediate. One of these is the organisational urgency that is felt for an early resolution. The style of mediation adopted might be regarded as a function of the necessity to expedite a resolution. For example, in an international armed conflict, an early cessation may reduce loss of life and injury. In a commercial mediation, large sums of money may be saved by pushing through a face-saving compromise. In the workplace, a successful solution may improve organisational performance, allow the commissioner to feel that mediation costs have been well spent and the mediator to feel justified in taking their fee.

First Case Study: Commentary, Analysis and Interpretation of Facilitative Role-Play

The mediators have been called in to help Chris, the manager of a local Community Advice Centre, and one of her staff, an advisor called Paul, who seem to be at loggerheads over work policy and practices. The conflict is souring relationships more widely in the office.

In workplace mediation it is not untypical for first visits to each party to be followed on the same day by the joint meeting.[4] First visits typically take an hour. These two role-played first visits ran for approximately eighteen minutes and twenty-two minutes respectively. On this occasion the first visits were held to enable the parties and the mediators to familiarise themselves with each other, so that they felt as comfortable as possible in the subsequent role-play joint meeting. This accords with a real mediation in which mediators aim to build rapport with the parties.

First Visit of the Two Facilitative Mediators with Paul

The speech text below has been edited for ease of reading. Some punctuation has been included and many repetitions, hesitations, pauses, 'you knows' and many of the fillers (such as erm and uhm) removed.[5] Some 'uh hums' and 'umms' have been retained to indicate acknowledgement or assent within the flow of the interactions.

First extract, (0 secs to 1 min 34 secs)

(1) Mediator 1: My name is (forename plus surname) this is my colleague (forename plus surname) and we are both mediators with (organisation name) okay. We've been doing the role for quite a while now and so hopefully we'll be able to give yourself and Chris some support and help today. Our understanding is that this mediation has been referred to us by your board of trustees of your charity, the local advice centre, it's about a dispute between yourself and Chris. Is that correct and are you happy to be, well happy is
(2) Paul: well I understand why we are here
(3) Mediator 1: okay so you're here voluntarily?

---

[4] Source: Workplace mediation training run in London by TCM Ltd in 2006. TCM Ltd aim to schedule a short second visit with each party separately during the morning as part of the preparation for the afternoon joint meeting.
[5] See Seaman (2010) for the original data laid out in a more literal fashion.

(4) Paul: uh hum
(5) Mediator 1: okay so you want to try and resolve the situation?
(6) Paul: yeah I can't really see what the problem is but I'm happy to kind of try and do whatever needs doing
(7) Mediator 1: okay that's cool, do you have any understanding what mediation is all about?
(8) Paul: not really no
(9) Mediator 1: shall I just sort of explain a bit and then maybe you can chip in with any questions if there is anything I've left unanswered?
(10) Paul: um hum
(11) Mediator 1: well mediation I suppose is almost like a problem solving process, we're here to help build dialogue or to help you build dialogue with Chris so that you can each better understand what the issues are and you've just said that you don't really know what the problem is
(12) Paul: uh hum
(13) Mediator 1: so that's our role, to help you maybe understand what the problem is at least from Chris's point of view and to help her understand what the problem is from your point of view, the actual process is...

Commentary and Analysis

Within the above interlocution several subtle rules of this particular mediation are courteously, yet rapidly, established. In line (1) the introduction is quite formal; the mediators' organisation is named and their own and their organisation's expertise is asserted. The mediator then emphasises her own and her colleague's experience explicitly. A clear message is conveyed that the mediators are experts and they say 'we'll be able to ... support and help ...', implying that they will help to find a form of resolution. Whether or not they always succeed, this is their trajectory. Their authority to do this is further underscored by noting that it was the board of trustees who referred the dispute to mediation. Hence 'subject positions' are established for both the mediators and the party (Torfing 1999; Fairclough 2001; Howarth 2005). The mediators view themselves as experts who have been appointed to do a job. Their expert position derives from their experience, their employing organisation and their authorisation by the party's employer. The party is placed in the 'subject position' of receiver of the mediators' help. As such, a relationship of power is established (Fairclough 2001), forming an enunciative modality (Howarth 2005). This is not the position of a humble mediator.

An alternative opening approach could have been to suggest that the purpose of the meeting is to find out if the party would like to make use of a mediation process and to discuss what that might be, i.e. to pose the question of whether mediation, and what type of mediation, would be of use to the party. Such an 'act of saying' (Howarth 2005) might have subverted the 'interactional routine' and its enveloping 'situation type' (Fairclough 2001) played out within this workplace mediation. The party might have still felt constrained to comply in accepting an invitation to a mediation process but the mediator could nevertheless have been able to position herself as a follower of the emergent expressions and apparent needs of the party. Thus, the opening session could have aligned much more with practices described by Bush and Folger (2005).

In line (3) the mediator asked 'so you're here voluntarily'. She presents Paul with a rhetorical question based upon her own assumption that Paul is here voluntarily. Alternatively, she could have inquired about how he feels about being here, again as a transformative practitioner would have (Bush and Folger 2005). She then continues in this questioning mode in line (9) to assert that Paul wants to resolve the "situation". By leading this interaction she has asserted a condition of the meeting. This further reinforces the operation of a particular 'interactional routine' (Fairclough 2001) in which one party holds a role of authority, if only as referee. Furthermore, within this 'routine' it can be seen that 'mediation' has been meaningfully equated with 'resolution' of a problem.

Thus, in a very few seconds the mediator has established her authority, that there is a dispute to be resolved, that Paul wants to resolve it and that she can help to do this. Paul has had very little opportunity to speak other than to say that, on the one hand, he understands why he is here but on the other he doesn't really see what the problem is (line (6)). As noted above, there is a courteous facade to these opening moments but they can also be interpreted as a coercion of Paul into acceptance of a 'subject position' (Fairclough 2001; Howarth 2000) as a more or less willing receiver of the mediators' help. The mediator has correspondingly adopted a 'position' as an authority in resolving the dispute.

In line (11) it transpires that Paul is to be part of a problem-solving process in which he is going to be helped to understand the issues and the problem from Chris's viewpoint (line (13)). Conversely she will be helped to see his viewpoint. In some way the mediator is going to orchestrate a dialogue (line (11)). Paul has barely uttered a few words before the mediator continues to lay out a process and the ground rules that govern it. If one concept of mediation is to place parties in control of their own conversation then this 'facilitative' approach has started in a directive manner. Such an underlying directiveness contradicts an espoused intent to be neutral helpers.

Second extract, (2 mins 12 secs—3 min 14 secs)

(1) Mediator 1: the purpose of mediation is to help you and Chris come to a resolution of your problem yourselves and as I say we do that by sort of helping you to communicate better together but we we're not here to actually say well we think you're wrong and Chris is right or Chris is wrong and you're right and this is what we think the solution should be. We're here to actually help you to sort of build your own solutions and agreements. All right we might play devils advocate sometimes
(2) Paul: um hum
(3) Mediator 1: and we might with your permission make some suggestions for how you could take things forward
(4) Paul: uh hum
(5) Mediator 1: but at the end of the day its up to yourself and Chris to kind of move things forward and go back into the workplace and work together in a way that you both feel comfortable with
(6) Paul: uh hum
(7) Mediator 1: okay so we're totally impartial but for the purpose of testing out your understanding and the same for Chris, we might kind of challenge you a bit and play our devils advocate bit

(8) Paul: umm
(9) Mediator 1:   in bid to really sort of get to the nub of the …
(10) Paul: okay
(11) Mediator 1: I hope that will be okay with you? Right
(12) Paul: umm

Commentary and Analysis

In line (1) the mediator states 'the purpose of mediation' is to help the disputants to 'come to a resolution of your problem yourselves'. This is an expression of the mediator's belief in her own neutrality. However, this statement assumes that there is a definable problem and that it will be resolved. The term 'your problem' places the causation firmly with the individual parties. They are the seat of the problem. The mediators are there to help deal with this problem. Hence, the mediator has effectively set an agenda and a goal for the first party. The mediator has thereby reinforced the underlying 'rules for engagement' and extended them to preclude consideration of conflict causation (Lederach 2003; Cloke 2001) and wider responsibility for conflict that does not reside with the individual. As in the first extract, the disputant is being talked to, rather than engaged in setting the scene for the mediation meeting that follows. In this 'act of saying' (Howarth 2005) the mediator is positioned as the authority overseeing the party as transgressor. It is as if she were saying, 'you made the problem, you must fix it' and that this is what your organisation requires.

The mediator continues in line (1) to say her role is not to judge or decide how to resolve the conflict but to be impartial and to just help with communication. However, at the end of line (1) and in line (3) she undermines this stance by proposing a role as devil's advocate and suggestion maker. She has thus contradicted her own opening assertion about 'purpose' made seconds earlier and assumed a position which would necessitate a more overt exercise of judgement and opinion.

In line (5), there is a clear agenda and pressure to 'move things forward', to 'go back into the workplace' and to 'work together'. Again in line (7) a contradictory statement is made in which total impartiality, itself an impossibility, is conveyed along with the mediator's decision that she will 'kind of challenge you a bit' and play devil's advocate in order to 'get to the nub' (line (9)). The mediator has assigned herself the role of identifying and judging what the nub of the problem is. She has seemingly migrated from, a role of helping others to consider and maybe solve their conflicts themselves, to that of a person who solves conflicts.

So far a 'situation type' (Fairclough 2001) has been established in which a mediator is positioned with authority to direct an interactional routine as problem assessor with a pre-set, desired outcome of a harmonious return to work. The party is being subjected to a mediation process in which it is assumed that they accept responsibility for conflict and for its resolution, as if there are organisational mores suggesting conflict represents some sort of failure. The desired "back to work" outcome (line (5)) suggests a more material and economic basis. As noted above, it is almost as if the disputant has transgressed and the mediator is the authority assigned to rectify the situation for the benefit of the organisation rather than the parties.

A Sequence of Extracts

After checking that Paul has no further questions about the mediation process the Second Mediator invites Paul to tell his story of the 'problem'. At 3 mins 48 secs she says 'well Paul what I'd like you to do is would you be able to tell us what the situation is for you, what's been happening for you…'

Paul then tells his story. At 4 mins 15 secs Paul says that 'recently I've been getting a lot of problems from Chris about my record keeping and you know she's really been on my back, to be honest really being difficult with me, about what I have to say I regard as fairly minor and kind of trivial things…'

During Paul's explication the mediator acknowledges him by nodding and saying yeah, uhm and okay, but does not intervene until, at 5 mins 25 secs, she moves the story on by posing a question. She asks 'and what have you done about it so far with Chris because you've been here for a short while, what has happened between yourself and Chris and between then and now?'

Third extract, (5 mins 32 secs—6 mins 45 secs)

(1) Paul: yeah well we had a formal review meeting about a month five weeks into my employment and you know I'm sure she'll say herself things were running really well, I was getting good reports
(2) Mediator 2: umm
(3) Paul: and the work was getting
(4) Mediator 2: umm
(5) Paul: done and so on but you know she started to make these kind of noises about the paperwork being sorted
(6) Mediator 2: right
(7) Paul: and you know I tried to keep on top of it for a bit
(8) Mediator 2: umm
(9) Paul: and I did my best but really there's too much of it and that's the real problem with—its just nonsense it just gets in the way
(10) Mediator 2: umm—gets in the way of?
(11) Paul: doing the job, doing the business that we're there for
(12) Mediator 2: right, which is what as far as you're concerned?
(13) Paul: well you know we get people in the advice centre in dire straights with real employment issues and real housing issues
(14) Mediator 2: umm

Paul expands this point, and then at 6 mins 36 secs Mediator 2 says,

(15) Mediator 2: it seems to me as if what you're saying is that if this was a set of scales, the people would be way down here and the paperwork you know
(16) Paul: Uh hum—that's how it feels absolutely yeah that's it exactly how it feels

Paul continues to explain his dislike of form filling at the expense of serving the clients and his resentment at suggestions from other advice centre workers that he does paperwork at home in his own time.

At 7 mins 38 secs Mediator 2 asks,

(17) Mediator 2: okay so you said that you've been here for just quite a short time what would you say your relationships has been like with Chris since you started?

Paul explains that he thinks that it has been okay, that he has sympathy for Chris's position but that he thinks she should manage the problem about the paperwork.

Commentary and Analysis

Up until this point Paul is being led through an exploration of his situation, in terms of issues and relationships, from his standpoint, by prompts and questions from the mediator, such as in lines (10), (12) and (17). She sums up his concern about the balance of paperwork versus advice giving in line (15). Paul is given space to relate his account of the situation, both the practical and relationship aspects. Nevertheless, by being gently questioned in this way he is being called to account. This style of interviewing can be seen to arise from a need to map out the issues and relationships of the conflict so that solutions may be subsequently generated, whether by the parties or by the mediators. The questions in lines (10), (12) and (17) are directive in order to serve the mediator's need for assessing the 'problem'. This is, not surprisingly, a characteristic of a 'problem-solving' discourse. Furthermore, the mediator's questions in lines (10), (12), and (17) display an unnamed authority to interrogate Paul so that he becomes 'positioned' as having to give account, as if he had broken some unspoken code of behaviour, as described above.

Thus, an interactional routine (Fairclough 2001) continues to unfold in which power resides with the questioner. This style of interaction tends to reinforce and naturalise the subject position of the mediator as one of authorised expert in conflict resolution. The party seems to fall into line with this arrangement and to take direction from the mediator. It is difficult to challenge a questioner who poses as a 'helper' and this difficulty is magnified if there are subliminal social pressures upon the party to feel shame for being in conflict.

A transformative mediation alternative to the above interrogation would have been to follow Paul's unfolding story and reflect back moments of dis/empowerment or recognition that it contains (Bush and Folger 2005). For example, at line (10) a transformative mediator may have remained silent or possibly reflected back Paul's expressed feelings and asked if he would like to say any more about how paperwork 'gets in the way' or whether he might want to talk about 'noises' made by Chris or whether there was anything else that was important to talk about? An explorative mediator might proceed in a questioning manner not dissimilar to this facilitative mediator but ensuring that questions at this stage are very open. In following the party's lead a transformative or an explorative mediator would not select a new subject and pose a closed question as in line (17).

Fourth extract, (8 mins 19 secs—11 mins 44 secs)

(1) Mediator 2: so what you are telling—{turning to the Mediator 1} have you got anything you would like to ask (Mediator 1's name)?
(2) Mediator 1: well I was just interested to see what your day might look like
(3) Paul: umm
(4) Mediator 1: I've kind of got this impression, you said there's lots of people wanting your advice
(5) Paul: yeah
(6) Mediator 1: I've got this impression that you maybe having an interview with someone however long it needs to last, you help them sort their
(7) Paul: uh hum
(8) Mediator 1: problem out and then there's someone else waiting immediately
(9) Paul: yeah typically yeah very typically
(10) Mediator 1: yes, so tell me
(11) Paul: I mean it comes in fits and starts but yeah that's the typical pattern really

(12) Mediator 1: right so are you are you sort of customer facing, I mean is there that much demand that you are customer facing all day long
(13) Paul: uh hum
(14) Mediator 1: from when you start to when you end or you could be?
(15) Paul: yes I can be, I mean there are other volunteers in the advice centre as well but you know I'm the kind of specialist who deals with the kind of more complex issues and so on, so I often
(16) Mediator 1: right
(17) Paul: get referrals from them so they're asking me things
(18) Mediator 1: so is the suggestion that you should be dealing with a referral or dealing with a customer and then filling up paperwork and then
(19) Paul: uh hum
(20) Mediator 1: dealing with the next customer and filling out the paperwork so you
(21) Paul: yes
(22) Mediator 1: so you should be doing it as you go along?
(23) Paul: that seems to be the kind of view, yes because
(24) Mediator 1: right
(25) Paul: I can understand that point of view because when you get to the end of the day if you've been seeing people all day long you just need time to do the paperwork, you just want to go home and that's often how I feel about it
(26) Mediator 1: do you find you can remember each of the cases when its time?
(27) Paul: I think I can, sufficiently. Obviously one takes notes when
(28) Mediator 1: right
(29) Paul: one's, we have a standardised referral form you know
(30) Mediator 1: yes
(31) Paul: I take notes and so on but yeah then there are these returns
(32) Mediator 1: uh hum

(33) Paul: I don't know if you understand, there's a system that we have
(34) Mediator 1: yeah
(35) Paul: this contract with the (funding agency) we have these returns that need to go back to them
(36) Mediator 1: right
(37) Paul: Chris will tell you all the details, I try and keep away from all that as much as I can but there are these kind of aggregated returns that need to go back
(38) Mediator 1: and what's the purpose of those?
(39) Paul: they're about funding, they're about providing evidence to get funding
(40) Mediator 1: okay so
(41) Paul: so this very much evidence driven funding
(42) Mediator 1: so if they don't get filled in the funding stops?
(43) Paul: well that's what they say
(44) Mediator 1: right {laughter}
(45) Paul: {laughter}
(46) Mediator 1: okay right that's one of the reasons that's been given is it for why you have to fill out the stats?
(47) Paul: yeah
(48) Mediator 1: okay just one more question. Do you have kind of targets
(49) Paul: uh hum
(50) Mediator 1: for the amount of time that you are expected to spend with each client or targets for the number of clients you're expected to see in a day?
(51) Paul: no
(52) Mediator 1: no okay
(53) Paul: each case is as long as it takes
(54) Mediator 1: yeah okay
(55) Mediator 2: so Paul what would be an ideal situation for you that would come from this mediation?
(56) Paul: hum
(57) Mediator 2: what do want from it?
(58) Paul: just for someone else to do the unnecessary work really
(59) Mediator 2: uh hum

(60) Paul: as I said I've suggested that there's an administrative assistant in the office and I can't see why she can't do some of this kind of work, this from filling. It just seems to be more of a kind of administrative task, I just can't see the point in employing a specialist skilled debt worker and then spending, paying hard earned money, its difficult to get money for these things, on form filling
(61) Mediator 2: so how would you describe your relationship with Chris right now?
(62) Paul: well until this really, I mean until this came up I thought we were fine...

Paul and the mediators continue talk about the bad atmosphere that arises from this conflict.

Commentary and Analysis

The problem-solving focus is very marked in this extract. Mediator 1 begins by asking for a picture of Paul's day in line (2). She proceeds to quiz him, making many interventions, to build up a picture of his work activity, almost analysing his working practice. In line (22) she proffers a normative assessment of a detail of this work practice and again quizzes him on his response in line (26). Another example of this investigative probing appears in line (38). There is a high incidence of mediator intervention, and the questioning remains within a narrow management domain and terminology. An opportunity to explore any wider causes of the conflict (Cloke 2001) perhaps in the form of the function of the funding agency or of Paul's working history may have been missed.

In contrast, Mediator 2 interrupts with a different line of questioning in line (55). This question, 'what would be an ideal situation?' is a standard question from the repertoire of a facilitative, problem-solving mediator. It subtly invites the party to adopt a focus on the future and on what needs to happen so that the current conflict can be left behind but not necessarily addressed. After Paul's reply it could have been possible to reflect back his answer and invite further exploration of his views (Bush and Folger 2005). Instead Mediator 2, a little abruptly, directs attention to a new subject, that of Paul's relationship with Chris.

In both Mediators' otherwise different lines of questioning (the practical and the personal respectively) the mediator is very much directing the exchange rather than seeking to follow where the party might wish to take a more open-ended discussion. Hence, the exchange becomes an interview with the party positioned as interviewee and the mediators as interrogators (Fairclough. 2001). Roles and positions already established for both mediators and the party are maintained and reinforced. In this way Paul is effectively positioned as a member of staff with respect to the mediators as 'managers'. Mediator 1 could be regarded as a line manager concerned with practical tasks and Mediator 2 as a personnel manager concerned with well-being and relationships in the workplace. 'What is said' by the mediators is accepted by Paul. Their 'subject positions' as authority figures occupying an enunciative modality within the workplace mediation setting is reinforced by Paul's acceptance of their adopted role (Howarth 2005). But these mediators have also become proxy managers. They are no longer tentative, humble helpers, or radical explorers of conflict. Instead, they are solvers of conflict. Hence, there is an apparent dove tailing of a standard workplace 'discourse' around task achievement, implicitly premised upon harmonious relations, with a problem-solving mediation 'discourse'. The power of the mediators, is to an extent, hidden or, at least, unconsidered (by themselves and the parties) in what superficially appears a natural and reasonable form of engagement in the course of their work (Fairclough 2001).

Fifth extract, (13 mins 4 secs—13 mins 40 secs)

(1) Mediator 2: so in an ideal situation what would be happening as a result of this mediation?
(2) Paul: well as I say you know we would have some system whereby I can be relieved of the of the burden of the paperwork. That's what I want
(3) Mediator 2: okay
(4) Mediator 1: is that practical?
(5) Paul: I think it is. I can't see any reason why if I fill out the referral forms at the same level of detail in which I'm doing it now.
(6) Mediator 1: right

(7) Paul: then I don't see any reason why those can't be passed to another person
(8) Mediator 2: uh hum
(9) Paul: an administrative assistant
(10) Mediator 1: to put onto the returns?

Mediator 1 then continues to ask several questions of fine, technical detail around the form filling before Mediator 2 brings back the question of 'how would you like your relationship with Chris to be as a result of this mediation?' At 15 mins 15 secs Mediator 2 summarises Paul's description of the issues and what he wants to happen. This first visit ends after 17 min 52 secs.

Commentary and Analysis

At the end of this first visit of the mediators to Paul, the overall impression is that Paul has been subjected to an interrogation, albeit a courteous one. The mediators seem to have adopted a stance as benign proxy managers who, in the search for understanding necessary to identify possible solutions, feel it within their remit to challenge Paul's beliefs about his work, as evident in line (4) above. The mediators' problem-solving disposition combined with the discursive environment of the workplace seems to have produced a 'subject positioning' that is a blend of interviewers/HR managers and interrogators/supervising managers. The whole discursive trajectory of this 'interview' has been towards an organisationally inspired resolution of practical and, to an extent, relational, work based problems.

First Visit of the Two Facilitative Mediators with Chris

First extract, (16 secs—2 mins 2 secs)

(1) Mediator 2: have you managed to have a read of the leaflet that we sent out to you about mediation?
(2) Chris: yes I have
(3) Mediator 2: okay would it be useful for me to go over it again just to explain what it is would that be okay?

(4) Chris: yes if you wouldn't mind thank you
(5) Mediator 2: well what mediation is its about us helping you to help yourselves basically okay. There's an issue that's going on between you, we've been led to believe and what its about its about helping you to find your own solutions. (Mediator 1) and I are not going to judge you in any way or to make decisions for you or to offer up solutions and say Chris you have to do this and Paul you've got to do that
(6) Chris: uh hum
(7) Mediator 2: because if we were to do that then it probably wouldn't work anyway its about you finding your own solutions it is confidential so the discussions that we have in here today are confidential between us. We wouldn't pass any information on to Paul unless you gave us express permission to do that
(8) Chris: right
(9) Mediator 2: now we've had the meeting already with Paul
(10) Chris: uh hum
(11) Mediator 2: we're going to have the meeting with you, the next stage is if you're both still happy to do this will be to have a joint meeting and this is where we sit around the table and each party will have time to have uninterrupted time, to have their say about what their issues are. We'll set some ground rules obviously beforehand and that's simply to create a safe environment for you, not that I'm suggesting its going to be unsafe {chuckle} but you know its where people can express their views because we know that a lot of the time people when they communicate they just stop communicating or communicate in a way that's not as useful as it could be
(12) Chris: uh hum
(13) Mediator 2: so its about us all sitting around the table helping to find solutions and then if there are solutions then agreement is reached and we write an actual agreement is that okay?
(14) Chris: yeah that's fine …

Chris goes on to describe the 'problem' as she is experiencing it, which centres upon her requirement for Paul to keep records of his time spent giving debt advice to clients of the Bureau. These records then enable funding support for this work to be drawn down from the funding agency.

Commentary and Analysis

These few lines of speech cover the principles of a facilitative/problem-solving mediation meeting; that is, the objectives, the process and outcomes, as well as the mediator's role. In line (5) Mediator 2 affirms a 'neutral' disposition saying we 'are not going to judge you in any way so or to make decisions for you…'. Also in line (5) she says that 'there's an Issue that's going on between you', implying that there is a problem to be solved. She states that mediation is 'about helping you to find your own solutions'. This latter message is repeated again in line (7). Hence, four messages are quickly imparted, that there is a problem, you can/should solve it yourself, but we, the mediators, will help you, without judging or proposing a solution. This is all re-emphasised again in line (13), in the statement that, 'its about us all sitting around the table helping to find solutions'.

The internally, contradictory tension of mediation has emerged straight away, being the desire to help without intervening. Any intervention will disrupt the parties' scope to find their own path through the conflict. The more the mediator 'helps' the greater is the departure from the mediation ethic of being non-judging, since the mediator's decision about how to help must arise from their judgement of the issues presented. In 'transformative' mediation this tension is addressed by only 'helping' with the communication between parties, the aim being to support an escape from an interactional crisis. In 'narrative' mediation parties are also helped to reconstruct the conflict story. A more directive element thus creeps in. In this 'problem-solving' approach, in which the aim is by definition to find a solution, it becomes impossible to proffer help without influencing the outcome.

In line (11) there is a glimmer of the possibility that the parties can decide to opt for a joint meeting or not. Within the rest of this section there is presumption that the meeting will take place. It is common in workplace mediating that the whole process takes place on one day. The parties are asked to agree an agenda entailing first visits before lunch and the joint meeting after lunch. Also in line (11) the processual parameters of this style of mediation are described, noting 'uninterrupted time' and 'ground rules', justified on the basis of making the process safe. Such procedures have long been criticised from a transformative perspective for their inevitable impact upon how the 'content' of the mediation unfolds (Rifkin et al. 1991; Folger 2001). Finally, in lines (10) and (11) it is inferred that mediation is about helping people to communicate, to then arrive at solutions and document agreements. A workplace discursive model of problem definition, solution finding, action planning, and monitoring, thus emerges as a conditioning force around the work of the mediator.

The form of broad influence most apparent in these opening remarks is found in the construction of a 'situation type' and an 'interactional routine' (Fairclough 2001) that positions (Fairclough 2001; Howarth 2005) the 'helper' as 'director' of the process and 'manager' of the attempt to discover a workable solution. This is evident in the adoption by the mediator of the role/position of 'manager' of the process and then enacted in the way information about the process is imparted to the party. 'What is said' underscores the mediators' 'subject position' and then the 'doing in saying' further fixes the constitution of this position (Howarth 2005). The mediator demonstrates their very expertise by electing to tell the party all about the process at the outset. There is an organisational expectation of the hired mediator to live up to a certain professionalism enacted through the adept management of a process. In this way, the discourse of a workplace, managerial competence insinuates itself into the mediation space. In this context the role of mediator as 'manager' of the process becomes naturalised (Fairclough 2001), serving to obscure the enormous power of influence over solutions that is held by the mediator.

The overall impression is that the party is to be subjected to a process and that this is likely to close down options and ranges of outcomes that might otherwise be explored. That which might be contingent i.e. other outcomes arising from different interactions that may have considered other ethical and political dimensions (Glynos and Howarth 2007), may be blocked or diverted. An alternative approach would be to invite the parties to manage the process of the meeting themselves. Mediators would adopt a humble position and could explain more transparently how and why they would intend to make interventions in order to support the conversation of the parties. This counterfactual style will be developed further below in Chaps. 6 and 7.

Second extract, (5 mins 29 secs—7 mins 37 secs)

(1) Chris: … but in this situation we just don't seem to be getting anywhere with it
(2) Mediator 1: so he's well aware of the importance of the time recording?
(3) Chris: yes and he was told before he applied for the post at the interview at the time of the appointment and subsequently, so I mean that everyone in the Bureau is aware of how crucial the (funding) is to the Bureau, so there's absolutely no question
(4) Mediator 1: right
(5) Chris: that he doesn't know
(6) Mediator 1: right
(7) Mediator 2: could I just ask a question Chris has was Paul promoted from within?
(8) Chris: yes
(9) Mediator 2: oh right okay
(10) Chris: yes
(11) Mediator 1: and is he aware of the implications of not filling out, not recording his time in terms of the funding stream?
(12) Chris: he understands that that's how, I mean basically when we had the contract at the Bureau everyone is part of everything that goes on so everybody needs to understand about it because sometimes the debt worker will be asking other members of staff to do things which they might think is bit strange, but its because we have to fulfil certain criteria to get the money and the time recording is one of them and yes he was and has been told
(13) Mediator 1: and how immediate are the funding implications?

(14) Chris: probably about three months, so what's recorded one month is usually processed in probably three months, before it would actually be obvious that
(15) Mediator 1: so in practical terms if for example he'd spent seven hours one day doing debt work and he'd not recorded all those clearly and so he'd only got say credit for four hours
(16) Chris: uh hum
(17) Mediator 1: are you saying that in three months time there's
(18) Chris: we would see the result of it
(19) Mediator 1: a very direct link there? Half, practically half of that day
(20) Chris: yes you get four hours of money rather than seven hours
(21) Mediator 1: okay and he is aware of that?
(22) Chris: yeah
(23) Mediator 2: how do you know that he is aware of how crucial it is?
(24) Chris: well because we have a contract …

Commentary and Analysis

In this exchange the mediators question Chris in detail about the requirements for time recording and about Paul's understanding of the implications for funding of not fulfilling these requirements. They seem to be adopting a position of line manager to Chris, or, at least, supportive management colleagues. Rather than let Chris speak for herself and simply listen and check for understanding, they seem to want to unravel the technical details of the issue to be able to mentally assess and judge it. Even at the 'first visit' they appear to be motivated by a need to own the problem and the prospect of finding a practical solution.

They have adopted an inquisitorial stance (very marked for example in line (23). An interactional routine (Fairclough 2001) is operating in which the mediators lead the questioning and direct the conversation. The party has thus become subordinate to the mediators' intentions to seek out a solution. The mediators here seem to retain all the power to manage the conversation and the process of the interaction. Were the mediators more concerned to support the party in exploring her own conflict a different situation type (Fairclough 2001) could have been set up at this early stage. Transformative mediation (Bush and Folger 2005) aims to support the party in arriving at their own clarification of the conflict by yielding power to the parties. In the more directive and evaluative, problem-solving approach, the possibility for conflict to disturb a 'subject position' (Torfing 1999; Howarth 2000) and open it up to possible change, would seem to be smothered. Thus, the potential 'political subjectivity' of the parties is also contained (Howarth 2000, 2005).

A Sequence of Extracts

Third extract, (9 mins 47 secs—10 mins 37 secs)

Chris and Mediator 1 are discussing Paul's previous role at the Advice Centre.

(1) Chris:	I mean that the alarm bells did ring I mean they did ring in terms of, is he going to want to work like this and we had that conversation
(2) Mediator 1:	okay
(3) Chris:	we had this specific conversation
(4) Mediator 1:	you did mention something about him improvising the information then that the paperwork and process type information, although it was important for audit purposes it wasn't so crucial to the funding and that you said that you could sort of work around it a bit. I was just wondering and you know shoot me down if this isn't correct at all
(5) Chris:	uh hum
(6) Mediator 1:	is that he maybe sort of felt that well that he'd managed to work round the system in that role and you'd kind of catered for that, for his particular way of working.
(7) Chris:	umm
(8) Mediator 1:	Do you think he might have expected that to happen now? I mean
(9) Chris:	it's not impossible …

Fourth extract, (11 mins 23 secs—12 mins 1 sec)

(10) Mediator 1: what does his job. description say?
(11) Chris: it covers the general roles of providing advice …{gives full details}
(12) Mediator 1: so it does cover all those admin things?
(13) Chris: oh yes
(14) Mediator 1: and the time recording and all that, is it couched in similar terminology to his previous job description?
(15) Chris: no
(16) Mediator 1: so it does make it…

Fifth extract, (12 mins 19 secs—12 mins 32 secs)

(17) Chris: point one, you would need to record every hour, minute you spend with the client. Point two, files must be
(18) Mediator 1: so again as far as you're concerned it has been clearly communicated to him okay? So why do you think he's not doing it? I know you've sort of touched on this

Commentary and Analysis

With a focus still upon the main 'problem', Mediator 1 asks a very detailed, leading and closed question about what Chris thought Paul's job expectations were concerning time keeping records in lines (4), (6) and (8). This way of assessing a work problem seems to be rooted in a 'situation type' (Fairclough 2001; Howarth 2005) of the office environment, as one manager speaks to another or as a senior manager speaks to a junior manager. The question in lines (4), (6) and (8) represents a search for an explanation why Paul feels his behaviour to be reasonable despite Chris's pleas to the contrary. This probing is followed up further in line (14). Mediator 1 is thoroughly checking Chris's belief that she has communicated the job requirements to Paul. In line (18) she cuts Chris off to move on to probe Chris's beliefs about Paul's motivations. (This point is picked up in the next extract.)

Mediator 1 and Chris 'identify' (Fairclough 2001; Stavrakakis 2005) with each other as managers grappling with a 'problem' that is a result of Paul's behaviour, although Chris is positioned in a subordinate role as she is asked to justify her opinion. Wider causes of the conflict such as the demands of the funding agency or other working pressures on Chris have been effectively excluded from consideration.

The 'problem' is delineated as Paul's behaviour and defined in terms of work role and performance, evaluated against a job description. As such the 'discourse' in play is that of the workplace and the 'discourse' of problem-solving mediation becomes aligned with it. This occurs as the mediator and the party mutually conform to a relationship implicit in the interactional routine (Fairclough 2001) of a manager and her staff. Again 'subject positions' are both acted and simultaneously constituted as the interaction unfolds (Howarth 2005). What might appear 'natural' (Fairclough 2001) in the workplace now occurs, as if also 'natural' within the mediation encounter.

Sixth extract, (14 mins 52 secs—15 mins 42 secs)

(1) Mediator 1: … are you suggesting that the there there's almost a sort of stubbornness there? That he feels very strongly that his time should be spent customer facing, helping the client?
(2) Chris: that would be my, I mean that may be very unfair
(3) Mediator 1: It shouldn't be spent filling in these bloody forms, they're a waste of time?
(4) Chris: well he's actually said those words {laughter}
(5) Mediator 1: okay{roars of laughter}
(6) Chris: we've actually had that conversation, so yes that is it
(7) Mediator 1: okay
(8) Mediator 2: so it's getting the balance between the customer facing and the paper work to keep it there?
(9) Chris: one is necessary for the other, that's the difference but

(10) Mediator 2: yes
(11) Mediator 1: yes
(12) Chris: I mean I really don't think he's doing it deliberately, I don't think he's setting out
(13) Mediator 1: no, okay, well from what you know, I think that that's a very helpful point to start off from. That point of sort of feeling that it's not deliberate, I mean. So what is your working relationship with him like at the moment?

Chris goes on to describe how she feels frustrated with the situation and is running out of ideas to resolve it to her satisfaction.

Commentary and Analysis

Mediator 1 is working sympathetically with Chris to assess the problem for herself from Chris's perspective. She has positioned herself as owner of the problem, as if she were a manager in Chris's organisation. In lines (4) and (5) Mediator 1 and Chris share empathetic laughter as they concur in their judgement of Paul's behaviour. Paul's behaviour is now the problem. In line (8) Mediator 2 says 'its getting the balance between the customer facing and the paperwork'. She thus suggests a practical or material solution to this interpersonal conflict. Then in line (13) Mediator 1 asks 'So what is your working relationship like with him at the moment?' One reading of such a question is that the mediator wishes to invite the party to reflect upon her own feelings about the situation. However, the question is very direct, specific and closed. In doing this she demonstrates she is satisfied with her own exploration of the technicalities of the 'problem' thus far and decides to dictate the next area of her inquiry into the 'problem' of the working relationship.

Once more the 'subject positions' of the mediators as intervening managers are strongly reinforced, in contrast with the declared intent of mediation not to judge, to remain impartial and to help the parties to find a solution themselves.

Summing Up the First Visit with Chris by Mediator 1

Final extract, (18 mins 51 secs—21 mins 1 secs)

(1) Chris: I don't manage by, I'm in charge and you'll do as I say
(2) Mediator 2: uh hum
(3) Chris: but I have to have done what I have to have done
(4) Mediator 1: okay
(5) Mediator 2: shall we summarise?
(6) Mediator 1: yes, I mean I think in one sense its almost quite simple, that Paul's, just from your point of view, not doing the job that you feel he was employed to do, that there's a lack of understanding or almost in a sense a sort of refusal to understand
(7) Chris: uh hum
(8) Mediator 1: I think is sort of the way you put it, that you know that he needs to get this balance between his customer facing and giving advice and actually filling out the time recording sheets so that you can actually get the funding and that for you that's taking up, it's beginning to take up quite a lot of your time and effort
(9) Chris: uh hum
(10) Mediator 1: and you're almost to the point of needing to go through a disciplinary process because it's just been going on for quite a long time now and you feel that he does understand what's required of him. The job he was doing before and the way that the new job has been communicated to him and the job description was sufficiently well set out that it distinguishes from what he was doing before and he does understand. It is different and the importance of actually filling out the time sheets to get the funding and your concern that it is having a negative impact on the rest of the team
(11) Chris: yeah

(12) Mediator 1: and its actually affecting the atmosphere and your relationship. You've clearly had a good working relationship with him for a number of years now and you've got a lot of respect for him and you think he's a good debt worker but that this situation is actually causing some friction between you and it's just not a very good environment to work in, okay?
(13) Chris: yep right
(14) Mediator 1: is there anything that you want to add to that?
(15) Chris: no I think that's about it
(16) Mediator 1: so basically from this you want him to do his job properly and you want to get back to how an easy going relationship
(17) Chris: everybody just getting on with what their doing and what their supposed to do
(18) Mediator 1: yep okay thank you
(19) Mediator 2: thank you Chris
(20) Chris: okay thanks
(21) Mediator 1: okay so the next steps are …

Commentary and Analysis

The distinguishing feature of this extract is how Mediator 1 speaks for Chris at some length. She demonstrates her mastery of the situation. The phrase from 'your point of view' in line (6) is a little like paying lip service to a notion of impartiality. Alarmingly, Mediator 1 even introduces the possibility of the need for disciplinary process in line (10). The first visit with Chris has more of the tone of a business meeting than a mediation encounter and in line (16) a conclusion is reached in the recognised need for Paul to 'do his job properly'. The notion of 'from your point of view' becomes, in effect, from our point of view, that is, the mediator's and Chris's. The whole session has been driven by questioning to understand the 'problem' and is consistent with how an HR manager might probe and assess a staff relationship that had broken down. It is the HR manager' job to expedite recovery of harmonious relationships in order to get people back to work. The problem-solving mediator seems to have a similar primary ambition.

This highly directive, problem-solving interrogation of Chris results in re-enforcing her identity as Paul's manager. Perhaps unsurprisingly, the order of the world within which the conflict has emerged is thus perpetuated by this practice, rather than opened up for exploration. Chris is 'positioned' as the manager and the Mediators are 'positioned' similarly as either supportive or superior managers with responsibility for finding a solution. Hence, the 'discourses' of the workplace (in which hierarchical power relations are the accepted norm) and the 'discourse' of problem solving mediation are interwoven. This type of mediation would seem to be more about control and conflict management to promote a quick solution. The alternative could be to use this dislocatory experience to explore, dialogically, party differences and wider webs and patterns of causal factors, from which the subjectivities of the parties may be mutually considered and a sense of the 'contingent' nature of the conflict apprehended (Glynos and Howarth 2007). To attempt this would require a disposition of 'undecidability' by the mediators to allow a more open conversation that is driven along by the parties (Bush and Folger 2005).

Joint Meeting Between Paul and Chris and Two Facilitative Mediators

Opening Welcome to the Joint Meeting

First extract, (6 secs—3 min 9 secs)

(1) Mediator 2: Welcome Paul and Chris. We're now having the meeting, you both agreed to meet together and thank you for doing that. I know that its quite a brave thing to do, it takes a good few good steps to agree to mediation so I do thank you for agreeing to come today because I do think it is an intention of your commitment to resolve the situation that you have. What we're going to do today if you remember with (Mediator 1) and myself,

we're going to have a meeting now where we're all sitting around the table and you'll both have time, uninterrupted time, to have your say about the situation that's happening between you, which means that there's no asking questions or interrupting the other person its just complete time because this as you know is an opportunity for the other person to hear the other parties situation from their own mouth and probably in a way that they have never ever heard it before. So we'll both have time to do that and then what we'll do is, we'll get into listening to when we've sorted out the agenda we'll go into joint discussion okay and then hopefully we'll get to be looking for solutions and then reaching an agreement okay. The agreement if we do reach one will be in writing, it's not legally binding in any way it's more or less a gentleman's agreement if I can use that terminology. Ground rules that you would like to set before we start, are there any ground rules at all that you would like to have to help the mediation flow?

(2) Paul: What kind of thing have you got in mind
(3) Mediator 2: I was thinking about things like maybe not shouting, maybe not getting aggressive, listening to each other
(4) Paul: uh hum
(5) Mediator 1: maybe trying to be as open as possible but without kind of focussing the blame on the other person, you know trying to be as constructive and honest as possible
(6) Paul: I don't have any problem with that
(7) Mediator 1: if that's okay
(8) Chris: I think also it might be it perhaps might be helpful if we could have something about confidentiality because I think its very important that what we talk about between us doesn't
(9) Mediator 2: yes
(10) Chris: get out to other members of staff
(11) Mediator 2: yeah

(12) Mediator 1: absolutely
(13) Mediator 2: absolutely yes and as (name of mediation organisation) mediators we're not going to report up to your management to say what's happened in the mediation. We will probably say yes it has been successful or no it hasn't and that is all that we will say. One or two of the previous mediations that I have done, part of the agreement has been that you show the written agreement to the HR person, is that okay? But that's obviously up to you to decide (Mediator 1) and I might make a few notes, that's simply just to jog our memory. We will destroy them at the end of the day, we won't give any notes at all okay
(14) Mediator 1: just
(15) Mediator 2: eh
(16) Mediator 1: go on
(17) Mediator 2: I was just going to say, any questions about the process that we talked through …

Commentary and Analysis

This opening statement follows routine mediation practice in its introductory coverage of the mediation process and implied mediator's role, ground rules and confidentiality (the last in this case raised by one of the parties). The 'enunciative modality' (Howarth 2005) of the mediators, their authority to set up and manage the encounter is, in practice at least, accepted by the parties. Furthermore, if the mediators and parties are viewed as autonomous, fully responsible individuals, an initial reading of this introduction might find the mediators' approach to be courteous, reasonable and devoid of overt political persuasion. Sarup (1993, p. 6) succinctly describes such a Cartesian psychology that,

> portray[s] the individual as a rational, conscious actor who could understand the basis for his or her action. … rooted in a philosophy of individual autonomy and rational choice.

However, a closer scrutiny that assumes the mediation meeting is a site for the co-construction of social realities and identities (McNamee and Gergen 1999; Torfing 1999; Fairclough 2001; Phillips and Jorgensen 2006) and in which 'language constitutes us as a subject' (Sarup 1993, p. 6) enables an alternative reading to be made. The above particular 'modality' of mediation may then be contested.

The first mediator's opening introduction to the meeting in paragraph (1) begins with the assertion that 'you both agreed to meet together'. This may be seen as a simple fact but it is possible that their willingness to attend is more ambivalent. This statement would seem to fix the parties in the role of volunteers to a process. It could also imply the mediators are there at the parties' direct behest, which is often not the case. This assertion is quickly followed by an assumption, that we, the mediators, have 'your commitment to resolve the situation that you have'. Later, this is referred to as the 'situation that's happening between you'. Thus, the parties are being directed to resolve the 'situation' that is a problem of their own making, for which they are jointly and individually responsible. The role or 'subject position' of the parties has been immediately delineated by the task of resolving the situation for which they are responsible.

Next in paragraph (1) the meeting process 'with (Mediator 1) and myself' is outlined, starting with uninterrupted time, followed by agenda setting and discussion, then 'looking for solutions', followed by agreement making and writing. It is noted that any agreement if reached is referred to as 'not legally binding ... more or less a gentleman's agreement'. The mediators' 'subject positions' as conductors of the meeting process, setters of an agenda and seekers of solutions is further affirmed by the expression 'what we're going to do today' (6th line of paragraph (1)). This attention to an 'agenda' and to 'solutions' brings a discourse of mediation (Beer and Stief 1997; Crawley and Graham 2002) into alignment with a more general discourse of the workplace (Clegg et al. 1999; Clegg and Hardy 1999). Moreover, the process is compared with an alternative legal process. This gives an unintended quasi-legal connotation to the proceedings, ironically creating an opposite effect to mediation's stated private, confidential, self-regulating character. This locates the mediator, albeit on the margins, within a hierarchy of authority that assesses or judges parties in conflict. The reference to gentlemanly practice carries a patriarchal notion of fair play and good behaviour, setting out the parameters against which the parties' ability to resolve the issues is to be judged by the mediators as representatives of certain social norms.

Such required good behaviour is then echoed in the mediators' recommendations about ground rules, e.g. not shouting; listening; not blaming; being honest. This last behavioural norm suggests that the mediator will take the role of arbiter of honesty and truth with respect to the future utterances of the parties. These ground rules also position the parties as relatively passive agents, who have misbehaved, or are liable to misbehave, and who are now expected to listen to each other and work towards a solution under the mediators' guidance.

Thus, this opening statement by the mediator may be read as an entreaty to the parties to stop behaving like children and make an agreement to resolve their conflict. The mediator is firmly cast in the role of authority figure, as both expert conflict manager and arbiter of social mores. Arguably, such entreaties are unnecessary because when parties volunteer to sit down in the presence of relative strangers, social and workplace conventions of behaviour usually condition them to moderate any anger or tendency towards extremes of emotional outburst.

The pronouns 'we', 'you', 'your' and the phrase 'we're' (Fairclough 2001) are used powerfully throughout this brief opening statement to effect a delineation of the mediators from the parties. An 'us' and 'them' 'situation type' (Fairclough 2001) is constructed with very distinct roles for each side. The parties are given little choice but to accept this opening statement, that conditions the format of the ensuing encounter and consequently forced to continue to engage in the proscribed process. The format of this process and its language are akin to a very business- oriented problem-solving process, typically concluded with written statements of agreement and 'action plans'. This suggests the need to escape from this model of workplace mediation if the ethic of mediation is not to be colonised by the dominant workplace discourse of objectives, efficiency, productivity and persons objectified as units of production or cogs in the machine.

In lines (8) to (13) the confidentiality of the mediation process is underscored. One of the aims of the mediation policy of confidentiality is to effectively quarantine the mediation process. Thus, parties are meant to be able to come to it voluntarily, to feel it is safe to express themselves openly and without prejudice to any other, subsequent formal processes e.g. an employment tribunal or a disciplinary process. This idea of confidentiality seems to draw its validity, in part, from the reductive, individualistic concept of the parties and the mediators as responsible agents. Behind the wall of confidentiality it is easier to imagine that the mediators are neutral, impartial, non-judging third parties able to support party self-determination. However, no forum can be socially hermetically sealed. Workplace mediations very often occur before or part way through disciplinary or employment tribunal proceedings (Gibbons 2007). Hence, claims about confidentiality require careful qualification in discussion with the parties.

In line (13) the promise that the mediators will report back to the mediation referrer (usually an HR manager) to 'say yes it has been successful or no it hasn't and that is all that we will say', apart from undermining the promise of confidentiality, alludes to the make or break, problem-solving nature of this approach to mediation. In transformative mediation it is emphasised that there are an infinite number of outcomes that parties may choose to take away from a mediation encounter and that the mediators are there to support the parties in finding their own outcome (Bush and Folger 2005).

Like many approaches to mediation this opening statement hints at an aim to promote an opportunity for conflicted parties to develop a dialogic exchange, i.e. for there to be a mutual shift in perspectives so that the views of the other person may be, at least, contemplated. To achieve this it is often argued that control of the process and structure of the joint meeting must be managed by the mediators as this is critical in creating a safe, secure environment for people to speak and listen to each other without risking a regression into angry, open conflict. Yet it is this very impulse to 'problem-solve' combined with control of process that has been criticised for removing the parties' power to choose their own modes of engagement, determine outcomes and decide upon future action (Folger 2001; Bush and Folger 2005). Under a 'problem-solving' approach, the already constraining setting of the mediation meeting may become even more constrained. In a workplace setting, where disparities in power are usual and where it may be assumed that voluntary participation is not always wholehearted, the control of process deemed necessary for engineering successful 'problem-solving' is even more likely to limit scope for party self- and co-determination. The above opening statement by Mediator 2 seems to place a discursive straightjacket around the ensuing encounter that anchors it firmly within an organisational hegemony.

The mediation encounter presents an opportunity to allow the disturbance of relatively stable, sedimented, subject positions to release a more fluid 'political subjectivity' (Torfing 1999; Howarth 2000) in which the contingency of the conflict may be apprehended through dialogic exchange. If the facilitative approach constrains scope to work towards an open dialogue, an alternative, entailing a more humble role for mediators prepared to shrug off a mantle of authority, would be to trust the parties to manage their own process of engagement (Bush and Folger 2005) and use the meeting as a chance for exploration of a conflict. Rather than make assumptions on behalf of the parties or assertions about their intentions, the mediator would wait until the parties proffer information and occasionally ask them very general, open questions and thereafter seek to stimulate the exploration of difference. This explorative approach, supporting a 'group' co-determination, with the agency of the parties being relatively dominant with respect to the mediator, could prove democratic and potentially yield more just outcomes.

Joint Meeting 'Uninterrupted Time', Selected Extracts

At 3 mins 53 secs into the joint meeting Mediator 2 asked who would like to go first (with their uninterrupted time). Paul begins.

Second extract, (4 mins 20 secs—4 mins 56 secs)

Paul: I really don't see what the problem is. I think that the situation is quite manageable really. I don't really see why we have to be here. I'm willing to kind of try and work things out but I don't really see it's a major problem and I just think if Chris could kind of agree to, you know, remove some of the kind of administrative load on me, I think we could walk away … its just I'm hired to do a job and I'm spending most of my time doing not doing a job …

Paul spoke for less than 3 mins.

Third extract, at 7 mins 4 secs Mediator 2 summed up and reflected back Paul's opening statement thus,

Mediator 2: So to sum up what your saying then Paul is that you don't see that there is a problem … you want to be able to do the customer facing work where you deal with the problem, you deal with the debt, you deal with the banks and you actually deal with what you consider to be the most important, which is the people factor … the job your paid to do okay and there's this weight there that's hanging around you which is all this paperwork that needs to be done that you think needs to be passed on to somebody else …

Mediator 2 then invited Chris to speak.

Fourth extract, (7 mins 49 secs—8 mins 44 secs)

Chris: Well I just wish I could feel that it was quite so simple. I think the thing that concerns me is that if Paul really believes that the job that he's paid to do is to only help the clients then I really don't understand where that's come from, because the post was very clearly explained and it's written down and there's a job description. There are other parts of it which involve statistical recording and time recording and things like that and that's the part that I have issue with. I don't have any issue with Paul. Your debt work in terms of the clients or anything like that. You're excellent at what you do but the problem is that we've got to have the time recording and we've got to have the statistics and we've got to have the administration done.

At this point Chris paused and Mediator 2 came in to ask at 8 mins 48 secs,

5 Instrumental Mediation 133

Mediator 2:   Chris do you want to tell us a bit more about the administration and about how important that is?

Chris went on to explain in great detail the technicalities of the paperwork, complaining that she has explained all this to Paul many times. Both mediators continued to prompt Chris on several occasions to further explore the problem from her perspective. Chris spoke for 5 mins 28 secs.

Fifth extract, at 13 mins 17 secs, Mediator 2 made the following summary of Chris's statement.

Mediator 2:   What you're telling us is that you do feel quite uncomfortable at the moment in trying to balance the issues that are happening within the workplace. Your not sure how else to communicate to Paul how important the recording of the paperwork is. You do actually acknowledge that it is tedious it … takes up a lot of time … however that it is very, very important to the Bureau that this happens. What you have done is that you have actually acknowledged that Paul is excellent at his job, as an Advisor. So has that summarised …

Chris agreed and spoke some more stating her regret that she gave Paul the job. Once Chris had finished speaking Mediator 2 then gave a summary of both parties opening commentaries as follows.

Sixth extract, summing up 'uninterrupted time' (from 14 mins 55 secs – 15 mins 34 secs)

(1) Mediator 2:   So the issues between you appear to be the recording of time within the file and the making up of the files and recording the time so that that can then be claimed back from the (funding agency) and from Paul's perspective, your saying you don't know how or why you should have to do this work, this job or this piece of the work, can't it be done by somebody else?

(2) Paul:	Yeah I understand the need it's just the balance of the thing isn't it. It's just completely unbalanced, spending more time doing paperwork than doing the job that I'm paid for and I just don't see why that should have to happen.
(3) Mediator 2:	Okay okay.
(4) Paul:	Its a bit rich saying that she now regrets giving me the job.

Commentary and Analysis

In line (1) above, Mediator 2 has defined and delineated time recording and consequent claiming of funds as an issue 'between you'. The 'issue' has been both attributed to both of the parties and also given a life of its own separate from both parties. In contrast, Mediator 2 then attributes a 'perspective' on the problem to Paul in the phrase 'from Paul's perspective'. No 'perspective' is correspondingly attributed to Chris. The 'issue' and a 'perspective' on it, is now skewed towards Paul. Chris and the mediator have been amalgamated into a silent 'we' in opposition to Paul. This would subtly seem to imply that there is a problem and that Paul is the cause and that he could, if he wished, solve the problem for Chris by doing what she is asking him to do. At this very early stage of the joint meeting the mediator has set out the task for the parties as necessitated by the dictates of the 'business'. Consideration of the relational, interactional crisis (Bush and Folger 2005) or discussion of other or underlying differences (Winslade and Monk 2001; Cloke 2001), between the parties has effectively been closed off from exploration. That is, their respective discourses have neither been given equal weight by the mediators nor held up for consideration and discussion in a move towards a dialogic exchange. Paul seems to sense this imbalance and immediately reacts to this summary defending his position with the mediator in line (2) and then furthering the argument with Chris in line (4).

It is useful to refer to Torfing's definition of discourse as 'a differential ensemble of signifying sequences in which meaning is constantly renegotiated' on the basis of the deconstruction of the ideas of both totalising structures and atomised social elements (Torfing 1999, p. 85). We might see Chris's position as a defence of a 'meaning system' or 'structure' imposed from outside the Bureau by the funding agency and Paul's criticism of it as an attempt to displace the funding agency as the defining 'centre' of the Bureau's 'structure'. Chris's support for the existing 'structure' (imposed by the funding agency) is not delineated by the mediators, whereas, in a negative, exclusionary sense, Paul's resistance to it is. Thus, the 'structure' that accepts funding agency rule is normalised or naturalised in the discourse of the mediators, in that its existence and pervasive presence is unnamed and silent (Fairclough 2001). Later on the mediation meeting does serve to partially question the meaning system set up by the funding agency. As Torfing notes, the 'relative structural order is conditional upon the exclusion of a constitutive outside' (Torfing 1999, p. 86). Paul is 'outside' prompting questions. This exclusion arises because the mediators inadvertently do not give equal expression to these two positions because they are themselves absorbed in the relative structural order that prevails. Furthermore, their particular style of 'problem-solving' would seem to be contiguous with this structural order. It is the inherently judgemental 'problem-solving' disposition that traps the mediators within a discourse of 'business'. 'Problems' can only be defined from within such a 'totalising structure' that regards the parties as 'atomised social elements'; that is, as autonomous individual agents.

A first step in an attempt to momentarily suspend this totalising tendency requires the mediator to adopt a stance of 'follower' of the parties' stories, rather than 'leader' of a solution. This is to become less a 'solver', to be wary of 'helping' and to focus upon 'supporting' in a manner that is minimally invasive. From this standpoint, the mediators may be able to loosen the ties of cultural apperception and inevitable judgement and instead reflect back the different discourses of both parties. It may then be possible to yield a deconstructive consideration of each party's identification with the problem. This could start by inviting both parties to reflect upon or clarify their different positions, issues, feelings and needs. Such a more open engagement would, in part, be addressed by the transformative method of highlighting feelings of empowerment and disempowerment (Bush and Folger 2005) and then more fully met by an exploratory approach encompassing direct consideration of the conflict issues.

Joint Meeting Exchange Stage

Seventh extract, (17 mins 21 secs—19 mins 15 secs)

(1) Paul: … as I've said before I don't see any reason why I should be doing all that and I don't see any reason why an administrator can't do that kind of work. It just seems pointless me spending my time doing it.
(2) Mediator 1: What do other people do in the organisation, other advice, would you {looking at Chris} have other advice workers other than debt workers?
(3) Chris: Yes but none of them have to time fill
(4) Mediator 1: Right so its just this
(5) Chris: they statistic record and they have to file record but not time record.
(6) Mediator 1: okay.
(7) Mediator 2: So Paul, you both know this job better than Mediator 1 and I. How could you see this working with an administrative person doing that work? How possibly could it work?
(8) Paul: Well it's just a matter of simple recording and simply noting how much time people spend on work. So I mean just a matter of simple time keeping, simple record keeping isn't it.
(9) Mediator 2: So if I was the admin person and you were doing that task how would I know how to write down what work that you have done? How would I know how to complete the form in the right way?
(10) Paul: Well because I mean obviously the amount of time that I spend with each person could be noted quite easily.
(11) Mediator 2: All right.
(12) Mediator 1: You mean you could note that down?
(13) Paul: I could note it simply, yeah just keep a record of how much time I spent with each person during the day, just in a rough format and then they could do all the kind of bits that follow on from there.
(14) Mediator 2: So this is the part where it would be input into the computer

(15) Paul: yeah the inputting and all that.
(16) Mediator 1:   So when you say a rough format …
(17) Paul: I mean. There's a story isn't there that it all has to be precise every single minute, well it doesn't really have to be, it just has to be roughly worked out, it doesn't have to be so precise surely?
(18) Mediator 2:   Chris what do you think?
(19) Chris: Well the difficulty we have Paul if you don't make it fairly precise …

Chris and Paul continue to argue about the need and practice of precise time recording of each case.

Commentary and Analysis

After the opening 'uninterrupted time' Mediator 2 gives a rounding up summary. This is followed by a stage of the mediation encounter sometimes called the 'exchange' (Beer and Stief 1997). It is notable that at 17 mins 21 secs into the whole joint meeting and at just 2 mins 21 secs after the 'uninterrupted time', both mediators, in the above extract, have largely moved directly to a sequence of problem-solving interrogation with Paul. The subject positions they adopted in the first visits remain unchanged as the joint meeting gets fully underway. From this position the mediator is authorised by self-presented expertise, confirmed by the act of commissioning, to manage conflict via control of the process of the mediation interaction.

After Paul attempts to defend his viewpoint in line (1), Mediator 1, in line (2), decides to refer a question of detailed working practice to Chris to try to find a comparative model against which to measure Paul's position. She is thus immediately entering into an instrumental, business debate about comparative workplace practice. She is also apparently deferring to Chris as Paul's manager. Alternatively, she could have addressed this question to Paul or, very differently, at this juncture she could have sought to simply further explore the differences between Paul and Chris.

In lines (7) and (9), Mediator 2 takes up the probing of the 'problem' with Paul directly. It would seem that Mediator 2 and Mediator 1 are doing nothing other than managerial problem-solving. It is as if they have already decided that Paul needs to do more of what Chris is asking and so they are both trying to get to grips with the detail of this with Paul through lines (7)–(16). Then, at line (18) Mediator 2 arbitrarily directs a question at Chris. She invites her to judge Paul's assertions.

In this manner the Mediators start leading 'problem-solving' as soon as the 'exchange' commences. They thus overlook scope for exploration of the parties' feelings about their personal disagreement or any deeper reasons, social circumstances or value systems that may have influenced the parties' conflict. It would seem that it is easier to deal with the 'problem' from a narrow perspective of instrumental reason or 'technocratic consciousness' (Habermas 1971).

Almost Opening Up an Issue

Eighth extract, (28 mins 53 secs—31 mins 39 secs)

(1) Chris: ... well what's the difference in doing that, when you've got this thing drawn up, to just writing down when you leave the office 10 o'clock to go to the client and when you come back up to the office, writing 11.30 or 12.30, when you answer the telephone just write 10 o'clock you've got a clock on the desk

(2) Mediator 1: maybe we should explore what the difference is because I thought I heard you {looking at Paul} say something earlier on, or the impact on me certainly was around the fact that you kind of feel that this is quite controlling is

(3) Paul: yeah absolutely

(4) Mediator 1: because you're having to state precisely

(5) Paul: uh hum

(6) Mediator 1: the time started and the time ended, that you're finding it quite

(7) Paul: yeah I just don't see what the problem is I just don't see why we can't get to the end of each week and say okay we spent this much time, you know, let's just kind of, its not falsification is it, its just kind of breaking things

5 Instrumental Mediation 139

	down, on a kind a rough basis, instead of having to be so precise an
(8) Mediator 1:	so what happens?
(9) Paul:	managed, its all this management isn't it, I thought I'd left all that behind when I came to work in a place like this. I was in social services, it was all over managed, now we're getting the same thing, its just over manage ment all the time
(10) Mediator 1:	but is that Chris's fault?
(11) Paul:	I don't know if it's her fault but its certainly what she does
(12) Mediator 2:	do you know, you mentioned about Dunstable earlier on and I'm just wondering whether if they've lost their funding sometime ago, would it be worth them coming to talk with you to explain to you what happened and how that happened, if they could do that without breaching confidentiality? Because we know that some people like small detail and some organisations have to have small detail and there are some people, and it sounds Paul like you're very much one of them, is you don't like small detail
(13) Paul:	absolutely
(14) Mediator 2:	what you like is you're focus is on the people, that's what's most important to you
(15) Paul:	absolutely
(16) Mediator 2:	and for you its about bringing the balance in to accommodate what Chris needs, what the bureau needs, so that you can keep these evenly balanced so that the (funding agency) are getting this, that they need, so that you can maintain clients
(17) Paul:	well that's what I'm saying isn't it, we work these things out on a rough basis rather than counting every minute that we're spending
(18) Mediator 2:	but it might be so important from what Chris is saying and from what Dunstable's experience is, it might be that it is crucial that the (funding agency) may be laying down, and if they are the provider

(19) Paul: uh hum
(20) Mediator 2: of the service they are the ones that have got the purse strings
(21) Paul: yeah okay but I mean what Chris could do is to support...

Commentary and Analysis

In line (2) Mediator 1 attempts to open up an exploration of the different feelings about time recording between Paul and Chris by reflecting back Paul's sense of being controlled. Paul then starts to voice his resistance to what he perceives as an hegemonic discourse of accountability, or over-management, but this is not explored further in what could have been an attempt to stimulate a renegotiation of meaning (Torfing 1999; Howarth 2000). Instead, Mediator 1 seeks to defend Chris in line (10), thus apparently taking Chris's side. This elicits a counter-defence from Paul who responds with a direct accusation in line (11). Perhaps Mediator 1 sought to build some common ground for Chris and Paul by constituting a common enemy in the form of the funding agency. Thus, the mediator seems to be holding to several mutually irreconcilable 'subject positions': these are of impartial mediator; of manager/director of the mediation process; of proxy manager in search of a solution; of arbiter of a 'reality' that deems time recording a necessary requirement of the funding agency; of enemy of the funding agency; of defender of Chris as manager; and briefly, that of sympathiser with the over-managed Paul.

In line (12) Mediator 2 cuts across this confusion and Paul's answer (line (11)) to Mediator 1's question and closes down the issue of Paul's feelings about over-management. In lines (14) and (16) she attempts to invent a mutual purpose around the idea of 'balance'. She is thus creating a form of solution on behalf of the parties based upon her own reading of the situation they have described. However, this attempt at 'mutualising' the 'problem' becomes weighted or biased in favour of Chris because the funding agency hold 'the purse strings' (line (20)). Hence, Mediator 2 effectively supports the demands of Chris, the manager, and asks Paul to accept these also. The discourse of accountability is thus maintained and the dominant ideology naturalised (Fairclough 2001).

Opening Up an Issue

Ninth extract, (36 mins 57 secs—37 mins 33 secs)

(1) Paul: ...its not the (funding agency) is it, its just the micro-management that's going on there isn't it?
(2) Mediator 1: do you think its not the (funding agency) then, do you think its your organisation?
(3) Paul: I think that's just a kind of bogey man isn't it, just being used to kind of worry us, its just the micro-management that's going on, the things spoiled in some way
(4) Mediator 1: are you saying then that Chris is somehow or that the advice centre is somehow using the (funding agency) as an excuse to manage you too closely?
(5) Paul: that's what I think that's how I feel about it
(6) Chris: so if that's what you feel then why do you feel I've just started doing that now?

Commentary and Analysis

In lines (2) and (4) Mediator 1 reflects back Paul's sense of disempowerment and his dissatisfaction with what he perceives as 'micro-management'. In doing this she seeks clarification, gives him a chance to be heard and opens up this issue and the discourse it inhabits for exploration. In this way the discussion may be opened up to uncertainty so that potential for dialogue is created. If Paul feels this way, it would be a mistake if his feelings were not allowed to emerge, as the roots of the conflict would tend to remain buried and therefore liable to re-emerge later. For these moments one of the parties is more in control of the discussion with respect to the mediators. The mediators are listening and following the discussion. Mediator 1 has thus temporarily divested herself of a particular 'subject position' as either mediation process manager or proxy manager for the organisation.

There is a certain finger-pointing edge to phrases such 'do you think' (line (2)) and 'are you saying' (line (4)). However, such an almost (but not) 'transformative' turn, more following rather than leading the party that has enabled the power between the mediators and the parties to be more balanced, could have been extended to encourage an exploration of differences, causes and identities embroiled in the conflict. To do this, the mediator would seek to be 'knowing' about 'not knowing'. However, this may lead to an apoliticism in an environment replete with politics. In countering this apolitical tendency, the mediator may seek to bring a judgement to bear upon the political and potential ethical dimensions of the conflict interaction between the parties. In practice, this means that the mediator may observe/assess points of difference between the parties. In selecting these points for overt consideration by the parties, the mediator acts politically (from within a normative, cultural milieu) and invites an ethical reflection (Glynos and Howarth 2007) by the parties upon their own subjectivities and associated social norms. Thus, the mediator both judges the situation whilst endeavouring to remain open and unknowing about the course the interaction might take. Hence, a counterfactual mediation style may admit the consideration of new 'identifications' entailing, albeit perhaps only on rare occasions, the temporary politicisation of the subjectivities of the parties.

Closing Down Issues and a Compromise Agreement

Tenth extract, (40 mins 1 secs—40 mins 37 secs)

(1) Paul: well maybe she could do some of the filing stuff then if that's going to satisfy you and
(2) Chris: well I want it to satisfy you actually
(3) Paul: I'll be more accurate with the with the time recording if that's what you're offering, is that what you're offering?
(4) Chris: I said I'll look at it I'm not saying it can happen because Theresa isn't sitting there doing her knitting all day is she?
(5) Paul: well
(6) Mediator 1: do you both sense that there's possibly some, a bit of spare capacity there for her to be able to help out
(7) Chris: well there's possibly, but if we can't get Theresa to do it then we might be able to get a volunteer to work with you but if we do that you're going to have to make sure

that the volunteer does what is needed by the (funding agency) because…

Commentary and Analysis

Paul makes a qualified offer to comply with Chris's demands in line (1) and (3) but is met with resistance from Chris, and so in line (6) Mediator 1 invites Chris to move her position. Mediator 1 can scent a compromise agreement and so directs Chris towards this. From within the dominant discourse of a managerial culture that focuses upon task achievement, the mediator manoeuvres the parties towards a solution. Mediation, if practised in this way, will tend to remain an instrument of management, motivated primarily by reasons of cost-effectiveness. The mediator will inadvertently and unconsciously support a status quo and an opportunity, however slim, inherent within mediation for an 'ethical' engagement that seeks to uncover the radical contingency of social objects and relations will be missed (Glynos and Howarth 2007). Those offered recourse to mediation may just come to view it as another procedure for management control.

Eleventh extract, (42 mins 24 secs—46 mins 22 secs)

(1) Chris: … we've ended up with one form that records every single piece of information. Other organisations have got five forms but we don't
(2) Mediator 1: so your essential requirement is for Paul to be very, very clear about exactly the amount of time he spends on each case? {turning to Paul} Are you concerned about not wanting to be micro-managed? Is there any sense in which you're concerned that Chris might then turn round and say to you why did you take too long over that case?
(3) Paul: no, no I don't think there's any of that
(4) Mediator 1: no okay so, right
(5) Paul: I don't think that's the issue
(6) Mediator 1: right
(7) Mediator 2: so what is it then? What's the real issue?

(8) Paul: its just spending time doing things that just are not valuable in terms of what the work is for
(9) Mediator 1: okay
(10) Mediator 2: and I think
(11) Chris: it's the principle and you're principles are going to cost the clients the ability to be able to access advice which I think is really sad
(12) Mediator 1: so is there maybe, going back to what we were saying earlier on about challenging the (funding agency), is there maybe some compromise or short term solution to be found here in terms of you providing the information reluctantly that is required? But that actually there's a commitment by all of you to work together to actually challenge the (funding agency) and challenge this kind of micro-management type approach with a view to trying to get it changed in the future? But in the meantime not play poker with your actual job, do you know what I mean?
(13) Paul: all right yeah okay, well if I thought there was a real commitment to doing that then I'd think about how I'd do what I could, sure.
(14) Mediator 1: I mean I just get the impression that your sort of rebelling in your own sort of way
(15) Paul: yeah absolutely
(16) Mediator 1: against the process and Chris's concern is that that's all very well and she can see your point of view but she doesn't want to play poker with your job
(17) Paul: uh hum
(18) Mediator 1: because if we or you rebel too much and the information isn't provided the experience at Dunstable suggests that you
(19) Paul: uh hum
(20) Mediator 1: know funding could be withdrawn and then you won't have a job. Does that kind of sum up?
(21) Mediator 2: well I think perhaps the rebelling is quite a strong word, because of your values, your values
(22) Paul: absolutely

(23) Mediator 2: are with the people not with the paperwork to use
(24) Paul: I'm not being bloody minded as she says
(25) Mediator 1: you're standing up for what you believe in
(26) Paul: yes
(27) Chris: yes but then I think you're doing it, I don't understand, you explain to me then how you equate this, I will not do it, I'm not going to do it or I haven't been
(28) Mediator 1: I'm not sure we need to go there because I think that what you've just said that you are agreeable to the idea of trying to work together to actually provide the information in the short term whilst agreeing, whilst both committing to actually challenge the (funding agency) in the longer term as to actually how they require information from you and maybe looking into the admin
(29) Paul: I'd be willing to look into that sure
(30) Mediator 1: and you were talking earlier on as well about looking into some admin resourcing to help Paul
(31) Chris: mm yes that's fine but in the meanwhile we've got to have it happening because I can't have the trouble with this, it isn't something that we can just say oh well let's see how we go for a couple of months
(32) Mediator 1: yes okay so
(33) Chris: you know
(34) Mediator 1: yes absolutely. Are you {looking at Paul} are you okay with that, that if you're going to change and provide the information its got to start pretty soon? Do you want to sort of agree now that you may have a meeting tomorrow or this afternoon, something to actually work through how this is going to work in practice?
(35) Paul: yes I suppose so. It's just a sad state of affairs isn't it
(36) Mediator 2: sometimes these things happen, that within [naming her organisation] we have been asked to provide all kinds of information that we never provided in the past and believe me the number of people who are raving against it, me included…

Commentary and Analysis

In line (2) Mediator 1 summarises the difference between the parties over detailed time recording/micro-management and then seeks to explore Paul's concerns, positing her own assumption about them. When this assumption is denied in lines (3) and (5) Mediator 2 interjects in line (7) with a direct question to Paul about what is 'the real issue'. Such a direct question carries unspoken overtones of a directive desire to sort things out and represents more the relationship of an adult to a recalcitrant child.

Chris's anger (line (11)) at Paul's 'principles' is deliberately cut off by Mediator 1 who, contrary to the stated norm of mediation, proposes a compromise solution in line (12). Paul acquiesces to this compromise but only if there is 'real commitment' to challenging the micro-management he objects to (line (13)).

Mediator 1, in line (14), casts Paul as a rebel, indicating her judgement that Paul's behaviour is the problem. Paul identifies with this naming of him as a rebel against the process. Mediator 1 goes on to enforce the message that if you rebel too much your job is at stake. This leaves Mediator 1 with only one solution to pursue on behalf of the parties. Thus, the mediation has moved a long way from its starting premise of helping the parties to resolve their problem themselves. The mediators have investigated the problem and arrived at the solution that they are now shepherding the parties to agree upon. Both mediators in lines (21) and (25) (and again in line (36)) massage Paul's ego. This triggers an outburst from Chris in line (27), which Mediator 1 suppresses with a restatement of the proposed, compromise agreement. Both Chris's residual anger with Paul's stance (lines (8) and (24)) and Paul's belief in his right to rebel (line (22)), plus his sadness over the compromise (line (35)), are not explored. To do so would tend to disrupt the chance of an agreement that the mediators have manufactured for the parties.

In sum, this section displays the mediators, having glimpsed scope for a compromise solution, leading the conversation, controlling contributions, suggesting the solution and preventing the parties from further expressing their thoughts and feelings to each other. Thus, the mediators occupy 'subject positions' of conflict managers rather than supporters to an exploration of conflict. The difference is subtle yet profound. The motivation to manage conflict would seem to be an instrumental one of simply getting people back to work.

This motivation is consistent with many expressed utilitarian reasons for the application of workplace mediation, such as improving working relationships, reducing absenteeism or improving morale and productivity. Yet the practice of a 'problem-solving' approach, driven by a need to get people back to work, would appear to undermine the claims that workplace mediation affords non-judgmental support for party self- or co-determination.

Mediation is a process enjoined by parties who are, to some degree, searching for the possibility of a peaceful resolution. In a world of work where the act of employment is depoliticised and naturalised, we may expect mediators to work within dominant discourses in their pursuit of resolution. Social norms from which the conflict emerged are likely to remain unquestioned. However, an aspiration to neutrality and impartiality necessarily becomes a political act. In deciding not to decide we make a decision that has an effect upon our relationships with others. A stance of purported 'neutrality', in a situation of unequal power relations, may result in tacit support for the powerful. (Where minimal influence is more closely approximated as in the case of transformative mediation this problem also arises—see next chapter.) Claims of mediator neutrality infer non-interference in any dynamic of power between parties, whereas recognition of influence would suggest mediators cannot detach themselves fully from power relationship between parties. Paradoxically, it is necessary to be sensitive to the absence of neutrality to ensure resolutions can be decided by the antagonists to the largest extent possible.

It would seem that mediators thus have a choice at the start of a mediation of either overtly managing the development of resolution or party compromise or of supporting the potential for the emergence of temporary acts of dialogue.[6] These two appear mutually incompatible though both entail political action. The former depends upon an artful or skilled manipulation by a mediator that precludes any support for dialogue. As seen in the above 'problem-solving' approach, furnishing a compromise can become a very directive, task focused exercise in which the mediator's perception of the needs of the organisation come to supersede those of the parties (although one or both of the parties may identify with the mediator's interpretation of an organisation's needs). By definition, a clo-

---

[6] When an explorative approach is followed but turns out to be largely unsuccessful, the mediation will of course be concluded in a constructive way. The mediator will have built trust with the parties so that it is possible to hold a practical discussion concerning what to do next about the conflict.

sure of the conflict aligns with the organisational need for a return to a co-operative and 'efficient' working relationship.

In the latter choice, pursuing dialogue demands sensitivity to the impact of an intervention upon the parties, informed by uncertainty and tentativeness on the part of the mediator. Thus, a pursuit of dialogue indicates the need to support the parties in a possible uncovering of the radical contingency of social objects and relationships (Glynos and Howarth 2007) that inform the conflict. Whilst this 'uncovering' has a potential to give rise to a challenge to the political conditions surrounding the conflict, workplace mediators do not work as political agents imposing their own normative critique. However, such an approach to mediation, resting upon an ontology of radical contingency (Glynos and Howarth 2007), is inherently critical and yet seeks to retain a humility in which the parties' interactions are 'followed' rather than instigated. In a second role-play, considered in Chap. 6, this explorative mediation behaviour will be contrasted with 'transformative' practice. In Chap. 7 some proto-explanations for these divergent modes of mediator engagement, in terms of how either mode may be in the 'grip' of fanatasmatic logics and associated modes of enjoyment (Glynos 2008) will also be considered.

Final extract, (49 mins 22 secs—50 mins 23 secs)

(1) Chris: … we can work it so we keep the money, the clients, get the service and you've still got your job. At the end of the day that's my total goal with it, nothing else. I mean I don't have any other agendas
(2) Mediator 1: okay
(3) Mediator 2: so tell me what it is that you've agreed what is it that you are going to do Paul, what are you going to do?
(4) Paul: I'm going to make a greater effort to try and improve my time recording and work with Chris to find ways of trying to resolve the overall administrative load on the post I suppose
(5) Mediator 2: okay, and Chris what are you going to do?
(6) Chris: well I think we'll probably need to go and sit down and talk about how we're going to move it forward in term

of timescales … we probably need to start looking at the administrative tasks because maybe removing some of that from you

The role-play ended at 53 mins 5 secs.

Commentary and Analysis

In lines (3) and (5) the mediator directs the parties to restate the solution as to how they will behave in future to prevent problems arising again. This has a feel of the mediator as 'arbitrator' or even 'judge' and does not accord with the descriptions of workplace mediation promulgated by the industry (Crawley and Graham 2002; Gibbons 2007; Acas 2005; Acas and CIPD 2009).

Summary Interpretation of the Facilitative Mediation Role-Play

In the above examination of the work of the mediators, it is clearly possible to discern an overt direction of a resolution to the conflict. A picture of the exercise of power emerges. It is the power of the mediators' enunciative modality that fixes the parties as subject to the mediators' authority. This authority is derived from a self-declared and institutionally-backed, professional expertise of conflict management. The mediators are thus afforded a 'natural' right and obligation to control the mediation meeting process and interrogate the parties within it. By these means mediators acquire an obscured power to direct parties towards solutions of their own imagining or devising. They are able to transform themselves from 'supporters' of the parties to 'leaders' of solutions whilst retaining the rhetoric of mediation as a non-judgmental, self-determining process. 'Positioned' as proxy managers, the act of mediating becomes subsumed within a prevailing organisational discourse of a necessarily desirable, efficient outcome. The mediators, beneath a pretence of impartiality, appear to be intent on persuading Paul to accept the views and demands of his manager. 'Solving' the conflict for the parties aligns with getting people back to work. Espoused values of neutrality and impartiality shroud an instrumental directiveness. Acquiescence by parties, atomised by an underlying acceptance of individual responsibility for success or failure, (Glynos and Howarth 2007, p. 172) completes the naturalisation of an ultimately hegemonic process. From within an assumption of the transparency and homogeneity of social power and action (Laclau 1990, p. 130) the mediators deploy the attributes of general mediation; listening, reflecting back, summarising, but these become distorted by naturalised beliefs about appropriate norms and practices in the workplace.

Hence, the mediation has seemed to focus mostly upon the material issues of the conflict rather than upon the personal interrelationship between Paul and Chris and the underlying discourses, beliefs and identities out of which this relationship is formed. Causal webs and patterns of power surrounding the conflict have not received much consideration. In a sense, the 'conflict' has been regarded as an aberration or a problem in need of correction, arising between two autonomous agents. As noted in Chap. 4, conflict is viewed as arising from an antagonistic clash between individuals 'with fully constituted identities and interests' (Howarth 2000, p. 105). Moving from a political analysis of antagonism at a social level analysed by Howarth, (2000) we may extrapolate that antagonism arises at the interpersonal level because one's sense of identity is challenged and interests linked with identity cannot be fulfilled. The adversary is then blamed. We can interpret the dislocatory experience, i.e. the conflict between Paul and Chris, as a blockage to the attainment of their respective identities. Chris's role, as a firm but considerate manager, has been challenged by Paul's apparent insubordination and refusal to comply with a procedure. Paul's identity as a skilled debt worker, valued by his clients and colleagues, is being threatened by unreasonable and bureaucratic demands for form-filling. The 'blockage' (form filling), is common to both of them; a demand by one versus a refusal by the other. In this opposition, they each become the other's 'enemy'.

Howarth describes the discourse analyst's task as

> to describe ways in which the identities of agents are blocked, and to chart the different means by which these obstacles are constructed in antagonistic terms by social agents. (Howarth 2000, p. 105)

Whilst the workplace mediator is not a discourse analyst and is working with 'individuals' rather than surveying social movements, she/he may derive an insight from this definition and regard the mediation meeting as an opportunity to support the parties in gaining an understanding of their own and each other's identities and subjectivities. This would necessitate that the mediators place people qua people ahead of people qua human resources/ units of production. Yet the above focus upon the 'material' aspect of conflict seems to lead towards the objectification of the parties as mere human resources. Notwithstanding this analysis, mainstream mediation espouses an exclusive concern for people, but for people as individual, sovereign agents. This suggests the operation of a doubly layered fantasy. Firstly, in this stance of humanism, in denial 'of an awareness of the socially constructed character of identity' (Stavrakakis 2005, p. 70) and secondly, in the belief that problem-solving mediation can elevate this humanism above a discourse of workplace task achievement that primarily serves the needs of the organisation. In the above case study the reverse is apparent.

Drawing upon a view of identity and identification that rests upon the Lacanian concept of ontological lack and also upon Laclau's concept of the radical contingency of identity and social formation, reviewed above, Howarth further explains that,

> antagonisms reveal the boundaries or political frontiers of a social formation, as they show the points where identity can no longer be stabilized in a meaningful system of differences, but is contested by forces which stand at the limit of that order. (Howarth 2000, p. 106)

Although this theoretical analysis again refers to broad socio-political forces it has a resonance in the microcosm of the mediation encounter. The stabilisation of identity in a 'meaningful system of differences' encapsulates a central theme of mediation, very closely echoing the objectives of transformative mediation in particular. The aim of transformative mediation is to restore calm and harmony through the stabilisation of identity and mutual recognition. However, if the system of differences maintains an oppressive hegemony, mediation may be accused of acting regressively in harness to such a system. A progressive form of mediation would, at first glance, seem to require a counter-intuitive act of possibly exacerbating the conflict to disturb this system of meaningful differences. It would appear to be madness to contemplate exacerbating conflict and therefore conflict must be suppressed. It is from this reasoning that the discourse of problem-solving mediation, that holds a 'negative vision of human conflict' (Bush and Folger 2005, p. 239) becomes naturalised.

In contrast, Bush and Folger argue for an 'essentially positive vision' (2005, p. 239) of conflict. In a similar vein, but with a different trajectory, it may be argued that it is possible to work through conflict, risking exacerbation, to create a reconfigured system of differences that may be less oppressive and conflictual than before. For Bush and Folger this 'working through' is found in their therapeutic method that aims to induce moments of recognition of the 'others' individual humanity, irrespective of contextual social and political norms. Drawing upon the logics of explanation developed by Glynos and Howarth (2007), it may be suggested that 'recognition' might go beyond Bush and Folger's idealistic humanism to a more material sensitivity to one's own and the other's subjectivity, brought into relief by awareness of the contingency of prevailing social and political norms. That this is not the case in either the 'facilitative' role-play above or the 'transformative' one examined in the next chapter may be partly explained if we regard the mediators as being in the 'grip of fantasy'. Glynos and Howarth explain that,

> [t]he role of fantasy in this context is not to set up an illusion that provides a subject with a false picture of the world, but to ensure that the radical contingency of social reality—and the political dimension of a practice more specifically—remains in the background. (Glynos and Howarth 2007, p. 145)

Glynos and Howarth define an ethical practice as one in which the radical contingency of social reality is brought to the foreground and the fantasy of the absence or insignificance of the political dimension is punctured. In considering the approach of Mediators 1 and 2 in the above role-play, it is possible to conclude that there is an unawareness, tantamount to a fantasy, of leading the parties to a solution that has been framed in the minds of the mediators themselves. This may be because the solution is obvious to all within the discursive frame of the contemporary workplace in which certain patterns of behaviour have been normalised. There are also implicit assumptions that both the conflict and the application of mediation practice have no political dimension. In the words of Glynos and Howarth it is placed in the background. Above all, there is a presumption that the subjectivities of the parties innately grow from their essential, human identities. It is as if the conflict may have brought on a momentary emotional disruption of their sense of wellbeing, but a solution, if it can be found, will restore 'normality'.

The mediators seem to have identified themselves with the role of peacemaker (or dealmaker in Dolder's critique) and, by deriving 'enjoyment' in this role, they become sedimented within a naturalised world of the work organisation that is found in a market economy (Fairclough 2001; Glynos 2008). Their own employment, as mediators, rests upon this sense of identity. This is how the 'subject position' of facilitative mediator becomes merged with the 'subject position' of proxy manager.

A counterfactual stance, what may be termed explorative mediation, would recognise that conflict is inherently political and that subjectivities are largely socially constructed and in a sense arbitrary. Therefore, this explorative approach would seek to give space for the parties to express themselves without the interference of an interrogative disposition. In this way it may be possible to open up a view of that which is contingent and thereby to afford an opportunity for exploration by the parties of their own 'modes of subjectivity' (Glynos 2008, p. 276).

A transformative or an explorative mediator would try to avoid equating party reconciliation with a success for the mediator. This is a matter for the parties and many different yet 'successful' outcomes are possible. In contrast, it is also possible that the mediators in this role-play tried even harder to achieve a successful outcome because they may have felt 'watched' or 'tested' by the 'observing' researcher, and even by the parties as actors. Approaching the act of mediating, 'enjoyment' (Stavrakakis 2005; Glynos 2008) may be obtained from an expectation of an expert performance, and then subsequently, in the believed achievement of peacemaking; of re-stabilising the same 'meaningful system of differences' that prevailed before the conflict flared.

However, all of these motivating emotional/ affective factors may be subsumed under the simple humane desire to help those in distress.

Mediators may believe, on rare occasions, that collective making of meaning within the group has occurred, illusorily or otherwise. There is a risk that the mediator may feel they have become a hero in the wise, Socratic mould, without awareness that dialogue may have been suppressed and the status quo upheld.

As noted, this same fantasy could equally well apply to a mediator practising in the explorative style. However, if parties are able to arrive at a new and critical understanding of the same system of differences, or even to glimpse an altered system of differences from which they can question social practices, their own subjectivities and 'realities', the mediator may be permitted some enjoyment. Such enjoyment is derived from sharing with the parties in an ethical detachment from fantasy as defined above (Glynos 2008, p. 291).

Mediators who are aware of choices in how they mediate may adopt a transformative or an explorative style. Nevertheless, underlying motivations, such as fear of not generating a successful outcome, or a humane, compassionate desire to help those in distress, may yet lead to a relapse into a more facilitative, problem-solving approach. A fear of 'failure' to achieve reconciliation may powerfully lead any mediator to compromise an 'ethical' practice and opt to shepherd parties toward such reconciliation. (This psychology of mediator motivation will be examined in more detail in Chap. 7.) We shall now turn to a consideration of how relational mediation and transformative mediation in particular address the problem of an inherent tendency to directiveness found in much facilitative mediation.

References

Acas (Advisory, Conciliation and Arbitration Service). (2005). *The Acas small firms' mediation pilot: Research to explore parties' experiences and views on the value of mediation*. Acas Research Paper Ref: 04/05. London: Acas. Retrieved from http://www.acas.org.uk/index.aspx?articleid=4701&q=small+firms+pilot

Acas (Advisory, Conciliation and Arbitration Service). (2014). *Reframing resolution—Managing conflict and resolving individual disputes in the contemporary workplace*. Acas Policy Discussion Papers March. London: Acas. Retrieved from http://www.acas.org.uk/index.aspx?articleid=4701&q=reframing+resolution+policy+paper

Acas & CIPD, (Advisory, Conciliation and Arbitration Service & the Chartered Institute of Personnel and Development). (2009). *Mediation: An employer's guide*. London: Acas. Retrieved from http://www.acas.org.uk/index.aspx?articleid=4701&q=mediation+an+employers+guide

Beer, J. E., & Stief, E. (1997). *The mediator's handbook* (3rd ed.). Gabriola Island, British Columbia, Canada: New Society Publishers.

Billig, M. (2001). Discursive, rhetorical and ideological Messages. In M. Wetherall, S. Taylor, & S. J. Yates (Eds.), *Discourse theory and practice: A reader* (pp. 210–221). London: Sage Publications.

Bush, R. A. B., & Folger, J. P. (2005). *The promise of mediation: The transformative approach to conflict*. San Francisco: Jossey-Bass Inc.

Clegg, S. R., & Hardy, C. (1999). *Studying organization: Theory and method*. London: Sage Publications.

Clegg, S. R., Hardy, C., & Nord, W. R. (1999). *Managing organizations: Current issues*. London: Sage Publications.

Cloke, K. (2001). *Mediating dangerously: The frontiers of conflict resolution*. San Francisco: Jossey Bass Inc.

Crawley, J., & Graham, K. (2002). *Mediation for managers: Resolving conflict and rebuilding relationships at work*. London: Nicholas Brealey Publishing.

Dolder, C. (2004). The contribution of mediation to workplace justice. *International Law Journal, 33*(4), 320–342.

Fairclough, N. (2001). *Language and power* (2nd ed.). Harlow, England: Longman.

Fairclough, N. (2005). Discourse analysis in organisation studies: The case for critical realism. *Organization Studies, 26*(6), 915–939.

Fairclough, N. (2006). *Language and globalization*. Abingdon, England: Routledge.

Folger, J. P. (2001). Who owns what in mediation?: Seeing the link between process and content. In J. P. Folger & R. A. B. Bush (Eds.), *Designing mediation: Approaches to training and practice within a transformative framework* (pp. 55–60). New York: Institute For the Study of Conflict Transformation, Inc.

Gibbons, M. (2007). *Better dispute resolution: A review of employment dispute resolution in Great Britain*. An independent Report commissioned by DTI (Department of Trade and Industry), published on March 21. London: DTI.

Gilbert, P. (2010). *The compassionate mind*. London: Constable and Robinson Ltd.
Glover, J. (1991). *I: The philosophy and psychology of personal identity*. London: Penguin Books.
Glynos, J. (2008). Ideological fantasy at work. *Journal of Political Ideologies, 13*(3), 275–296.
Glynos, J., & Howarth, D. (2007). *Logics of critical explanation in social and political theory*. Abingdon, England: Routledge.
Greenberg, J., & Eskew, D. E. (1993). The role of role playing in organizational research. *Journal of Management, 19*(2), 221–241.
Habermas, J. (1971). *Towards a rational society*. London: Heinemann.
Howarth, D. (2000). *Discourse*. Buckingham: Open University Press.
Howarth, D. (2005). Applying discourse theory: The method of articulation. In D. Howarth & J. Torfing (Eds.), *Discourse theory in European politics: Identity, policy and governance* (pp. 316–349). Basingstoke: Palgrave MacMillan.
Laclau, E. (1990). *New reflections on the revolution of our time*. London: Verso.
Lederach, J. P. (2003). *The little book of conflict transformation*. Intercourse, PA: Good Books.
McNamee, S., & Gergen, K. J. (1999). *Relational responsibility: Resources for sustainable dialogue*. London: Sage Publications.
Phillips, L., & Jorgensen, M. W. (2006[2002]). *Discourse analysis as theory and method*. London: Sage Publications.
Rifkin, J., Millen, J., & Cobb, S. (1991). Towards a New Discourse for Mediation: A Critique of Neutrality. *Mediation Quarterly. 9*(2), 151–164.
Sarup, M. (1993). *An introductory guide to post-structuralism and postmodernism* (2nd ed.). London: Harvester Wheatsheaf.
Seaman, R. J. (2010). *Locating the mediator within workplace discourse: Supporter of the status quo or humble "midwife" of dialogue? Developing and alternative workplace mediation practice*. Ph.D. thesis. Retrieved from http://eprints.bournemouth.ac.uk/17117/
Stavrakakis, Y. (2005). Passions of identification, discourse, enjoyment and European politics. In D. Howarth & J. Torfing (Eds.), *Discourse theory in European politics: Identity, policy and governance*. Basingstoke: Palgrave Macmillan.
Torfing, J. (1999). *New theories of discourse: Laclau, Mouffe and Zizek*. Oxford: Blackwell Publications Ltd.
Winslade, J., & Monk, G. (2001). *Narrative mediation: A new approach to conflict resolution*. San Francisco: Jossey-Bass Inc.

6

Relational Mediation

Building upon the critique of facilitative mediation above, this chapter will examine the two styles of mediation known as 'narrative' and 'transformative' and dubbed by Kressel (2006) as 'relational mediation'. These two schools of practice, as indicated by the name, focus on the recovery of relations that are non-conflictual and thereby give emphasis to an overtly moral dimension in addition to any instrumental and practical objectives of facilitative workplace mediation. By assessing the potential of relational styles to privilege an aspiration for dialogue, this examination will then afford a basis for the delineation (in Chap. 7) of an explorative style that places an aspiration for dialogical behaviour at the centre of mediation practice.

In the standard problem-solving approach to mediation, mediators help individuals to understand and prioritise their respective interests (i.e. their underlying concerns and needs) in order to discover a mutually acceptable compromise position that will largely satisfy their principal interests. From a transformative perspective, it has been convincingly argued that, because facilitative mediators take full control of the mediation process, including managing turn-taking and agenda-setting, they inevitably become too involved in the content of the conflict (Folger 2001). Furthermore, mediator tendencies of 'problem' evaluation and of direction towards resolution seem to be inherent in this facilitative, settlement-driven model of mediation, at least when it is applied inside organisations. Indeed, when facilitative mediation is deployed within the workplace, these directive tendencies are found to be knit together with an instrumental purpose of minimising disruption and re-establishing a pre-conflict status quo. However, in the 1990s a very different approach to mainstream problem-solving mediation was promulgated by Bush and Folger (1994, 2005), one called transformative mediation. Then, with the publication of 'Narrative Mediation' in 2001 by Winslade and Monk, yet another style of mediation was offered to practitioners. These new 'relational' approaches have arisen, not surprisingly, from critiques of problem-solving mediation and in particular of the problematic widespread assumption of neutrality.

These will be examined below to assess how their founding purposes extend beyond the limited but, in many senses valuable instrumental intent of problem-solving mediation. The transformative school explicitly affirms a moral purpose of supporting respectful communication for the very specific mediation technique it defines. Perhaps the moral dimension peculiar to narrative mediation lies in its intent to help parties understand 'complex social contexts' and 'cultural stories' (Winslade and Monk 2001, p. 11) and in its openness to alternative stories. Also, narrative mediation, like the transformative approach, is concerned with the creation of a 'relational climate' (p. 71) by which communication may be recovered in the midst of conflict.

Narrative Mediation

In a narrative turn, Cobb and Rifkin (1991) addressed questions of mediator neutrality from a perspective of poststructuralist theory, stating that conflict stories are constructed and that mediators 'manage the social construction of disputes and settlements' (p. 50). They go on to describe neutrality as, a practice *in discourse*, specifically, the management of person's positions in stories, the intervention in the associated interactional patterns between stories, and the construction of alternative stories (p. 62).

This suggests that mediators sit within discourse alongside the parties but are also somehow able to stand apart and manage the unfolding of discursive meaning construction in the mediation session. So rather than deny influence, in a stance of neutrality, the mediator engages in a cocreation of alternative stories. But it is implied that this is done with some considerable influence, attributing a certain professional detachment to the mediator. It is questionable whether the mediator who is said to be part of discourse can operate influentially and dynamically at a meta-level simultaneously above discourse. By definition we are all drawn into discourses, 'symbolic systems and social orders' (Howarth 2000, p. 5), and whilst meanings are continuously negotiated, we yield to an acceptance of prevailing 'realities'. How the identities of things and people are thus formed is often masked through language and other social processes. Far from being able to 'manage' discourse from 'above', the mediator is more likely to be drawn into alignment with dominant discourses threading through the mediation space. (This will be illustrated in the second case study below).

The quote from Cobb and Rifkin above mirrors the mediation process developed by Winslade and Monk (2001), who explain that their approach is based upon social constructionist principles and arose in part due to others' critiques of problem-solving mediation. They note that the mainstream mediator is characterised as an objective, neutral third party operating in the scientific tradition in the search for a universal 'truth'. However, they prefer not to cast the mainstream school as in some way 'wrong' (p. 35). Rather, the 'mainstream' represents for them but one of many culturally and historically situated methods. Nevertheless, they cite the disquiet of many who question assumptions of neutrality and the possibility for impartial detachment of a 'process facilitator' (p. 36) from the content of the mediation. Narrative mediation is proffered as a 'theoretically robust and intensely practical' (p. 37) alternative. The mainstream 'inside-out' model, locating the emanation of conflict within the individual's 'desires, interests and needs' assuming that 'the individual is unitary and context-independent', is contrasted with narrative mediation's '"outside-in" phenomenon' (p. xi). Here conflict is understood as a social product in which meanings and stories are socially contested.

Thus, narrative mediation seeks to grapple directly with the parties' stories about their conflict, and mediation is defined as a task to tease out narratives 'in order to open up possibilities for alternative stories to gain an audience' (p. 53). This approach, which has grown from narrative therapy (Monk and Winslade 1996), embraces three main elements. The first is 'engagement', entailing listening, building rapport and storytelling. This is followed by 'deconstruction' of the conflict story, involving the externalisation of parties' language and the identification of alternative stories. Lastly, the mediator works with the parties to 'construct' a new, non-conflictual story. Winslade and Monk note that '[e]very story offers people positions to take up in relation to each other' (p. 72). The mediator's deconstructive thrust seeks to 'make visible the relative positions that each version of the conflict story offers' (p. 74). Further, '[b]y asking questions, the mediator tries to make visible the workings of the dominant problem discourses' (p. 78). Then these positions are named to isolate 'sticking points' (p. 82) between parties. Also, the narrative mediator selects, or elicits through questioning, experiences left out of the conflict story, termed 'unique outcomes', in order 'to build on them a counter story of the conflict-saturated story' (p. 84). Thus, 'the mediator asks questions that draw forth the parties' knowledge about how to resolve the dispute' (p. 75). The mediator also aims to 'facilitate the development of personal agency' (p. 87) by the parties, and to 'invite people into positions of partnership in the development of preferred resolutions' (p. 70).

From these descriptions of practice we may deduce that narrative mediation commences 'relationally' in that it deals with parties' accounts of the conflict rather than focusing upon problems to be solved. Yet it would appear to move towards a form of 'problem-solving' as the mediator works to free parties from their conflict stories and build a new story, which is a 'resolution' ultimately led by the mediator. Hence, the process has an end in view in the mind of the mediator, which is to create a new account of the conflict that is not conflictual or to escape a 'conflict-saturated relationship' (p. 82). Winslade and Monk do echo Bush and

Folger in arguing that '[s]ometimes the development of an attitude of cooperation and respect may be more important than any substantive agreement' (p. 82) but there is a clear trajectory implicit in their method. This is evident in their explanation that the 'narrative orientation might be described as an effort to join the parties to a dispute in an alliance against the effects of the conflict' (p. 71).

It is apparent from this type of questioning and intervention that the narrative mediator is required to exercise considerable influence and even directiveness (however transparent) from a base of substantial expertise. We may therefore infer that narrative mediation is a top-down, expertly led, therapeutic intervention, possibly enacted with limited acknowledgement of the wider political dimensions of conflict despite claims to an underpinning social constructionist philosophy. As a more top-down intervention it is ultimately unlikely to be conducive to the emergence of dialogue.

However, contrary to this assessment, Winslade and Monk argue that through an interest in the micro-politics of mediation they are at pains to avoid 'practicing down' (p. 122). Recognising the mediation encounter as a discursive event, Winslade and Monk warn against mediators placing themselves in an 'expert knowing position' or getting drawn emotionally into the participants' stories (pp. 74–75). They argue that reflexive practice by the mediator can 'render transparent the practices of power in the mediation relationship' (p. 122) so that their power is shared with the parties. This is said to be achieved by making 'position calls' more transparent so as to justify 'the right to be an author in others' life stories' (p. 121). This phrase is pivotal to the narrative approach. To author another's story is certainly a description of mediator influence and power, even if this power is apparent to the 'other' and accepted by them. As the mediator steps into this role of authorship, contingent stories from whatever source may be shut out. Therefore the timing (at whatever stage of the mediation) of any acts of 'authorship' becomes important. Thus, there are at least two overlapping dimensions of power of the mediator in play. The mediators may, unconsciously or otherwise, influence the outcome from within their own evaluation of the conflict and, secondly, they may either enhance or inhibit access to other contingent narratives irrespective of their own 'opinions'. If such access is inhibited, this technique might reduce conflict to a superficial matter of language differences between individuals, detached from underlying social antagonisms or wider contextual concerns. But although a risk, this may be unlikely to be the case where the mediator is skilled and sustains openness to many stories for as long as possible. Winslade and Monk do imply that parties may be helped to name power relations, which could lead to exploration of contingent stories, although it is not made clear how this could happen.

Concerning the relative power of the parties, they point to a dilemma for mediators who hold an essentialist understanding of power (p. 50), in the sense that power is viewed as a commodity residing in the individual. This is because such mediators want to maintain their status as 'neutral and impartial agents' (p. 50) and therefore they are unable to support obviously weaker/oppressed parties and prevent mediation becoming a site of abuse by more powerful parties. But Winslade and Monk are fully aware that this neutrality is a mirage that belongs in the realm of 'folklore' (p. 48). They also reject 'static pictures of power belonging to and resting with individuals' (p. 50). They thereby avoid what they term a dilemma by adopting a poststructuralist Foucaultian interpretation of power in which power operates not as a commodity adhering to a hierarchical position, but 'in and through discourse' (p. 50). This being so, they argue that mediators do not even need to seek to support weaker parties. This all seems to point to some confusion about their philosophy of power and agency. If mediators are not neutral they must have a certain power to influence parties, inadvertently or otherwise. Indeed Winslade and Monk accept that some people (parties and mediators) may be positioned in places of influence (p. 50) and that power can be oppressive and 'operate systematically' (p. 51). They further note that people engage in struggles and resistance, as 'relations are constantly being produced and reproduced, even in the middle of a mediation' (p. 51). By resisting, they argue, people may develop a sense of agency. Retaining this notion of 'agency' they explain that their poststructuralist

> analysis moves away from a globalized notion of powerlessness and sensitizes persons to their ability to act, even in some modest way (p. 51).

This reinforcement of a concept of agency is seemingly inconsistent with their claim to Foucaultian poststructuralist credentials. As already touched upon in Chap. 4, Foucault decentres both power and agency, limiting capacity for intentional action (Caldwell 2007). Willmott (1994) finds in Foucault 'a refusal to clarify the normative criteria for distinguishing more or less acceptable forms of power' (p. 115) and notes that resistance by a Foucaultian agent to subjection appears 'restless … capricious, individualistic and ultimately nihilistic' (p. 115). So on the one hand, Winslade and Monk seek to deny the problem of manifestations of hierarchical and structural power in keeping with Foucault's analysis, thus potentially depoliticising mediation, yet on the other they appear to reconstitute a dualism in which agency is counterposed to oppressive power operating systematically. Agency is both denied and asserted in a practice avowedly underpinned by Foucaultian theorising.

Perhaps this confusion betrays a wider apoliticism in their work. The concern of narrative mediation to exclusively focus upon rewriting the parties' stories, with reliance upon mediator 'authorship', may lead to directive attention at the micro-political level and a lack of attention to macro-political dimensions. These wider political dimensions may be rendered as unspoken or unacknowledged hinterlands to many conflict situations. However, negating an overly harsh critique, this tendency to lose sight of the 'political' might be almost innate to any small-scale (two party) mediator engagement. This is because parties and mediators alike bring their relatively fixed identities and subjectivities, which have already been shaped in the discourse of their culture, into the mediation meeting. Furthermore, we all tend to interact with an overpowering sense of our individuality (however illusory) and parties often feel they are wholly responsible for their *own* conflict.

Theoretically at least, it may be possible to escape this facet of mediation practice by finding a base for mediation philosophy and practice in the discourse theory of Laclau and Mouffe (Howarth 2000; Torfing 1999). This theory can help us resolve some of the confusion over the relative balance of forces between, on the one hand, the deterministic aspects of structural power and on the other the voluntaristic implications of 'agency' that are evident in the narrative project. Far from finding 'structure' and 'agency' antithetical or dualistic, the social significance of interrelated and interconnected concepts of agency and structure (of the individual and the organisation) are theorised 'as the outcome of political articulations' (Willmott 2005, p. 751). Willmott (2005) finds that Laclau and Mouffe's theory posits neither voluntarism (privileging agency) nor determinism (privileging structure). Acquiring identity represents an inescapable decision made in circumstances of undecidability and such a decision results in an imaginary closure of structural possibility, which nevertheless remains precarious and subject to dislocation. There is always an excess of meaning (and of possibility/impossibility) beyond the temporary yet necessary closures in which forms of identity and structure are articulated in the social and political domain. As Laclau (1990) explains, 'the same precarious character of any structuration that we find in the domain of the social order, is also found in the domain of subjectivity' (p. 92). The practical inference of this dynamic discursive reality, found in the mediation meeting, is that the mediator should suspend interpretation of readings of the conflict, thereby withholding 'mediator-led' decisions arising from any such interpretation, including the authoring of new stories. It remains uncertain how the narrative mediator, required to deploy considerable expertise in teasing out a non-conflictual story, could maintain such a suspension of interpretation that would seem necessary to better allow space for the flourishing of dialogue.

As a therapeutic, counselling-based intervention, narrative mediation that leads parties towards a reframing or rewriting of their conflict stories is surely of great value. But if Winslade and Monk follow Cobb and Rifkin by ambitiously placing the mediator as orchestrator of 'discourse' and arbiter of 'meaning', their approach may be criticised as being based upon a vulgarised interpretation of a social constructionist discourse theory. Having said this there is great significance for the field of mediation in Winslade's and Monk's identification that

> Discourse exploration in mediation is a useful tool for depersonalizing conflict. It helps us see how systems of meaning, or fields of knowledge and belief, shape not only people's perspectives, agendas, and desires but also the very nature of a conflict. (2001, p. 42)

In recognising discursive power, narrative mediation broadens the instrumental remit of facilitative approaches to admit a political dimension even if this dimension remains undeveloped. All mediation may be said to hold a moral intent in that it seeks to diffuse conflict. Perhaps narrative mediation may be said to enhance this moral dimension through the recognition of the social and political context of conflict, which is lacking in the mostly instrumental disposition of facilitative workplace mediation. Transformative mediation, which will be considered next, does not take inspiration from an understanding of discourse but does have an overtly moral message. Moreover, transformative mediation raises the mediator's suspension of any interpretation or evaluation of the parties' stories to something of an art form.

Transformative Mediation

Overview of Theory and Practice

Bush and Folger unequivocally state the consequence of a problem-solving approach is a failure to realise the 'Promise of Mediation' (1994; 2005), one amounting to a lost opportunity:

> In our view, the potential that mediation offered to foster and support positive human interaction within conflict was being squandered. Instead mediation was being used to shore up institutional processes that operate to control, contain, and settle conflict (Bush and Folger 2005, p. 1).

It is argued that problem-solving inevitably inhibits the goal of mediation to create an environment that enables party self-determination and the recovery of a positive human interaction. Furthermore,

> [s]olving problems *for* parties is not transformative mediation, because it fails to support—and probably undermines—genuine party empowerment (p. 71).

Despite a feeling of squandered potential, and with echoes of Winslade and Monk's slightly tangential critical stance, they do not state that other mediation approaches are invalid. However, they proffer an alternative that rests upon a 'coherent viewpoint' (p. 45) of conflict and conflict intervention. Party empowerment, self-determination yet interconnectedness and mediator neutrality are interwoven, central concepts of Bush and Folger's transformative mediation project. In their consideration of the specific 'problem' of mediator neutrality, they have reconceptualised 'neutrality' thus:

> Neutrality means that the mediator's only interest is the interest in using his or her influence to make sure that the *parties maintain control* of decisions about outcome. … By adopting the transformative approach, the mediation movement gains a solution to the problem of the inevitability of influence (Bush and Folger 1994, pp. 105–106).

Hence, they argue that using the transformative technique to empower the parties, the necessary influence of the mere presence of a third party can be completely channelled into the support of self-determining interactions. The mediator thus effects a certain, almost radical detachment from the parties. This approach to mediation is rooted in Bush and Folger's theory that conflict is primarily an 'interactional crisis' (2005, p. 46).

Deeper than possible causal concerns of power, rights or needs, Bush and Folger see conflict more significantly as a disturbance to human beings' 'sense of their own strength and their sense of connection to others' (p. 46). Thus, disputants feel powerless and self-absorbed and view their antagonists with hostility and anger, eventually demonising them. Hence, for the transformative mediator, mediation is not about containment or negotiation but about a way to foster a qualitative transformation of human interaction (p. 9). Bush and Folger's theory is that the negative spiral of conflict interaction can be reversed if the parties make shifts towards greater self 'empowerment' (p. 56) to re-stabilise a sense of their identity, which then releases an innate human ability for understanding and reconnection or 'recognition' (p. 56). These behavioural responses of 'empowerment' and 'recognition' are the twin pillars of their philosophy and their technique. They define empowerment as 'the restoration to individuals of a sense of their own value and strength and their own capacity to make decisions' (p. 22). In an ironic sense, the individual becomes again the self-determining person who entered into conflict but is now balanced by acquisition of 'recognition'. Recognition is defined as 'the evocation in individuals of acknowledgement, understanding, or empathy for the situation and views of the other' (p. 22). This is clearly a precursor to any possibility for the emergence of dialogue. Hence, Bush and Folger advocate a technique of mediation intervention designed to support parties in these shifts of 'empowerment and recognition' in order to effect a 'transformation' of the conflict interaction (p. 56). This is what they mean by the term 'transformative mediation'.

To this end, as much of the transformative mediation process as possible is placed in the control of the parties with the mediator supporting their conversation to enhance the realisation of opportunities for empowerment and recognition, thereby helping the parties listen to each other and to themselves (p. 135). In the course of the meeting the mediator will intervene to summarise, paraphrase, reflect back dialogue or check intentions, with the aim of ensuring clarity of communication. But most importantly, interventions are designed to support the small shifts in empowerment and recognition that may be occurring. Thus, transformative mediators proactively 'listen intently for cues that offer opportunities to work with empowerment and recognition' (p. 221). They 'encourage the parties to engage in a constructive dialogue' (p. 221), and importantly, 'they *follow* the parties along their path through empowerment and recognition' (p. 222, italics added).

The key word in this description of a proactive practice is 'follow'. The parties pursue their own course through the meeting and the mediator follows them closely, with a 'microfocus' (p. 233) on the moment-by-moment interactions. Hence, they do not pay close attention to the content or substance of conflict stories that unfold. Again this enables the parties to be much more in control of the process, the content and the outcome. Parties expressing high emotion are not, in general, reined in. Mayer (2004, p. 103) explains that in conflict 'the fundamental need that people have is to express strong feelings in strong ways.' An absolute trust is placed in the capacity of the parties to transform their own conflict rather than spiral down into anger and recrimination. However, this places a heavy burden of self-determining responsibility for the conflict upon the parties, while the mediator remains aloof from the issues of conflict content or context. This being said, a form of interaction that may be described as bickering might arise in both community and workplace mediations, although it is less likely to occur in the more contained environment of the workplace. Bickering usually takes the form of rapid-fire exchanges of accusations and denials. Both parties become highly defensive, justify their own positions and simultaneously attack the other party for being offensive, injurious and wrong. To prevent the mediation from breaking down completely, the mediator will typically intervene to cool things down. In the transformative case this might be achieved by a quick sequence of interventions picking up on the statements in which both parties express disempowerment, by requesting fuller explanations of the various accusations being thrown about. Thus, whilst the transformative style hands process control to the parties, it yet retains a supportive structure, as the very interventions underscoring shifts in empowerment and recognition afford a framework for holding parties on a track and away from a possible descent into a negative spiral of bickering.

The power exercised by the transformative mediator is not that of an expert facilitator, reframing statements otherwise imbued with blame, focusing on the future and shepherding parties through a conversation, away from discord, to common ground and towards material choices about ways of finding a necessary, workable settlement. Rather, their more circumscribed skill and power rests with the intervention timing and the choice of party dialogue she or he summarises or reflects back, or the questions of clarification that are posed. For Bush and Folger,

> [t]he promise that mediation offers for transforming conflict interaction is real, because skilled mediators can support the parties' own work, create a space for that work to go on, and—most important—stay out of the parties' way (2005, p. 83).

This style of mediation is comparable with the basic technique of the client-centred therapy and group learning methods of Carl Rogers (2001). As Winslade and Monk point out 'by using paraphrasing to summarise and reflect the feelings, … expressed by the client', mediators are using skills 'advocated by Carl Rogers' (2001, p. 64). In the case of narrative mediation this enables the mediators to demonstrate their understanding of the client to the client. But paraphrasing and summarising in transformative interventions, whilst highly reflective of what the parties have recently contributed, maintains a sole focus upon shifts in 'empowerment' and 'recognition'. As noted, the narrative span of the conflict story is not of immediate concern to the mediator and is regarded as a distraction or a temptation to make judgments or assessments and evaluations of the parties and their conflict. In a purist commitment to interventions that only address the 'interactional crisis' (Bush and Folger 2005, p. 52) Bush and Folger absolutely reject the notion that transformative mediation practice could be 'combined or integrated' (p. 45) with other approaches. Others have questioned this purist stance (Gaynier 2005; Pruitt 2006; Seul 1999; Williams 1996) and it would be a shame for the mediation field not to benefit from the work of Bush and Folger through the integration of different approaches. The purist application of transformative mediation appears to be grounded in its supporting philosophy. The following critique of transformative mediation arises from its overly optimistic view of the social in the form of its particular *relational worldview* (p. 252) and from an apoliticism discernable in the corresponding social philosophy underlying this worldview that will now be examined.

Critique of Transformative Mediation

One contribution of the transformative technique that is of enormous value is the mediator's ability to learn to listen more clearly to his or her own mental formulations of alternative (non-transformative) interventions, which carry, however obscured, the assumptions, evaluations or subtle directions of the mediator. By remaining exclusively focussed on shifts of empowerment and recognition, assumptions and evaluations may be controlled and self-censored, providing an antidote to any tendency towards the innate directiveness of a 'problem-solving' disposition. The mediator is unable to make comments containing judgements of the parties, as these would not be supportive of shifts in empowerment and recognition. The transformative approach may be viewed as potentially a much more reflexive and reflective practice (Rothman 1996; Kingdon 2005) than problem-solving mediation. As Bush and Folger argue, adopting the transformative approach to mediation would help solve the problems of problem solving: by offering a solution to the problem of mediator influence. (1994, p. 107)

However, they add that this major practical advantage is surpassed by transformative mediation's greatest strength, that of 'capturing the priceless opportunities for moral growth' (1994, p. 107). They regard moral transformation as the 'ultimate purpose' (1994, p. 107) of transformative mediation. Bush and Folger use the term transformation to connote '*individual moral development*, although this kind of change will very likely lead to changes in social institutions as well' (Bush and Folger 1994, p. 24). This claim is based upon a belief that mediation can produce 'stronger and more compassionate human beings out of the crucible of human conflict' (1994, p. 25). In their 2005 book they offer a more measured definition of individual moral development, supported via the transformative mediation process, as the ability to balance 'the claims of the self and the other and the relation of the two' (2005, p. 74). Such claims seem to be rooted within forms of ego-based psychological therapy, again bringing to mind the Rogerian techniques noted above. As Rogers explains,

> [e]xperience in therapy seems to bring about another change in the way our clients live in their family relationships. They learn something about how to initiate and maintain real two-way communication. To understand another person's thoughts and feelings thoroughly, with the meanings they have for him, and to be thoroughly understood by this person in return—this is one of the most rewarding of human experiences, and all too rare. (Rogers 2001, p. 323)

The intent of transformative mediation points in the same direction as the form of communication described by Rogers, and yet the technique of an exclusive micro-focus upon moments of 'empowerment' and 'recognition' does seem to constitute a restrained detachment of the mediator from a form of communicative, mutual understanding. This combination of purpose and style effects a certain measure of 'neutrality' but as Cloke observes 'neutrality implies objectiveness and distance from the source of conflict' and 'places a check on our ability to unravel the sources of conflict' (2001, p. 14). Gaynier (2005) further argues, '[i]t is not enough to limit mediator behaviour for fear of mediator bias' (p. 406).

Stepping beyond the limits of transformative practice, if the mediator is free to engage with parties in exploring the substance of their conflict embedded in a social domain, a potential for dialogic communication may be realised. This is because the mediator elects to listen avidly to the parties' stories, trying to deeply understand, without judgement, both parties' positions, interests and needs. The understandings and insights gleaned may then be reflected back to the parties. This generates a broader social and political engagement and as noted, opens the possibility for dialogic exchange. This form of compassionate engagement does entail a risk of influence or bias in going beyond a narrow, detached focus upon speech interactions that are only demonstrative of an agency of either empowered self-identity or considerateness. The search after dialogue must surely go further than respectful intercommunication and is more messy than the idea of a coolly distant mediation can admit, requiring not self-determination but a co-determination of outcomes, ultimately by all the individuals in the mediation space. This is not to say that mediator influence should not be kept to a minimum and made transparent. The potential and limits on achieving this are discussed in the next chapter.

In common with Winslade and Monk, Bush and Folger are concerned to discuss their underlying philosophy. They recognise that no mediation practice can be 'value free' (2005, p. 1) and will have an ideological foundation. The particular detached, individualising positioning of the transformative mediator seems congruent with their philosophical foundation that views mediation as an opportunity for individuals to attain moral self-improvement. This possibility for 'moral growth' (p. 73) is in turn based upon Bush and Folger's espoused dualistic worldview of 'autonomy and connection' (p. 254) in which the needs of both self and other come into harmonious relation. However, they display a strong leaning toward the former, that is, towards an idea of autonomously empowered self-identity. Although Bush and Folger also emphasise 'the inherent human potential for social and moral connection' (2005, p. 38) nevertheless, as with all such dualisms, there is a tendency to give more weight to one pole, in this case that of individualism and the unity of an individual's identity. Such a determination of the 'self' by the 'self' would seem to foreclose a potential within mediation for the exploration of collective experience. It is a concern with the autonomous individual that repeatedly surfaces as the more prominent preoccupation in their work. This can be discerned in the expression of their beliefs about human identity. Antes and Saul (colleagues of Bush and Folger) list the following transformative mediators' beliefs about humanity:

- A person's reality is unique to that person and based upon his/her life experiences.
- People have inherent needs for both advancement of self and connection with others.
- People are capable of making decisions for themselves.
- People are capable of looking beyond themselves. (Antes and Saul 1999, p. 3)

People, persons and individuals are very much centre-stage. Bush and Folger demonstrate a deep humanism, asserting that transformative mediation is 'not a magical vision, nor naive; its belief in human strength and decency carries the deepest truth within it' (2005, p. 83). It is difficult not to attribute an essentialist humanism and even utopianism to their worldview. This is not dissimilar to the philosophy underpinning the humanistic and individualistic stance of facilitative, problem-solving mediators Beer and Stief (1997, p. 9) who claim that '[T]he parties speak for themselves, think for themselves, decide for themselves.' Taking it to the extreme, this set of beliefs brings to mind the critical 'idea of a society of individuals where each person shuts himself up in his own subjectivity, and whose only wealth is individual thought' (Fanon 1985, p. 36). However, in contrast, Bush and Folger proclaim a relational worldview,[1] suggesting that the transformative dimension of mediation is

---

[1] The humanism of Bush and Folger would seem to fall into the category of liberal humanism, against which Harvey (2015) counter-poses a revolutionary humanism that 'refuses the idea that there is an unchanging or pre-given "essence" of what it means to be human' (p. 287).

connected to an emerging, new vision of self and society, one based on *relational connection* and understanding rather than on individual autonomy alone. (2005, pp. 23–24)

They argue that it is possible to conceive of society as an integration of individual freedoms and relational connections and that transformative mediation is one concrete realisation of this vision. They simultaneously stress autonomy, observing that people hold a sense of personal authorship of their lives and an 'essential' social connection (p. 60). Thus asserting that the two combined form the 'very essence of human consciousness' (p. 60). Whilst they cite McNamee and Gergen (1999) as one of their philosophical sources, they hold back from a radical, social constructionist understanding of identity or indeed other 'de-subjected' (Willmott 1994) or 'contingent' (Glynos and Howarth 2007) understandings of subjectivity and identity. These writers would view the notion of personal authorship as illusory. McNamee and Gergen debunk a notion of subjective agency that has a 'capacity for internal deliberation and control of one's actions' (1999, p. 6). Bush and Folger's dualistic concept of 'individuality and connectedness' (p. 60), whilst superficially attractive, slides into an ego psychology of an essential humanism that reinforces the idea of autonomous authorship.

Although Bush and Folger's (2005) theorising does not seem to have any roots in Critical Theory, they do cite Habermas as a secondary source (p. 253) and reinforcing earlier claims, suggest that transformative mediation might 'help transform the quality of social interaction and, ultimately, social institutions' (p. 14). This seems to hold out the possibility of incremental change by means of creation of multiple 'ideal speech' situations (Habermas 1984, 1987). There is no apparent recognition of the need for radical political change that redistributes power as a precursor to end point social conditions that might vaguely approximate an ideal speech situation (and arguably never will). The humanism found in Habermas and also echoed throughout the transformative mediation project fails to 'recognise how the pursuit of humanist ideals tends to foster and promote unacknowledged disciplinary effects' (Willmott 1994, p. 115). To explain this tendency Willmott highlights a 'paradoxical freedom of modernity' (1994, p. 104) in which, the sense of self-determination opened up by modernity is simultaneously regarded as a precious defining characteristic of what it is to be human *and* experienced as a painful burden from which individuals are motivated to escape. (Willmott 1994, p. 104)

Thus, such humanism may lead to a mirage of a 'universal' set of beliefs about how *things should* and *must* be as people conform (via moves of empowerment and recognition) in order to feel secure within dominant, accepted norms of attitude and behaviour. In a sense, reflecting the thinking of Winslade and Monk (after Foucault), '[t]he domination and disciplining of self [are] internalised within the individual' (Harvey 2015, p. 204). Herein, Bush, and Folger proffer a defence against the anxious freedom of modernity, afforded by their concept of individual human decency, identity and uniqueness, the latter being stabilised through the 'transformative' technique of re-empowerment. Bush and Folger's theory of 'recognition' that purportedly leads to relational connection fails to recognise the prevalent distortion of relationships caused by inequalities in wider society. Their dualism coupling individuality with relational connectedness relies more upon a psychology of emotion and empathy and does not sit neatly with an espoused social constructivist theory.

This observation may be tempered by admitting that it is valid to bring many different theoretical lenses to illuminate subjects as complex as conflict and mediation. However, an optimistic humanism driving the tightly delineated and detached transformative method may foreclose the possibility for all parties (including the mediator) in mediation conversations to collectively glean shared understandings of how *things are* leading to a consideration of alternatives—these alternatives being always radically contingent (Glynos and Howarth 2007).

The detachment of the transformative mediator thus has two major effects. On the one hand the mediator makes more real than ever before the aspiration to 'neutrality'. By means of this containment of influence and of the greatest significance to the field of mediation, transformative practices teach mediators how to become reflexively aware of their overt and hidden influence loaded into their spoken interventions. But perhaps in the achievement of an approximation of neutrality, by default the relatively aloof mediator defers to the status quo by emptying the process of potential for a more wholehearted embrace of the political and a more far-reaching consideration of conflict causation. Hence, the consequent pursuit of dialogue must tend to be impaired. Bush and Folger's defence of a pure technique that should not be corrupted by other methods is understandable but also understandable is a desire by other mediators to use elements from different approaches as noted above. The transformative method helps disputants recover an ability to communicate where this has been lost in the heat of conflict, but a broader approach that can engage fully with the content of the dispute would seem necessary to move beyond basic communication towards dialogue. Mediation is not just about respectful exchange but as Gaynier reminds us, it is about 'meaningful exchange between two parties' (2005, p 406) in which moments of dialogue may emerge.

The next section provides extracts from and analysis of a second role-play exercise in which a professional workplace mediator adopted a transformative style. She met with the same disputants as in the first role-play. This second transformative role-play was set up to draw an analytical contrast with the first facilitative one.

Second Case Study: Commentary, Analysis and Interpretation of a Quasi-Transformative Role-Play

As noted above, the mediator in this role-play has worked as both a professional facilitative, workplace mediator (and trainer)[2] but she is also a volunteer transformative community mediator. Thus, it was possible to invite her to play a transformative mediator in a workplace setting. Interestingly, to an extent demonstrating the 'realism' of the role-play, this proved to be quite a difficult task and facilitative workplace practices emerge in the data below. For this reason the following extracts are certainly not offered as fully representative of transformative mediation. This would have required finding an experienced transformative

---

[2] This mediator was employed by a different workplace mediation service provider from the mediators in the role-play in Chap. 5.

workplace mediator to participate so that a much more purist enactment of the transformative method could have been the subject of analysis.[3] However, the text below does reveal many facets of transformative mediation mixed with some more facilitative interventions. Recall that Bush and Folger are adamant that their method cannot and should not be used in combination with other techniques and that to do so would invalidate the transformative approach. Nevertheless, the following case study offers an instructive object for analysis in its own right and brings aspects of transformative and facilitative techniques comparatively into relief. It also helps to imagine another explorative approach that builds upon the developmental insights of both the narrative and transformative schools. This explorative approach values the concept of neutrality whilst recognising its impossibility. It therefore has the ambition of minimising mediator influence on the one hand but also, paradoxically, consciously deploying a certain form of influence on the other. This latter intent comes about through the mediator's commitment to engage in attempting to understand the parties' perspectives, which may also result in an engagement with them both that becomes empathetic. Scope for an explorative approach will be signalled occasionally in the following case study and then developed more fully in principle in the next chapter.

In transformative mediations it is not assumed that first visits will lead to joint meetings.[4] First visits can be long, depending upon the needs of the party. Because of the accepted intent to hold the role-play joint meeting, the following first visits were very brief. Again, the first visits were held to enable the parties and the mediators to familiarise themselves so that they felt as comfortable as possible in the subsequent joint meeting. As in the previous chapter, the dialogue has been edited to improve readability and many of the hesitations, repetitions and fillers found in everyday speech have been removed.

---

[3] To the author's best knowledge such practice is currently found in the USA but not the UK.
[4] Most contemporary mediation practice in the UK adopts a process of face-to-face first visits with each party separately. It seems that it is common in the USA for 'first visits' to be carried out by telephone. This is done in the 'Purple House' example (Bush and Folger 2005).

First Visit of the (Quasi) Transformative Mediator (TM) with Chris

Extract, (0 secs—1 min 54 secs)

(1) TM: Chris welcome, its good to meet you. We've spoken on the phone. We've just got a little bit of time together now so I want to check in with you, see how you are and see if you've got any questions before we actually get together with Paul later on today

(2) Chris: right okay

(3) TM: how are you feeling about being here today?

(4) Chris: fine I think this is sort of the end of the line as it were because we've tried, well no its not the end of the line, its the step before the end of the line, because I've tried various different ways to try to resolve this that haven't been successful. So this is another opportunity to see if we can sort it all out

(5) TM: so you've tried quite a few things already?

(6) Chris: yes when I say things I mean things that I have done or that I've tried personally

(7) TM: so you've tried to find coping mechanisms if you like

(8) Chris: uh hum

(9) TM: to deal with the solutions but you've decided that mediation is going to be something worth trying

(10) Chris: yes definitely

(11) TM: today

(12) Chris: uh hum

(13) TM: okay do you have any questions about the way mediation works, about my role about the process that you want to cover?

(14) Chris: what exactly do you do?

(15) TM: well my role is I suppose most importantly to say that I'm here to be impartial and objective and I'm not here to try and judge criticise or give suggestions or recommendations as to what you and Paul should do. So my role is really to support you in understanding and making sense of the situation and how it's affecting both you and Paul and to become clearer about what you want to do in order to move it forward

(16) Chris: right
(17) TM: the kind of things that I might be doing when we get together this afternoon would be reflecting back to you what I'm seeing and hearing, checking that you are comfortable with the way that the thing is going and seeing if there are other ways that you want to use your time. Does that make sense?
(18) Chris: yes okay
(19) TM: okay
(20) Chris: that's fine

The meeting ended a few seconds later.

Commentary and Analysis

In line (3) the TM checks how Chris is feeling and in line (5) she reflects back Chris's contribution to allow Chris to steer the opening part of the meeting. In this way the TM can take her cue from Chris. Hence, she immediately demonstrates her intent to place control of the meeting process and content in the hands of the parties. In lines (7) and (9) the TM reflects back what Chris has said and then moves on to invite questions about mediation. This reflecting back has the effect of inviting Chris to express herself without any leading assumptions being made by the mediator.

However, the use of the term 'solutions' in line (9) is worth remarking upon. Although Chris has spoken of something to 'resolve' in line (4) the word 'solutions' appears almost like a Freudian slip, as if the word has forced itself into the dialogue. In a similar manner, at the end of line (15), the TM says 'in order to move it forward'. This implies that some form of resolution is an aim. This is not in keeping with the principles and practices of transformative mediation, as to talk of 'moving forward' may prejudge what the parties might decide to do (Bush and Folger 1994, 2005). Moving forward from a negative, destructive interaction to a more positive interaction is an aim of transformative mediation, whereas moving forward to find a settlement or solution is not, although it may be a by-product of the former. In defining conflict as a crisis of human interaction, Bush and Folger argue that, 'help in overcoming that crisis is a major part of what parties want from a mediator' (2005, p. 46). 'Overcoming' of course can be equated with a forward movement so there is an ambiguity in the term chosen by the TM but its meaning is usually apparent when viewed in context.

When asked about this terminology afterwards, the mediator suggested a more transformative phrasing could have been 'where would you like to go from here,' which, she said, 'sounds less like pressure to "move forward"'. A 'future focus' is typical of much workplace and commercial mediation. This aim seems to have seeped into the mediator's concept of her role here, and again below at several points. It appears that this mediator's facilitative, workplace experience has blended with her otherwise 'transformative' disposition.

First Visit of the Mediator with Paul

Extract, (15 secs—1 min 14 secs)

(1) TM: ... I want to check with you if you have any questions about today or any concerns or anything at all that you want to raise before we're in a room together with Christine later on?
(2) Paul: I don't think so. Can you tell me a little bit more about what we're going to do?
(3) TM: sure well when we meet later on today the purpose of the meeting is for you and Chris to find out how you want to explore the issues that have brought you to mediation
(4) Paul: uh hum
(5) TM: and to find out how you want to take things forward
(6) Paul: right
(7) TM: I'm not going to impose much structure on that unless you ask me to
(8) Paul: okay
(9) TM: the way I work is much more to follow your and Chris's lead as to how you want to use the time and really work with you in a way that I can support you
(10) Paul: right

(11) TM: any other specific questions about my role or do you have any concerns about what's going to happen?
(12) Paul: no I don't think so ...

The meeting ended after a few more seconds.

Commentary and Analysis

The TM has stated an aim to work very openly without an imposed structure so that the parties may find out 'how [they] want to explore the issues' (line (3)) and 'to follow your and Chris's lead as to how you want to use the time' (line (9)). Although, again, there is an assumption of a desire to 'take things forward' in line (5), which betrays a more task oriented and problem-solving discourse.

Joint Meeting Between Paul and Chris

Opening Welcome to the Joint Meeting

First Extract, (7 secs—4 mins 38 secs)

(1) TM: just before we start I want to say a few things about mediation, if you like the spirit of mediation, to check that we're all here under the same understanding. The first thing to say is about confidentiality. I'm not going to pass on anything that either of you say to me to anyone else. Do you have, either of you, any concerns about confidentiality you want to raise with one another in terms of how what is said is used or passed on to any anyone afterwards?

(2) Paul: well as you know we're here at the behest of the chair of the trustee board and I just want to check with you what the relationship, what's going to happen about that? Is what's discussed here going to go back to the chair of the board or what?

(3) TM: okay so you want to understand whether what we discuss, what you discuss is going to be passed on to particularly to the chair

(4) Paul: uh hum
(5) TM: of the board. Well I'm not going to pass anything on to them at all and it's really for you both to decide if there's anything that you agree that you want to jointly pass on to them whether
(6) Paul: right
(7) TM: it's in a written form or whether verbally but I certainly won't and you can make a request of one another not to pass anything on without agreeing it between you if you would like to
(8) Paul: right
(9) TM: Chris any concerns or any questions
(10) Chris: yes I think my concern about confidentiality is that it doesn't get passed on to other members of staff. I don't think it's appropriate for other people to be involved in it
(11) TM: yes
(12) Chris: so there aren't any reasons as far as I am concerned why it should
(13) TM: so for you its important that nothing is passed on. You wouldn't like anyone to be aware of what was said here
(14) Chris: no
(15) TM: is that something that you would share Paul?
(16) Paul: yes absolutely of course yes
(17) TM: so how would you like to capture that agreement? Is it enough for you to have said it to one another or would you like to have that written in some form whereby you agree not to pass anything on and sign it?
(18) Paul: I don't think so
(19) Chris: no I don't think no
(20) TM: you're comfortable? Fine because that's the first thing. The second thing I would just like to raise, which is crucial to the mediation also, is that your presence here is voluntary. That's really the way it works best that you are both here in the spirit of trying to find a way forward that works for both of you. So I want to check that you're quite sure that this is the right place for you to be right now and you're okay to proceed? Just double check

(21) Paul: well I don't really see the need for it but I'm
(22) Chris: hum
(23) Paul: happy to kind of talk sure
(24) TM: okay so unsure about what the need for mediation is
(25) Paul: uh hum
(26) TM: but you're happy to talk. Okay if we need to unpack that and understand a bit more about that you see the need
(27) Paul: uh hum
(28) TM: let me know and we'll do so but for now that sounds like an okay? Yes I'm here in
(29) Paul: okay
(30) TM: principle
(31) Paul: yes, yes
(32): Chris: yes
(33) TM: Chris?
(34) Chris: I'm fine with that
(35) TM: fine okay and then the third thing is about I guess it's to do with my role which is that I'm a neutral here. I'm not here on anyone's side or with a particular agenda as to what should be the outcome. I'm really here to support you in having a productive conversation. I want to help you in making sense of the situation and how it's impacted on you both and becoming clearer about what you both want to do to move things forward. So the kind of things I might be doing is reflecting back to you, telling you what I'm seeing and hearing and checking that you are both comfortable with the way the mediation is going. If at any point you would like to make any suggestions or requests as to how we use the time, whether you want to break, that kind of thing, then please just let me know. I think that's it. Well one last thing I'd like to check actually is, if you at this stage have any request or suggestions about things that might make you both feel comfortable being here and talking to one another. Sometimes I find that people like to introduce ground rules about how you talk to one another, the language you use all that kind of thing. Is there anything of that nature that

springs to mind and we can always introduce them later if you think of them later but is there anything at this stage you want to raise?
(36) Chris: no
(37) TM: nothing okay
(38) Paul: no I don't think so no
(39) TM: okay

Commentary and Analysis

The TM starts by setting up a conversation about confidentiality in lines (1) to (19). She places control of and decisions about confidentiality with both parties, for her part promising to treat all discussion as confidential. Promises of confidentiality help the mediator gain the trust of the parties and create an environment in which it is safer to be open. But as noted above, behind the shield of confidentiality the mediator is also able to lay claim to a mythical ethic of the 'neutral' assistant. By reference to the need for confidentiality alone, the mediator locates her/himself at least at the margins of a hierarchy of authority that assesses or judges parties in conflict, albeit not as a fully-fledged member of this hierarchy.

The habit of workplace mediators to suggest documenting agreements, as in line (17), also hints at the potential prospect of these more formal, legal and statutory processes. This may indirectly confer status and authority upon the role of the mediator and so again may tend to subtly undermine the mediator's belief in the parties' capacity for self-determination. Even a 'fly on the wall' presence may induce acts of self-discipline that are believed consonant with social norms. The shadowy presence of more formal processes and adjudication systems gives an indication of the non-neutrality of mediators in that they are, in practice, unable to detach themselves from the cultural milieu of conflict in the workplace. This points to the necessity for mediators to recognise the myth of neutrality, implying the need for reflection upon the almost inevitable political agency inherent in the very act of mediating. Hence, such mediation discourses of 'confidentiality' and 'agreement-making' can be constraining but they may yet afford structure within which a certain freedom for dialogue might develop. In this transformative example they are offered as choices for the parties that can be explored, rather than enforced by the mediator as a matter of dogmatic practice.

In line (20) the TM invites the parties to consider the importance for mediation of the parties' voluntary attendance and to give them an opportunity to say if they feel they are there on a voluntary basis. The TM again associates voluntary attendance with a desire 'to find a way forward', a phrase more akin to a problem-solving discourse. As noted above, finding a way forward can be understood in different ways. Bush and Folger argue that:

> With or without the achievement of agreement, the help parties most want, in all types of conflict, involves helping them end the vicious circle of disempowerment, disconnection and demonization—alienation from both self and other. Because without ending or changing that cycle, the parties cannot *move beyond* the negative interaction that has entrapped them. (Bush and Folger 2005, pp. 52–53—italics added)

It would be antithetical to Bush and Folger to tell the parties that they must cease their negative interaction and move it forward, but that is their unspoken ambition. Bush, acting as a mediator, expresses it thus:

> I'm not going to, uh, make decisions for you in any way here really, uh, whether decisions about how to have the conversation or what to talk about or where to wind up. I see my role as helping you to have the conversation, listening to you, helping you listen to yourselves in a way, as well as to each other. (Bush and Folger 2005. p. 135)

The mediator follows the parties, intervening only to help bring more clarity to moments of 'empowerment /disempowerment' or 'recognition /non-recognition'. The whole purpose of transformative mediation is to support listening and the healing that comes from regaining 'empowerment' that opens potential to recover a capacity for 'recognition'. Thus, whilst it is for the parties themselves to decide to move beyond the crisis, the mediator holds an ambition for them to do so and makes therapeutic interventions to promote this possibility. Agreement may or may not follow. Success in transformative mediation varies from small gains in clarity and individual decision-making or small improvements in 'interaction' through to full mutual recognition and joint decisions that can sometimes flow from this recognition.

As noted above, Bush and Folger attribute a negative vision of conflict to the 'problem-solving' school. They themselves argue for a 'positive vision' of conflict (Bush and Folger 2005, p. 239) because, in moving beyond conflict, moral growth may be realised in which the 'claims of self and other' (2005, p. 74) are brought into balance. However, this also implies a negative view of the state of imbalance entailed by a crisis of interaction. In sum, Bush and Folger seek not to resolve specific 'problems' but to resolve the general problem of an interactional crisis. Whilst transformative mediators 'follow' the parties, Bush and Folger do describe them as pilots of a ship 'with a fixed point of orientation' (2005, p. 45). They are thus also 'problem-solvers' but of a different kind. Other mediators try to directly address 'problems' and hope subsequent communication will improve and ill feeling will be reduced.

From the transformative standpoint it is not 'issues' that bring people into conflict but a deficiency in relational skills. This polarisation would seem too extreme, perhaps another mistaken dualism. But in practice parties may pursue an argument about 'issues' while transformative mediators 'work' on the interactional crisis. It would seem more logical to simultaneously pay attention to both interactional behaviour and the substantial issues being presented. From the perspectives of post-Marxist and poststructuralist writers reviewed above (Laclau 1990; Torfing 1999; Howarth; 2000; Howarth and Torfing 2005; Glynos and Howarth 2007), antagonism, conflict and power demand a consideration of the social, political and psychoanalytic dimensions of life. An exclusive focus upon 'empowerment and recognition' would appear to suppress the political dimension of mediating as will be drawn out in this case study. As argued above, the work of Bush and Folger (1994, 2005) is marked by an apoliticism. This may be one reason why the TM is unable to prevent herself from slipping from the transformative style into a more mainstream, facilitative, problem-solving mode of mediation. Because the detachment of the transformative method effectively circumvents a confrontation with the political, it by default lapses into the medium of the dominant organisational discourse.

The beginning of the intervention in line (35) represents a contradictory mixing of 'problem-solving' and transformative mediation. It is as though the TM is unable to throw off the usual workplace mediator 'subject position' that entails a sharp focus upon the restoration of productive working relationships. She says she has no 'particular agenda as to what should be the outcome', and yet these very words, 'agenda' and 'outcome', are reminiscent of management control and echo a workplace 'discourse'. The TM then continues to say: 'I'm really here to support you in having a productive conversation. I want to help you in making sense of the situation and how it's impacted on you both and becoming clearer about what you both want to do to move things forward.' Apart from the presumption of moving things forward, these aims accord more closely with transformative practice and the TM goes on to describe ways in which she will hand control of the meeting process to the parties with the intent of supporting them through their present 'interactional crisis' (Antes and Saul 1999; Bush and Folger 1994, 2005; Folger 2001). However, and this is critical, even this demonstration of transformative practice, when set in the context of employee relations within an organisation, contains a presumption of reconciliation. Transformative mediation in principle, aims to surpass interactional crises. Whilst 'becoming clearer about what you both want to do' could include electing to initiate a grievance or a disciplinary procedure, this would constitute a failure of the workplace mediation process. Hence, in the workplace, the overall trajectory of a transformative mediation intervention will tend to inevitably become aligned with the needs of the organisation for reconciliation and a return to productive work activity. Of course, all workplace mediation interventions necessarily ultimately serve this agenda.

However, the fact that parties with the support of mediators seek to address and possibly resolve interpersonal conflict does not necessarily entail any capture of the mediator as a hegemonic agent of the organisation. A subtle shift of mediator ambition might limit it to supporting a search for understanding of the conflict and of the 'self' and 'other' within it. This is an ambition that broadens the transformative focus on the interactional crisis and embraces the subject matter of the conflict and its context, although healing might be expected to result if such greater understanding is found. A search for understanding does leave open the political undecidability (Torfing 1999; Howarth 2000) of the patterning of conflict causation and any possible forms of resolution. In the absence of any political awareness of power, the more prescriptive 'transformative' ambition of moral growth achieved by an autonomous, self-determining party would seem to suppress any sensitivity to an innate undecidability. However, a mediator aim to support the exploration (and not necessarily resolution) of conflict is also premised upon a belief that a conflict, though it may be instructive, is an episode to be healed. This might seem to equate to the temporary suturing of a dislocation (Torfing 1999. p. 115). Nevertheless, a search for mutual understanding could combine a subjective, or intersubjective, emotional healing with maintenance of political insight that holds to a continued sense of radical contingency and hence undecidability.

But such potential is dashed in practice when the aims to support a productive conversation, expressed in the above quote from line (35), are immediately followed by the words 'to move things forward'. Whether this aspiration is for resolution of specific issues or only about their 'interactional crisis' is ambiguous at this early stage. It may be the former, but if it is the latter, this is not an 'outcome' that a transformative mediator would set out as an explicit goal, even though it may be implicit. This is because the transformative mediator seeks to 'follow' the parties' conversation and not take a lead.

Throwing the Meeting Open to the Parties

Second extract, (4 mins 39 secs—13 mins 24 secs)

(1) TM: okay fine so that's enough talking from me, from now on I'll be doing much less talking and its really for you both to use the time as you see fit. How would you both like to start? Would you both like to start by telling one another what brought you here to mediation?
(2) Paul: um
(3) Chris: I think certainly that we both know there's been a problem
(4) TM: uh hum
(5) Chris: the trustee board suggested this as a possible way forward

(6) TM: uh hum, so a problem? You're both in agreement that this is the case and that the trustees are suggesting that mediation could be a way for you to find a way forward? Is that
(7) Paul: uh hum
(8) TM: how you see it Paul as well?
(9) Paul: umm, yeah as I said before I don't really see there is a major problem. I think it's a pretty minor thing, which has been blown up really out of proportion but I willing to concede the fact that things aren't right in the office. Obviously it's not a good atmosphere to work in.
(10) TM: okay
(11) Paul: I would want to solve that if I could.
(12) TM: So that's what you were referring to when you said that you're not quite clear of the need for this or that somehow the things
(13) Paul: yeah
(14) TM: been blown out of proportion but you see now that there is an issue
(15) P: uh hum
(16) TM: in terms of how things are in the work place
(17) Paul: yes, it's not a happy place at the moment obviously and I'd like that sorted out if it can be.
(18) TM: uh hum, okay so your looking really for a way of making the environment in the office a more happy place to be. Okay does that sound to
(19) Paul: umm
(20) TM: you Chris like the kind of outcome I guess you'd like to see from today's meeting?
(21) Chris: yes I think that I have two outcomes. One of them would most definitely be the one that Paul was saying and the other outcome is that we get some way of dealing with the fact that Paul's job is not being done in exactly the way that it needs to be done because of the role that he carries out.
(22) TM: uh hum
(23) Chris: I mean the atmosphere in the office is unpleasant and it's not nice and it's never been like that before. Something needs dealing with but I think the other thing runs alongside it.

(24) TM: um, so from your point of view Chris, really two outcomes
(25) Chris: uhm
(26) TM: that you'd like to see and one, which you share with Paul, is to try and improve the environment in the office which as you
(27) Chris: uh hum
(28) TM: say hasn't been like that before and so you would like to make a change to that
(29) Chris: umm
(30) TM: and the other is to see a change in the way that Paul's job is being done
(31) Chris: uh hum
(32) TM: which of those two would you {looking at both of them} like to start talking about first?
(33) Chris: I'm not sure. From my point of view until we deal with the way the job's being done I can't quite see how the other side of it can change because we've only had the problem of the atmosphere in the office since the job has not been done properly
(34) TM: okay
(35) Chris: umm
(36) TM: you used the words I think Chris that for you Paul's job isn't being done properly {turning to Paul} and then I mentioned that when you [Paul] first started talking you didn't mention that as one of the outcomes you'd like to see discussed. How does it strike you as a topic to talk about today and to address? Are you comfortable with that?
(37) Paul: yes I mean that's been the bone of contention between us. I don't think it's a problem in particular but Chris obviously does which is why we have the bad relationship currently. I think what seems to me to be a kind of minor kind of trivial administrative matter is being made a great deal of and being used as a kind of stick really to beat me with
(38) TM: right, okay
(39) Paul: and there's a lot of pressure on me now that I don't think needs to be there
(40) TM: um, it's really putting a lot of pressure on you the situation which as you see it as stemming from a minor administrative issue

(41) Paul: yeah!
(42) TM: and its being used you feel against you almost like a stick
(43) Paul: yeah I mean it's very simple isn't it? I do this job as a full time debt counsellor. I spend my time dealing with clients' debt problems okay
(44) TM: umm
(45) Paul: and I don't fill in some pieces of paper in enough detail and this is a problem but in my view these things are just trivial administrative matters. Anybody could do that. I don't see why I should spend my time doing them. Really it's just out of balance, the whole thing's come out of balance
(46) TM: okay
(47) Paul: the need for the work itself has become kind of secondary to the filling in bits of paper. It seems to me
(48) TM: so for you, you have a clear idea as to what should be some kind of balance between
(49) Paul: yeah
(50) TM: work that you are doing, the content of the work you are doing and the paperwork that sort of supports that
(51) Paul: yeah
(52) TM: is that right? okay
(53) Paul: absolutely
(54) TM: Chris how would you characterise that balance, how would you expect it to be?
(55) Chris: I think that its not so much how what I personally expect it to be. It's the way that it has to be in terms of the—its a bit complicated when you don't …

At 10 mins 45 secs, Chris explains the technicalities of the case and time recording paperwork needed to draw down funding, complimenting Paul on his 'excellent' debt counselling work but explaining that Paul has a problem with the processes and paperwork that are needed for the Advice Centre to 'get paid'. Then at 12 mins 6 secs the TM sums up thus, looking at Chris:

(56) TM: okay so if I try and look at the way you see you see this balance between these two parts of work. For you obviously not the paperwork but the content of the work itself is crucial

and your saying there's no problem with that and Paul is excellent at that. When it comes to the paperwork you see it as more important perhaps than Paul does because it is what enables you to get the money to keep the organisation
(57) Chris: yes
(58) TM: going okay. {Turning to Paul} whereas for Paul you feel that paperwork is interfering actually with the importance of doing the core work
(59) Paul: yeah absolutely
(60) TM: so and I realise I'm doing a lot of
(61) Paul: yeah
(62) TM: talking now and you're addressing what you're saying to me …

Commentary and Analysis

In line (1), in keeping with the transformative method, the TM passes responsibility for managing the meeting to the parties. However, she says 'would you both like to start by telling one another what brought you here'. This may seem innocuous as in general, mediations occur because people view the fact that they are in conflict as a problem to sort out. It is also unavoidable that in the workplace setting the employing organisation becomes an absent third party in the room. We might say that 'naturally' the employer positively wants a resolution to be achieved and has invested in the mediation process to that end. However, the phrasing of this invitation points to the conflict as a 'problem' and as your 'problem' of your making, which of course on one level it is. This is more directive than is usual in a transformative mediation and tends to 'position' the mediator as a referee, by directing the parties to tell one another what the problem is (whether this be in terms of their relationship, presuming a need for reconciliation, or of substantive issues between them). Any mediator, by definition, cannot escape from an 'enunciative modality' (Howarth 2005) as mediators speak from a position of authority but our concern is with the effective 'subject position' this mediator comes to occupy (Fairclough 2001; Howarth 2005; Torfing 1999) and the nature of the authority thus claimed by this position. Nevertheless, this opening is far less directive than in the facilitative case study and at this juncture the parties seem uncertain about what this mediator will do. This is a marked contrast with the facilitative role-play whereby the parties were quickly 'positioned' as interviewees by the mediators.

In line (6) the TM reflects back Chris's response to her opening question and proceeds to check that Paul agrees in line (8). Again such a direct prompt to Paul is not consistent with transformative practice. He is now being guided in his contribution by the mediator (Folger and Bush 2001). Nevertheless, in lines (9), (11) and (17) Paul agrees that he does want some sort of resolution. Whether contiguous with the other party's concerns and/or with those of the employing organisation, as already noted, parties usually agree with an aim to resolve conflict including some form of reconciliation. However, if the mediator adopts a similar ambition, as would seem 'natural', it is possible that this aim is likely to surface as a subtle but active pressure to reconcile. As already identified, to mitigate this tendency, the counterfactual explorative mediator may set an aim to only support the parties in exploring and understanding their conflict in a manner that follows the speech of the parties and does not seek to interpretively run ahead of them. To do this the mediator would need to remain open to all possible understandings and, with humility, hope that the parties develop their own understandings, mutual or otherwise, beyond any initial intransigence. This does entail a great deal of concentration and work by the mediator to support the parties in exploring the conflict.

In lines (12), (14) and (16) the TM reflects Paul's uncertainty about the need for mediation and his concern about the office atmosphere. This empowers Paul's contribution in line (17) which again, in keeping with transformative practice, the TM reinforces in line (18). But then at the end of line (18) and in line (20), she steps out of a 'transformative' practice and gives an overt prompt to Chris. This prompt both directs Chris to address this particular issue and also places a focus upon an 'outcome'. By putting Chris on the spot with a direct question that guesses at Chris's view, the TM, whilst following the information revealed by the parties, is also leading them in the definition of a normative problem to be solved, being a bad office atmosphere. A transformative intervention might have read as, 'so you both feel there has been a problem or an atmosphere, would either of you like to say any more about that now or is there anything else either of you would like to raise?' In this way the mediator would help to create space for an exploration of the unhappy office 'atmosphere' or space for possibly recognising each other's disempowerment whilst leaving decisions about the direction of the conversation equally with both parties.

The word 'outcome' (lines 20 and 24) is very much a contemporary term from a management discourse, one with strong connotations of solving problems or achieving results. It echoes the earlier notion of 'moving things forward', an outcome being something to be achieved in the future. By use of this one word the discourse of this partially transformative style of mediation has become woven together with a problem-solving approach and the meaning system of a managerial discourse (Fairclough 2001). After its use in line (20), it is immediately picked up by Chris in line (21). The TM then reflects it back in line (24) further embedding it in the discussion. This tends to naturalise the place of the mediator as a joint seeker after an 'outcome' (Fairclough 2001).

The TM returns to a reflective 'transformative' style in her summary in lines (24) to (32). She might have also added 'or is there something else you want to discuss' to the end of line (32), so that all options are open for the parties. However, whilst the TM is following the lead of the parties, the conversation, at this early stage, has become focused upon either the 'environment' in the office or the way Paul does his job. The TM seems to be practising partly in the 'transformative style', working reflectively with issues brought up by the parties, and partly in a more 'facilitative' mode, in that she has begun to shape an agenda with and for the parties. She seems to be constructing a 'subject position' of a purportedly enlightened 'leader' who seeks to empower staff but yet retains a positional authority (Knights and Willmott 2007) from which she can apply a partly obscured pressure to reconcile.

In line (36) the TM uses a deferential, inquiring approach but in effect directs Paul to respond to the issue raised by Chris of 'the job not being done properly'. The TM is thus suggesting that Paul respond to Chris's agenda. In a more rigorous 'transformative' practice he would have been given space to decide to respond for himself, as would likely have been inevitable. In 'transformative' terms he has been disempowered by the mediator (Jorgensen et al. 2001).

In lines (40) and (42) the TM again demonstrates a more 'transformative' mode by reflecting back disempowerment felt and expressed by Paul. This affirms Paul and empowers him to further explain his feelings and beliefs about his work. The TM continues in this vein through lines (48), (50) and (52) until in line (54) she again slips into a facilitative mode and puts Chris on the spot with a direct question. Since Chris is Paul's line manager, this has the possibly unintended effect of inviting Chris to judge Paul's views on the right balance between giving advice and completing the paperwork. Hence, such a directive intervention would seem to 'position' the TM momentarily in the role (subject position) of a manager overseeing a dispute between two subordinates. The mediator is thus drawn into the management fold. An alternative, less directive intervention at this point would have been to summarise Paul's and Chris's different perspectives and to invite them to either explore these differences or the problems that appear to arise from them, and to offer the option of introducing anything else they may have wanted to talk about. Such a counterfactual mediator tactic may go beyond the 'transformative', therapeutic technique if born of an *intention* to invite the parties to open up the radical contingency of their conflict situation (Howarth 2000). This going beyond the boundaries of transformative practice is born of a mediator desire to understand the parties and to reflect back this understanding (for confirmation or otherwise). There is a risk of imposing the mediator's cultural and political prejudices upon the mediation discussion but this may be mitigated if the mediator can remain open to the contingency of the parties' conflict. The more passive and detached reflecting back in the transformative mode, where the mediator acts as a selective mirror noticing only expressions of party empowerment/disempowerment or recognition, avoids such a risk of mediator influence.

Third extract, (15 mins 28 secs—17 mins 40 secs)

(1) Chris: … if you don't do what it is that we're supposed to do in order to fulfil the contract then they will take the contract away and there will be no debt advice
(2) Paul: I don't believe it
(3) Chris: well I'm sorry but it is

(4) Paul: I just don't think they'll do that
(5) Chris: well they did it in Dunstable, They took it away
(6) Paul: no there must have been something else
(7) Chris: well they did, they did take it away
(8) Paul: there must have been something else going on there
(9) Chris: no there wasn't they didn't have the time recording properly and they didn't have all the forms and things signed in the files, the exact things that you've got that you don't like doing and I know you don't like doing them and I knew you didn't like doing them when I gave you the job
(10) TM: so the...
(11) Chris: but you know it goes with the territory. You have to do what it is in order for them to give you the money and if you don't do what they want they don't give you the money
(12) TM: uh hum, I can see very clearly that, from Chris's point of view, you can see that doing that paperwork isn't much fun for Paul and
(13) Chris: no its not
(14) TM: and you said you've been in that situation before and you'd love to
(15) Chris: I know its not
(16) TM: spend all your time dealing directly with the clients but that for you it is a reality that in order to make the money, to keep the work and ultimately to be able to serve the clients, you have to do that paperwork, and you're saying Paul, well first of all there's got be some kind of balance and why would you employ a specialist such as yourself to do that work
(17) Paul: uhm
(18) TM: if you know half the time has to be spent on doing stuff that doesn't involve the qualifications presumably that
(19) Paul: uhm
(20) TM: you bring and so for you there's got to be some system, some other way, you're almost looking for some other way of doing
(21) Paul: uhm
(22) TM: of setting up this scheme
(23) Paul: uhm

(24) TM: and then of course you came to this issue of Dunstable where you're saying Chris that there was this real concern because funding can get taken away, whereas Paul, you're sceptical about that and saying there must have been some other reason for that
(25) Paul: yeah
(26) TM: so do you want to look more about that specific situation and understand what it was that meant the funding went away or see if there's another way of running the system as you perhaps were suggesting Paul?
(27) Paul: uhmm, well I've suggested …

Commentary and Analysis

This extract demonstrates the TM summarising and reflecting back both parties' concerns in an even-handed way, affirming both parties and clarifying and making time for each to listen to the other. In line (10) she starts to speak but stops as Chris wants to say more. Then, in line (26), she offers them both a choice about what to consider next. This 'choice' is focused upon the central 'problem' and towards a rational search for a solution. Thus, a problem-solving presumption indicating a need to reconcile emerges again. Also, the practicalities of their dispute and the discourse of 'workplace task' seem to hold a magnetic draw for the TM. However, she is letting the parties manage the meeting process by asking them what they want to do next. She is 'positioned' more as a 'follower' of their meeting and a 'supporter' of their engagement in the argument. She speaks as a concerned observer. This more transformative-like style contrasts markedly with the interactional routine (Fairclough 2001) that held sway throughout the above facilitative role-play and yet it still contains a subtle pressuring by the mediator to bring the parties to some form of workable reconciliation.

Fourth extract, (22 mins 56 secs—25 mins 38 secs)

(1) Chris: … you're not meant to be seeing nine clients a day you're only meant to be seeing six
(2) TM: it sounds as if there's something

6 Relational Mediation   197

(3) Chris: you can't do it, you know there's not enough time

(4) TM: I think it sounds as if what Paul was saying about this feeling of having pressure on him to work outside his normal working hours, you're saying that that actually gets to you quite a bit, that comment, because you're saying you do care a lot about peoples

(5) Chris: I think its very unfair yes I think its very unfair

(6) TM: yes and you're saying that you're the first person to say at five thirty leave the office and you see it's important that people have a good work-life balance. But for you it's not a question of the amount of time that Paul is spending, it's more to do with the level of organisation and perhaps it sounds as if you think he's trying to look after too many clients or contact too many clients?

(7) Chris: {Chris nods her head}

(8) TM: okay

(9) Paul: I don't contact them they come to the door. I'm not going to be turning people away to sit there and do paperwork. It's not me, it's not what I do, it is not what the job is

(10) TM: uh um it sounds that its almost like questioning you as who you are and who you want to be in your job

(11) Paul: yeah, absolutely

(12) TM: as someone who is available and accessible to people who come in to be able to serve them is that, have I understood right

(13) Paul: absolutely yeah that's what the job is, it's not a job it's a calling whatever, you know it's something more than a job isn't it. There's no money in it, you wouldn't do it for the money so it's what you do and I couldn't honestly turn people away from the door who are in need and spend my time filling in bits of paper. I couldn't do it, it's just not moral, it's not right

(14) TM: so for you

(15) Paul: and that's the problem you know, that's the problem with the office, there's something shifting there's this managerialism

(16) TM: sounds to me like now we're beginning to get beneath some of the surface of what's brought you here today and you're talking more about almost what's the purpose of having a

job. You're saying it's a calling, it's what it means about you as a person than just how you spend your days or make your money and you're saying there's some shift in the office away from that sort of
(17) Paul: uhm
(18) TM: approach to work to something
(19) Paul: uhm
(20) TM: different. Chris how do you respond to that? How do you see
(21) Chris: I don't actually disagree
(22) TM: uh huh
(23) Chris: my job as manager in the last five years has changed from one thing to something that's almost completely unrecognisable. I think the way that the nurses in the hospital, they don't have matrons any more do they, or the matron spends all her time filling paperwork in, she doesn't deal with clients …

Commentary and Analysis

In lines (4) and (6) the TM is reflecting back Chris's reactions, clarifying and creating space for them both to listen. She is working with the feelings presented and not being drawn into investigating issues or problems. The TM then underscores Paul's strong feelings about his sense of work identity. This type of reflecting back in lines (4), (6), (10) and (12) is consistent with the transformative model in amplifying empowerment (Jorgensen et al. 2001). Reflecting back is of course generally a part of mainstream facilitative work (Beer and Stief 1997; Crawley and Graham 2002) but here it is deliberately focussed around expressions of disempowerment.

In line (16), the TM underscores Paul's comments about his sense of vocation and changing approaches to work in the office. Here she touches upon two conflicting discourses of work, being what Paul calls 'managerialism' and his working values about serving needy people. Hence, his contribution in line (15) alludes to a much wider causality feeding the conflict between himself and Chris. At this juncture a transformative mediator might have made a summary of the discussion, checked if her/his understanding was correct and invited the parties to decide where to take the conversation next (Folger and Bush 2001; Bush and Folger 2005). In this way transformative mediators try to avoid injecting their own evaluations of the conflict into the conversation. Here, the TM does reflect back disempowerment but also engages in a more explorative manner with the substance of Paul's concerns, She then, in line (20), directs Chris to 'respond' to Paul's concern about the undermining of his sense of vocation that she describes as a 'shift in the office away from that sort of approach to work to something different'. Again it is as if she is blending a transformative and even an explorative approach with a style of workplace mediation that operates to overtly fix the interactional crisis. Whereas, transformative mediation has an aim of helping parties work out their crisis of interaction through a subtle therapy of support for moments of 'empowerment and recognition', the approach in this role-play more forcibly shepherds parties to confront and deal with their relationship breakdown. This is achieved by directing one party to 'respond' to the comments of the other party. This points to an underlying pressure upon them to overcome this hiatus so that they are able to return to a productive, working relationship. This is what the organisation requires of them. In the 'gaze' of the mediator, almost positioned as the overseeing manager, the parties are no longer just parties but also 'staff'.

In an alternative, explorative approach, a mediator could have developed the intervention in line (16) and stepped further beyond a transformative practice by making a 'political' choice (Glynos and Howarth 2007) to reflect back more explicitly the clash of 'discourses' and their origins as highlighted by Paul in lines (13) and (15). The parties could have been *invited* to consider this matter if they wished, i.e. the mediator would not go so far as to *direct* the parties to address this issue.[5] In fact Chris does pick up on Paul's concerns about a shift towards a more intrusive accountability.

---

[5] The transformative and explorative styles may both result in a similar intervention for different reasons and in this sense they may overlap. The explorative mediator may register the term 'managerialism' as having discursive political connotations whereas the transformative mediator may just sense a moment of disempowerment when this term is uttered. As noted before, there are many commonalities across all styles of mediation.

Fifth extract, (27 mins 24 secs—32 mins 41 secs)

(1) Chris: … but it's as good as it can be at this moment in these circumstances

(2) Paul: umm, it's just not good enough is it? I think its down to you to work the system better, to make representations to the funders and to try and find ways round, to tell the funders this isn't possible to do. You're funding us to do this work but we can't do all the work we want to do because we're having to jump through your hoops. You ought to be more of an advocate, you've lost touch with the reality of seeing clients, you've forgotten what its like to sit in rooms with people and see them in pain and want to get them sorted out. You've just become, the whole things just become too managerial.

(3) Chris: Well I mean that's not true. I haven't forgotten because I know what's going on all of the time and at the end of the day the reason I'm doing what I'm doing is because I can remember what it's like sitting in that room with those people who are in pain. Otherwise I'm not doing this for making a profit. I'm not doing this so I've got a company car and a holiday in the Bahamas. I'm doing this for the same idealistic reasons as you are. I'm trying to help people. That sounds very halo-ish but this is about doing it because it's the right thing to do. Because people should have access to advice and the only way at the moment, and I'm not saying this will be the same in six months or nine months or a year's time, the only way at the moment that I can get money for debt advice is to get it where I'm getting it and it comes with the strings. Yes I can say to them and I will say to them this is time consuming and could we do this and could we not do that and could we do something else, but there were thousands of these contracts all over the country. If they're all saying the same thing then they might change it but if I just go around bleating on about my debt worker said this and my debt worker wants to be seeing more clients, they don't want to be doing paperwork they don't want to be sending you statistics of who they've seen and how long they've spent

|||with them. In the long term maybe they will do something about it. I think probably they won't but I agree that's not a reason for not doing it so we can do that
(4) Paul: uhmm
(5) Chris: but it still doesn't alter the fact that there are thousands of these contracts all round the country and they are all running, having to conform in the same manner that I'm asking you to. Which doesn't make it right because you get a hundred people go and do something bad, at the moment it's what we're stuck with. It's not ideal
(6) TM: there's obviously a lot of frustration for you Chris at having to, it sounds like you've made that decision to accept that there are strings attached to getting funding this way
(7) Chris: uhm
(8) TM: and that that's a source of frustration for you. That you have concluded that that's the best thing to do
(9) Chris: well I didn't have any choice
(10) TM: umm
(11) Chris: I am choosing to do it. I could have just said no we won't have a debt worker we don't like their strings. Sorry all you people, go away with all your pain and suffering and debt. We can't see you. Well I can't do that because that would be ridiculous. So I have to say right well what can I do? This is the best we can do at the moment
(12) TM: uh hum, so in order to keep that (funding agency) contract alive and serve all those clients this is what you think is the best thing to do
(13) Chris: umm
(14) TM: and you were saying earlier that for you there's as much a conscious desire to help people who are in situations of debt and you {turning to Paul} express it very differently, because of course you're different people, and as to whether its idealism or whether it's a calling or use different terms for it, but there's something in there it looks to me from the outside that there's a clear similarity I guess between you and that you're here not because you want to earn lots of money but in order to fulfil a particular role

(15) Chris: well that's why people work in organisations like ours isn't it
(16) Paul: umm, certainly not for the money
{several seconds of silence}
(17) TM: so till this point it looks like we've talked about the issue of what this balance should be between paperwork and actually meeting and serving clients. Do you feel that you've got any clearer on this issue as to what one another thinks or what you want to do about it? How do you want to move forward now? Do you want to come to some kind of agreement over that as to whether to to try and make any change or not, or talk about the other issue that you both raised earlier on, which is the environment in the in the office?
(18) Chris: well I think one goes hand in hand with the other so I don't see
(19) Paul: I just don't see what I'm not being offered. There can't be any agreement as far as I can see. I'm just being told to do this and get on with it.
(20) Chris: well it is your job

Commentary and Analysis

In lines (6), (8), (10), (12), and (14) the TM reflects back her sense of Chris's frustration and the necessary decision to comply with the funding agency's strings. She also emphasises a similarity between Chris and Paul, in a sense directively 'urging recognition' (Jorgensen et al. 2001), noting that they both have a vocational 'desire to help people' rather than 'earn lots of money'. Chris and Paul concur in lines (15) and (16). Once again a pressure to reconcile may be detected. However, the TM completely overlooks Paul's complaint about managerialism in line (2). Then, in line (17), the TM mistakes a moment of subdued agreement (lines (15) and (16)) for a more significant shift in the parties' interaction and hints they may want to now 'move forward' and 'come to some kind of agreement'. This amounts to a premature forcing of a reconciliation that is not felt by either party, as expressed by them both in lines (18) and (19). Also, in line (17), Paul's concerns and earlier plea (line (2)) for Chris 'to be more of an advocate' are reduced to a matter of 'what this balance should be between paperwork and actually meeting and serving clients'. Here the transformative concern with the 'problem' of the relationship is conflated with the practical 'problem' of Paul's time recording. This corresponds with the approach of the mediators in the 'facilitative' role-play. The TM's intervention in line (17) has reduced the whole mediation to one 'problem' requiring a solution, i.e. being to find a 'balance' between paperwork and serving clients. The TM has thus adopted a 'subject position' as a problem-solving manager of conflict thus placing the parties in the role of 'staff'.

This contrasts with a counterfactual possibility for a mediator to contain their own 'subject position' to that of an 'explorer' so that she/he sees the parties as people and not as 'staff' or 'employees' or 'managers'. From this 'position' of 'explorer', it may be possible to retain an independence from the apparent, immediate needs of the organisation for a 'balance'. The mediator could thus have sought a kind of escape from a drift into a merged organisational and workplace mediation 'discourse'. This would have entailed continuing to reflect back the impasse between Paul and Chris over their differing assessment of how to respond to the dictates of the funding body. To do this the mediator would attempt to understand both parties' viewpoints and articulate these for both to hear again, from the lips of the third party as mediator. Hence, the mediator would try to maintain a space for the parties to explore the conflict and become aware, in themselves and each other, of a possible 'misrecognition' of their situation. Laclau (1990, p. 92) describes 'misrecognition' as 'the non-recognition of the precarious character of any positivity'. The conflict would thereby have been temporarily 'opened up' rather than immediately 'closed down'. The parameters of any power struggle between them may be mapped out and perhaps held at a metaphorical distance so the high emotion of conflict may be subdued. Parties may be able to move beyond a resistance to the other's viewpoint by suspending their own beliefs and looking momentarily through the eyes of their antagonist. In this way the mediator could support the parties in a mutual exploration of differences that holds potential to vitalise their 'political subjectivities' (Torfing 1999), albeit transitorily. In such a space there is a chance for dialogue to flourish even though parties are likely to return to existing 'discursive formations' (Torfing 1999). A partial re-fixation of identity and meaning would follow but not at the urgent behest of the mediator. In this case the funding agency's strings would still remain uncut but some dialogue might have occurred.

The potential for mediation to open conflict to deeper exploration of wider causes may appear counter-intuitive to the mindset that informs much contemporary, facilitative workplace practice in which a discourse of organisational problem-solving is 'naturalised' (Fairclough 2001). In this example, to strike a balance between necessary form filling, ('it's your job') and debt advice provision is the 'natural' conclusion arrived at by a transformative mediator. It may be expected, not surprisingly, that the hegemonic practices of the workplace may condition what is able to be said, making it difficult for the mediator to invite or amplify consideration of other discourses touched upon by the parties, however tangentially. This may be even more difficult if the mediator operates under a self-imposed, 'transformative' constraint following the parties shifts of empowerment and recognition (precluding a search for understanding to be able to re-articulate 'differences' and 'context') and if the parties' own discourse remains largely within the language of the workplace.

Sixth extract, (50 mins 12 secs—51 mins 25 secs)

(1) Chris: ... and its going to seriously affect the clients, the clients that you so much want to help because you won't be there to help any of them if that contract goes. So the six that you're only able to see if you do the paperwork properly or the nine that you do see without doing the paper work, none of them will have a debt worker because you won't be there and I don't think you want that any more than I do, do you?
{several seconds of silence}

(2) TM: Chris you're explaining what you see as your options. If you're to follow Paul's logic either you just say that you're not going to work anymore with the (funding agency) straight away, you just stop handing them that paperwork, the files and the records of time keeping and you think that in three or four months probably they will actually just take the contract away anyway, as happened in Dunstable and you said, Paul, that you just don't believe that and so it so it looks a bit like a sort of an impasse there. You're saying that's the way

	you {Chris} see it and you're saying {Paul} no, I know I don't believe you
	{TM has hands out, palms up, as if to say 'what are you going to do about this?'}
(3) Paul:	uhmm
(4) Chris:	do I normally lie?
(5) Paul:	I'm not
(6) Chris:	do I normally make things up?
(7) Paul:	I just think you're exaggerating ...

Commentary and Analysis

In contrast to the facilitative session the TM continues to 'follow' the parties and not manage or direct their interactions. At this juncture the TM has decided to highlight the impasse. It is not unusual for a mediator to reflect back an impasse and it may be merely to observe a momentary reality. But here it is baldly stated, as if the mediator is disowning the positions of both parties rather than trying to find an understanding of each of them. In a 'transformative' mediation it would be more typical to offer open-ended options for working through an impasse. In this situation it appears that the TM is gently 'knocking heads together', if this can indeed be done gently. Again, we could view this intervention as that of a manager saying 'you have got to sort this out' and thereby implying a judgemental disposition towards both parties equally. Obviously, this does not correspond with the aim of a transformative mediator to engender empowerment and does represent another slippage towards a presumption of a requirement for reconciliation. The result is for each party to continue to defend their own position. As noted in the previous extract commentary, the alternative could have been to help them pursue an exploration of the impasse and its causes if the parties are willing to do this.

Within a workplace discourse, the ambition to end the conflict and return to work will unsurprisingly appear as 'natural' and 'reasonable'. However, to accept it as such implies a role for the mediator as a powerful director of parties towards conflict resolution. Such an acceptance infers that workplace mediation could only be about engineering a return to work in which the mediator pretends to act as an unbiased referee, whilst making assumptions and judgements that are obscured or hidden within workplace and mediation discourses (Fairclough 2001).

Seventh extract, (61 mins 45 secs—62 mins 55 secs)

(1) TM: … there are a couple of points at which I see that you're still sort of slightly, I wouldn't say head to head, but let's say not in agreement. One is whether in fact there is scope perhaps to play around with the amount of time and precision that is put into time keeping? You're saying Paul
(2) Paul: uhmm
(3) TM: maybe they really don't need that much paperwork, and Chris, you're quite clear that they wouldn't have said it if they didn't really mean it and that's what's happening all around the country. So that's one point of difference between you. I guess there's also, Paul you think, well Chris is the manager, it's her responsibility to change something here
(4) Paul: uhm
(5) TM: and Chris, you're saying it's not your choice, that it's the way it is and there's nothing you can do to change it. I'm wondering how you want to move on from those points of disagreement. Do you want to agree to disagree or do you want to try and understand better why the other person can't understand you or?
(6) Chris: well I don't think we don't understand each other do we?
(7) Paul: no I think we understand each other very well
(8) Chris: yes I don't think there's any problem with that {laughter}

Commentary and Analysis

Paul and Chris are continuing to resist exploring each other's viewpoints. In lines (1), (3) and (5) the TM even-handedly restates their differences. At this point she could have invited the parties to look again at these differences and also asked if there was anything else that was of concern. As before, this could have kept the exploration of the conflict open, or silently left it to the parties to decide what to do about their impasse. Instead, in line (5), she again invites them to 'move on'. Her focus is now very much upon the parties as if they are two sovereign individuals locked in battle over issues rather than ideas tied to their own 'identifications' (Torfing 1999; Glynos 2008). But we can also see the parties as holding radically different views of the world, invested in their sense of identity, which prevent them from being able to see the other's perspective. Paul's identity as advice-giver to the needy resists an unnecessary micro-management born of distrustful accounting practices. Chris seems to see herself as a firm but fair manager of an agency that helps needy people but works with, and relies upon, other funding agencies.

Also in line (5) is the TM's suggestion 'do you want to try and understand better why the other person can't understand you'. This is a most relevant, rhetorical question and perhaps a leitmotif of any mediation exercise. Mediation can provide an opportunity for the parties to explore each others' 'realities', 'discourses', 'subjectivities' and 'identifications'. However, here it is too baldly and directly put to be understood at this moment by the parties. Stated so openly, it becomes another projection upon the parties to fabricate reconciliation.

The TM seems to have lost confidence in the 'transformative' method and has again lapsed into directing the parties towards the need for them to resolve the conflict. However, 'transformative' mediation, if practised more purely by eschewing problem-solving, only allows the mediator to follow the words and expressed feelings and emotions of the parties 'in the moment' in order to facilitate shifts in 'empowerment' and mutual 'recognition' from which a 'problem' may or may not be solved. Antes and Saul lay out a basic 'transformative' belief in '[h]umans and their capabilities' being that '[p]eople are capable of making decisions for themselves' (1999, p. 3). This implies that people can resolve their conflict *themselves* on their *own* terms, in their *own* way. It is taboo to make any evaluations of the parties' situation on their behalf. As Bush and Folger state,

> [t]he most important premises of the transformative theory are that parties have both the desire and the capacity for conflict transformation. Helping to support this desire and capacity is the 'valued added' that the mediator brings to the table. (2005, p. 62)

As such, transformative mediation seems to have its roots in an '[e]go psychology [that] asserts that "self-improvement" is possible without calling society into question' (Sarup 1993, p. 7). An explorative style of mediation can extend beyond the reflective parameters of this transformative model by prompting parties to explore the differences and the sources of those differences, either personal or social, that have led to the crisis of interaction. Note that in order to arrive at a point where differences may be explored the interactional crisis, that is the 'problem' transformative mediation sets out to resolve, must be surpassed, at least partially and temporarily. If this is achieved the explorative mediator then has a responsibility to the parties to assess and understand the situation presented and reflect back this assessment by inviting the parties to consider apparent differences of meaning and patterns of wider causality. In this way, it may just be possible for the parties to critique socio-political norms (Glynos and Howarth 2007; Glynos 2008) out of which their conflict has arisen.

However, in an important pivotal sense and as implied above, to move beyond the parameters of a transformative mediation discipline could potentially have two possible effects for a mediation, either to lapse into directiveness or to open up exploration of the discursive terrain of the conflict. Of course, the transformative critique of facilitative mediation asserts the former, suggesting that the mediator would risk taking over the parties' problem and become evaluative and directive. But by holding to the confines marked by transformative practice, as noted above, it is probable that both mediator and parties remain caught within the discursive formation of the workplace that conditions the language and relationships through which they express their conflict. They are subject to the constraining effect of what Fairclough (2001) terms 'members resources', that is, their learnt interpretive procedures based upon background knowledge 'socially determined and ideologically shaped' (p. 9).

This mediator also seems to be trapped by the discursive formation of the workplace and the ego psychology of transformative mediation. She starts her intervention with a balanced summary but then lapses into a push to reconcile. This pressure to reconcile, which collapses into a problem-solving mode of mediation, appears to necessarily embroil the mediator in the dominant work discourse that demands unquestioning observance of rules and authority. But even without this departure from a more strict application of transformative techniques, the hegemonic power of the workplace might seem irresistible and yet, logically, it is not. Torfing usefully makes the point that

> if the relational and differential logic [of discourse] prevailed without any limitation or rupture, there would be no room for politics. All identities would be fixed as necessary moments of one and the same discourse, and conflict would only be played out between different intradiscursive variations. (Torfing 1999, pp. 91-92)

Curiously, this encapsulates the danger for transformative workplace mediation and workplace mediation more generally. However, Torfing goes on to explain that the necessarily,

> *partial fixation* of meaning produces an irreducible *surplus of meaning* which escapes the differential logic of discourse. (Torfing 1999, p. 92)

He calls this surplus *the discursive,* 'being not extra—or non-discursive but … discursively constructed within a terrain of unfixity' (Torfing 1999. p. 92)

Translating this technical language, hopefully without loss of meaning or muddying the water further, the social and cultural behaviours and practices and ideological beliefs of people in the workplace are never, as it were, set in stone and immune from contestation. The development of one social system of practices over time, rather than another, is rooted in contingent conditions. Alternative systemic developments that might have been realised but were not are then left outside. It is this contingent outside that both made possible the system that is temporarily pre-eminent and makes impossible a petrification of the dominant system to the exclusion of all subsequent possibilities. Returning to the terminology of political discourse theory, the ontology of the social that Torfing's observations rest upon accepts that (as noted in Chap. 5, endnote 2) there is a 'constitutive failure of any objectivity to attain a full identity' (Glynos and Howarth 2007, p. 110). Thus, there are always alternative social and meaning systems and subjectivities inhabiting them immanent within the social fabric: this is what Torfing has termed *the discursive*. It is theoretically possible for parties supported by mediators to navigate and negotiate this space of *the discursive*. However, it is socially and politically extremely difficult and may rarely occur. Having said this, if a mediator seeks to press parties to reconcile or problem-solve more generally and shuts out any possibility of entering dimensions of the discursive in moments of dislocation arising from conflict, she or he is likely to contain the parties within an undifferentiated sameness of the extant workplace discourse. Perhaps a mediator can adopt a 'subject position' of humble explorer of conflict, enacting a compassionate concern to understand, in order to potentially leave open a discursive space for the parties. But such an explorative mediator cannot urge parties into this space. To do so would negate any humility and also result in a collapse back into another form of problem-solving in which different political prejudices of the explorative mediator may likely come into play. However, this is not to say that these prejudices may not be used to support the exploration of the conflict.

Eighth extract, (64 mins 19 secs—67 mins 20 secs)

(1) Chris: … the other issue which I hadn't even thought about until having this conversation is that you decide to do your guess-timating for record keeping for the funding agency and you get it mixed up and it suddenly becomes provable that it couldn't have been what it was. I'll be the one who probably gets the sack. You'll get the sack as well probably but I shall get the sack for fraud because I'm the supervisor of the contract
(2) Paul: umm
(3) Chris: the ramifications are absolutely dire
(4) Paul: yes I can see that
(5) Chris: I don't want you sitting with a clock on your desk that's not what it is. It's just about making sure that every time that you make a phone call or you do something with a client you write down some time for it and you have to write it down more or less when you do it because after you've seen three clients in a day you can't remember what you've done with whom and when you did it
(6) Paul: humm

(7) Chris: I can't
(8) Paul: no I can't, you're right
(9) Chris: sometimes I see three clients, when I used to be doing it, and by the time I get to the third one I couldn't remember which one had the children and which one didn't and everything else
(10) Paul: umm
(11) Chris: if you don't write it up in between
(12) Paul: I understand that certainly
(13) Chris: umm
(14) TM: it feels as if there's a little window of light here maybe. That's my optimism. I'm not sure but it looks as if the moods slightly changed. What would be the most useful thing right now? Would it be to take a short break? Would it be to just check that we are at the point at which we can move forward into looking at what might happen next by just checking that you've said everything you need to say to one another, about how the situation has impacted you, what's brought you here today, what really this is all about, making any requests of one another as to how to avoid getting here again in the future? What do you both need to say to one another at this point?
(15) Paul: no, I can see, I've heard all this before obviously but kind of hearing it again, I mean there isn't very much room for me to move is there? It's going to be very difficult isn't it? I feel like I'm being pushed into doing it, which I don't like pretty obviously. It's hard to see what else can be done isn't it?
(16) TM: so you feel a bit trapped a bit
(17) Paul: I do really. Yes I do and I resent it. I have to say
(18) TM: in a corner
(19) Paul: it's a difficult place to be isn't it? I mean it's not very comfortable but having heard it all again. Chris hasn't got anywhere to go either has she I suppose. She hasn't got any room for manoeuvre either
(20) Chris: well I don't want you to be uncomfortable if there's is anything I could do about it …

Commentary and Analysis

The TM continues with her, by now, mantra of 'moving forward' in line (14). In contrast, she adopts a thoroughly 'transformative' practice in lines (16) and (18) when she asks if Paul feels trapped. Given that Paul is extending an olive branch to Chris and a resolution is in sight, this intervention resists any temptation to quickly conclude the mediation, and exemplifies transformative practice of staying with the parties 'in the moment' to amplify 'disempowerment' (Jorgensen et al. 2001). Chris responds with 'recognition' in line (20). The TM thus demonstrates a highly non-directive intervention far removed from the facilitative practice analysed in the previous chapter. For a moment she becomes less a manager of conflict and more a humble 'midwife' of dialogue.

Final extract, (70 mins 35 secs—71 mins 42 secs)

(1) TM: So just to summarise what you've both said in those last few minutes. Paul you're saying you felt somewhat trapped in the situation being forced to do something that you don't really want to be doing but then you said you probably see that Chris is also trapped. There's not much she can do. Chris you're saying that you really would like to do everything you can do to make it more comfortable for Paul and you wouldn't be here today if you had already thought of something else that you could do. Neither of you welcome the fact that you are here. You've also both started to talk about how things might work out in the future. What do you want to do about that? Do you want to actually explore in more detail how things are going to work going forwards? When would be a good time to do that? Do you want to do that today or do you want to find a time tomorrow or another point to look at that?

(2) Paul: Yes, I'd like to hear how you could support me. I'd like hear something about that …

Chris then goes on to explain in detail what she wants Paul to do concerning time keeping, suggesting clerical methods he might use to do it more easily and better. The TM summarises and prompts the parties to

agree a time and place to sort out these details saying 'so you both think it would be useful to set up a session outside this meeting to go through all these issues. Do you want to fix a time for that or …?'
The meeting ends at 76 mins 14 secs.

Commentary and Analysis

The TM continues with her theme of 'moving forwards' and finally re-enforces her own 'subject position' as an authorised manager of their interaction 'problem' by suggesting they arrange a specific date to discuss how they are going to work together in future. It would seem that this 'moving forward' is code for a return to the status quo.

Summary Interpretation of the 'Transformative' Mediation Role-Play and Comparison with the Facilitative Mediation Role-Play

The overall style of this role-play demonstrates how transformative mediators follow the parties rather than 'lead' them or orchestrate their interrogation. In the facilitative role-play the parties were relatively passive participants, reacting to the direction of the mediators. Here, the more humble disposition of the TM requires an active engagement from the parties, who are given space to hold their own conversation. After the role-play the TM, speaking as a professional workplace mediator, said she enjoyed doing 'less of the of the decision making myself and passing over more of the responsibility to the parties … and that felt good'. The relation of power between mediator and parties was more evenly balanced than in the facilitative role play.

However, in this case study, the TM dilutes a pure transformative method and blends it with a much more facilitative technique that presses the parties to focus upon the future and 'move forward' towards a desirable outcome. This outcome may or may not be desirable for those in conflict but it is what is required for the benefit of the organisation and the trustees. This slippage into a facilitative workplace mode of mediating has brought the TM into alignment with a workplace discourse of outcomes and agreements.

Because of this intermingling of styles, the TM's 'enunciative modality' (Howarth 2005) varies between that of a directive, supervising manager, a (mythical) enlightened leader/ follower and, at moments, a more fully 'transformative' supporter of parties in conflict. Hence, there are moments within this role-play that demonstrate how transformative mediation supports parties without leading them to problem solutions that have been conceived in the mind of the mediator. As such it does afford a practical demonstration of the critique of facilitative, problem-solving mediation.

We are left with the question of why the TM was not able to hold to a more pure transformative practice? In subsequent discussion with her she explained that when being paid to work she felt an obligation to her commissioner to be effective which was not felt when working voluntarily in a community mediation setting. This points to the overwhelming power of workplace discourse exerting hegemonic influence over this particular mediator. For mediators in general (whether practising in the facilitative, transformative, narrative or explorative modes), it also suggests the possibility of an envelopment in a fantasy of identity as one who is skilled in manipulating the resolution of conflict, taking enjoyment and a thrill from this function (Glynos 2008). The mediator may thus have a self-image as a wise, emotionally intelligent individual (Goleman 1996).

It has been argued that an explorative mediation style, derived from an ontology of 'lack', would be able to extend the inherently reflective method of transformative mediation to the knowing consideration of competing discourses and causal webs of conflict presented, but perhaps not fully recognised, by the parties. The mediator could bring these discourses and webs of difference back to the attention of both parties. As explained, even such a marginally evaluative intervention radically departs from the guiding premises of transformative mediation. The latter method holds to a liberal humanism whereas the alternative, explorative mode suggested above, is concerned with the better understanding of each others' socially constructed subjectivities and realities. An element of assessment is entailed in the alternative which transformative mediation resists. It can be argued that awareness of such an element of critical assessment is born of a political consciousness, sensitive to the radical contingency of the social, on the part of the mediator. In the absence of such a consciousness it is perhaps not surprising that, as noted above, the TM slipped into a problem-solving mode of practice.

We can speculate about other causes of a departure from the transformative method. As already noted, these may be to do with a human desire to help or alternatively a fear of failing to get to a solution. Carnevale, cited by Noll (2001) above, considers a limited psychology of mediator motivation but the attitudinal aspects of behaviour he touches upon are outside the scope of this inquiry. Nevertheless, the above data yields a powerful picture of how even a relatively humble and non-directive style of intervention may bring pressure upon the parties to find a path to reconciliation, despite introductory promises to the contrary. This tendency seems to militate against any escape from the dominant workplace discourse. Alternative discourses of 'managerialism' and 'accountability and trust', raised by one of the parties, were not given space to be explored.

Another transformative mediator could well have maintained a more strict application of the transformative method. A study of transformative workplace mediation would be valuable to evaluate if there is a tendency for transformative, workplace mediation, with its goal of improving the parties' interactions, to be captured by an organisational hegemony. Such a tendency is indicated in the example from Bush and Folger (2005) referred to below.

However, it can be assumed, by definition, that neither transformative nor explorative mediation methods can ever fully escape from the discursive formations (Torfing 1999) of the workplace environment. We might imagine that the possibility of and potential for an occasional and partial escape from this tendency would more likely be realised by the above indicated explorative practice that extends beyond the diffusion of antagonism. This is because this style concentrates upon an ambition to support parties in exploring their conflict and no more. Such exploration may support the potential for the negotiation, not of needs and interests,[6] but of the *discursive*, being that 'irreducible *surplus of meaning*' (Torfing 1999, p. 300) that otherwise remains obscure.

---

[6] Explorative mediation is concerned with the *understanding* of needs and interests rather than their negotiation.

Closing Remarks

Narrative mediation resting upon certain philosophies of social construction has pointed the way towards a more rigorous consideration of discourse within mediation practice but perhaps transformative mediation has turned away from such consideration. The uneasy tension between the dualism of humanistic agency and social connection (if not construction) manifests itself in an internal contradiction of the transformative method. This is, that the mediator avoids social connection with the parties by emphatically desisting from any mental or expressive involvement in the interpretation of the substance or content of the parties' conflict. They restrict themselves to supporting perceived shifts in micro-moments of empowerment or recognition. They are thus a very detached presence, almost socially disconnected from the parties. An approximation of neutrality is maintained and the parties are left alone to self-determine the outcome. By exclusively focussing upon the interactional crisis and not acknowledging other presenting causes of conflict, any currents of power or the 'political' are overlooked or ignored by the mediator. This may result in a strange disconnection of the mediator from the world of the parties. If in contrast the mediator tries to deeply understand, without judgement, both parties' positions, interests and needs, she or he will be able to reflect these understandings and insights back to the parties. This generates a broader social and political engagement arguably opening the possibility for dialogic exchange.

Bush and Folger tell a story of a conflict between a formerly active union representative in the US Postal Service who applied informally to be considered as a potential first line manager but met with rejection due to his earlier activity. He submitted a complaint. After a mediation session, his supervisors agreed to take him on and the complaint was dropped (Bush and Folger 2005, pp. 26-34). From one perspective the mediation served to confirm this former activist's personal process of depoliticisation and we assume he was subsequently absorbed into management. If problem-solving mediation tends to generate solutions that accord with the constraints of institutional settings, the tendency of transformative mediation, to re-enforce or empower a humanistic belief in an essential selfhood, may similarly contain the conflict interaction within a cultural or social status quo. Ironically, the opportunity for parties to explore the sources of their differences may be missed in the orchestrated journey to 'recognise' the other's humanity. Thus, to put it another way, in Bush and Folger's quest for 'moral growth' (1994, p. 27) along a humanistic trajectory, the opportunity for self-learning that the dislocation of conflict affords may be lost. Bush and Folger are right to emphasise the vital need to heal the psychological and emotional fragmentation induced by conflict but not at the expense of smothering a possible, emotionally intuitive and also reasoned reflection upon notions of 'self' and 'other' in a social context. Milner's (1996) critique of Bush and Folger's earlier work that 'the political and economic context' (1996, p. 751) is sometimes ignored, would also seem to apply to this example of transformative mediation from the US Postal Service.

In facilitative problem-solving mediation, mediator neutrality is a construct needed to protect the notion that the parties themselves determine any outcome. This 'neutrality' is discredited and deemed impossible by many observers including Bush and Folger. However, Bush and Folger have developed an alternative definition of neutrality along with a technique that aims to ensure that the idea of party self-determination remains enshrined within the mediation process. Their own particular interpretation of a relational worldview steps back from a more radical belief in the social construction of identity or a similarly radical concept of relational responsibility (McNamee and Gergen 1999) and retains a heavy investment in the empowerment of an autonomous individual. The result is a reflective style of intervention, informed by an apolitical humanism, which holds little scope for any critical questioning of selfhood and the socioeconomic status quo surrounding any given conflict.[7] This tends to suggest that the very notion of party self-determination at the heart of contemporary mediation, whether 'facilitative' or 'transformative', is itself problematic. The alternative is to embrace a more thorough-going relational worldview as defined by McNamee and Gergen.

> Relational responsibility, then, lies within the shared attempt to sustain the conditions in which we can join in the construction of meaning and morality. (McNamee and Gergen 1999, p. 11)

---

[7] The apolitical as always is political in that to abstain by default lends support to the majority.

Thus, if the mediator regards her/himself and the parties less as autonomous individuals and more as persons whose identities are significantly dependent upon 'nurture' rather than 'nature', and if the mediator views identity as mostly constructed in social and cultural interaction, then the premise of self-determination may be altered to one of co-determination. From this more poststructuralist perspective, responsibility for the conflict then spreads beyond the persons immediately engaged in the mediation. This perspective also behoves the mediator to act purposefully within the domain of co-determination; in other words, the mediator should not shy away from giving something of her or his own experience to the exploration of conflict. In this situation the concept of mediator 'neutrality' may be replaced with an acceptance of 'influence'. It then becomes necessary to understand the types of influence that prevail in mediation encounters in order to be able to minimise influence as appropriate and/or to make such influence more transparent and amenable to acceptance or rejection by the parties. How this role of the co-determining mediator might be defined is the subject of the next chapter.

References

Antes, J. R., & Saul, J. A. (1999). *Staying on track with transformative practice: How do we know if mediators have internalized the framework?* Paper presented at the Hamline University 1999 Symposium on Advanced Issues in Conflict Resolution—"Moving to the Next Level in Transformative Mediation: Practice, Research and Policy." St Paul, MN, October 16–18. Retrieved from www.transformativemediation.org

Beer, J. E., & Stief, E. (1997). *The mediator's handbook* (3rd ed.). Gabriola Island, British Columbia, Canada: New Society Publishers.

Bush, R. A. B., & Folger, J. P. (1994). *The promise of mediation: Responding to conflict through empowerment and recognition.* San Francisco: Jossey-Bass Inc.

Bush, R. A. B., & Folger, J. P. (2005). *The promise of mediation: The transformative approach to conflict.* San Francisco: Jossey-Bass Inc.

Caldwell, R. (2007). Agency and change: Re-evaluating foucault's legacy. *Organization, 14*(6), 769–791.

Cloke, K. (2001). *Mediating dangerously: The frontiers of conflict resolution.* San Francisco: Jossey Bass Inc.

Cobb, S., & Rifkin, J. (1991). Practice and paradox: Deconstructing neutrality in mediation. *Law and Social Inquiry, 16*(1), 35–62.

Crawley, J., & Graham, K. (2002). *Mediation for managers: Resolving conflict and rebuilding relationships at work*. London: Nicholas Brealey Publishing.

Fairclough, N. (2001). *Language and power* (2nd ed.). Harlow, England: Longman.

Fanon, F. (1985). *The wretched of the earth*. Harmondsworth, England: Penguin Books.

Folger, J. P. (2001). Who owns what in mediation?: Seeing the link between process and content. In J. P. Folger & R. A. B. Bush (Eds.), *Designing mediation: Approaches to training and practice within a transformative framework* (pp. 55–60). New York: Institute For the Study of Conflict Transformation, Inc.

Folger, J. P., & Bush, R. A. B. (Eds.). (2001). *Designing mediation: Approaches to training and practice within a transformative framework*. New York: Institute For the Study of Conflict Transformation, Inc.

Gaynier, L. P. (2005). Transformative mediation: In search of a theory of practice. *Conflict Resolution Quarterly, 22*(3), 397–408.

Glynos, J. (2008). Ideological fantasy at work. *Journal of Political Ideologies, 13*(3), 275–296.

Glynos, J., & Howarth, D. (2007). *Logics of critical explanation in social and political theory*. Abingdon, England: Routledge.

Goleman, D. (1996). *Emotional intelligence: Why it can matter more than IQ*. London: Bloomsbury Publishing Ltd.

Habermas, J. (1984 [1981]). *The theory of communicative action volume one: Reason and the rationalisation of society* (T. McCarthy, Trans.). Boston: Beacon Press.

Habermas, J. (1987 [1981]). *The theory of communicative action volume two: Lifeworld and system: A critique of functionalist reason* (T. McCarthy, Trans.). Boston: Beacon Press.

Harvey, D. (2015). *Seventeen contradictions and the end of capitalism*. London: Profile Books Ltd.

Howarth, D. (2000). *Discourse*. Buckingham: Open University Press.

Howarth, D. (2005). Applying discourse theory: The method of articulation. In D. Howarth & J. Torfing (Eds.), *Discourse theory in European politics: Identity, policy and governance* (pp. 316–349). Basingstoke: Palgrave MacMillan.

Howarth, D., & Torfing, J. (Eds.). (2005). *Discourse theory in European Politics: Identity, policy and governance*. Basingstoke: Palgrave Macmillan.

Jorgensen, E. O., Moen, J. K., Antes, J. R., Hudson, D. T., & Hendrikson, L. H. (2001). Microfocus in mediation: The what and the how of transformative opportunities. In J. P. Folger & R. A. B. Bush (Eds.), *Designing mediation: Approaches to training and practice within a transformative framework* (pp. 133–149). New York: Institute For the Study of Conflict Transformation, Inc.

Kingdon, C. (2005). Reflexivity: Not just a qualitative methodological research tool. *British Journal of Midwifery, 13*(10), 622–627.

Knights, D., & Willmott, H. (2007). Management and leadership. In D. Knights & H. Willmott (Eds.), *Introducing organizational behaviour and management* (pp. 259–310). London: Thompson Learning.

Kressel, K. (2006). Mediation revisited. In M. Deutsch, P. T. Coleman, & E. C. Marcus (Eds.), *The handbook of conflict resolution: Theory and practice* (pp. 726–756). San Francisco: Jossey-Bass Inc.

Laclau, E. (1990). *New reflections on the revolution of our time.* London: Verso.

Mayer, B. S. (2004). *Beyond neutrality: Confronting the crisis in conflict resolution.* San Francisco: Jossey-Bass Inc.

McNamee, S., & Gergen, K. J. (1999). *Relational responsibility: Resources for sustainable dialogue.* London: Sage Publications.

Milner, N. (1996). Mediation and political theory: A critique of Bush and Folger. *Law and Social Inquiry, 3,* 737–759.

Monk, G., & Winslade, J. (Eds.). (1996). *Narrative therapy in practice: The archaeology of hope.* San Francisco: Jossey-Bass Inc.

Noll, D. E. (2001). A theory of mediation. *Dispute Resolution Journal, 56*(2), 78–84.

Pruitt, D. G. (2006). Some research frontiers in the study of conflict resolution. In M. Deutsch, P. T. Coleman, & E. C. Marcus (Eds.), *The handbook of conflict resolution: Theory and practice* (pp. 849–867). San Francisco: Jossey-Bass Inc.

Rogers, C. R. (2001). *On becoming a person: A therapist's view of psychotherapy.* London: Constable.

Rothman, J. (1996). Reflexive dialogue as transformation. *Mediation Quarterly, 13*(4), 345–352.

Sarup, M. (1993). *An introductory guide to post-structuralism and postmodernism* (2nd ed.). London: Harvester Wheatsheaf.

Seul, J. R. (1999). How transformative is transformative mediation?: A constructive-developmental assessment. *Ohio State Journal on Dispute Resolution., 15*(1), 135–172.

Torfing, J. (1999). *New theories of discourse: Laclau, Mouffe and Zizek*. Oxford: Blackwell Publications Ltd.

Williams, M. (1996). "Can't I get no satisfaction?" Thoughts on the promise of mediation. *Mediation Quarterly, 15*(2), 143–154.

Willmott, H. (1994). Bringing agency (back) into organizational analysis: Responding to the crisis of (post) modernity. In J. Hassard & M. Parker (Eds.), *Towards a new theory of organization*. London: Routledge.

Willmott, H. (2005). Theorizing contemporary control: Some post-structuralist responses to some critical realist questions. *Organization, 12*, 747–780.

Winslade, J., & Monk, G. (2001). *Narrative mediation: A new approach to conflict resolution*. San Francisco: Jossey-Bass Inc.

7

Explorative Mediation: An Instrumental, Ethical and Political Approach

In the introduction, the instrumental, moral and political aspects of mediation were differentiated. As noted, there are of course elements of all three aspects in all types of mediation, given that mediation is fundamentally about people in conflict sitting down together to talk and find ways of resolving their differences. But it has been argued above that facilitative styles of mediation, at least in the workplace, tend towards the instrumental, and the relational styles bring a more marked moral dimension into relief. The relational styles are underpinned by explicit philosophies of the social and theories of conflict that yield particular understandings of how people, when in conflict, may potentially communicate better. This is especially so in the moral philosophy of Bush and Folger's work. The conscious adherence to a particular philosophy and theory seems to drive out a given style of practice. Although, as noted earlier, it may be argued that a temperamental predisposition to a style will be justified by reference to a selected grounding theory.

The styles of both facilitative and narrative mediation appear more 'top down', with procedures being led by the mediator. The former addresses the presenting 'problems' (underlying issues and needs), while the latter addresses the way in which these problems are presented, i.e. the stories.

The former seems to function without acknowledgment of organisational hegemony and the latter theoretically views power through a Foucaultian prism. In these ways mediators may appear apolitical but become inadvertently political; that is, they potentially direct resolutions but very possibly do so without an overt awareness of either their influence or of 'the political' context of mediation. Transformative mediation, in contrast, might be described as a 'bottom up' approach whereby the mediator yields process control (mostly) to the parties and follows their discussion. Again, there would seem to be an apoliticism in this method where the act of 'following', constrained by parameters of 'empowerment' and 'recognition', tends to preclude a more direct engagement with the necessarily political subject matter of the conflict.

In this chapter an argument will be made that mediation practice can retain this 'follower' style, can be distinctly ethical, and can be informed by a particular sense of the political that appears in many ways absent in either the facilitative/problem-solving or relational models. This alternative practice recognises that conflict, being situated within a given political setting of prevailing social and cultural norms of identity and behaviour, affords opportunities for reflection upon the contingent nature of this setting. This practice is termed 'explorative' because it is centred in an openness to dialogical communication that may reveal the contingency of any social setting via a deeper *exploration* of conflict. The mediator should support such an exploration as humbly and as non-judgementally as possible. The key elements of this approach will now be outlined, followed by a discussion of its practical limitations from the perspective of the mediator (being the primary focus of this book) and also finally from certain party-oriented perspectives as well.

A Description of Explorative Mediation

The main aim of explorative mediation is to support those in conflict as they attempt to hold a dialogue/conversation in which parties may look at and listen to each other and themselves. Although Bush is similarly quoted above as saying he is there to help people listen to each other and themselves, the pursuit of dialogue represents a step beyond a 'transformatively' supported recovery from a crisis of interaction. Recognition of and for the other must be a prerequisite for seeking a dialogue, but whilst necessary it is not sufficient. To recover respectful communication and to resolve conflict are moral aims, but it is the pursuit of dialogue that carries the additional ethical and political impetus of this approach to mediation (as discussed in Chap. 4 and further below). Solutions tend to arise from dialogical conversation but these might not constitute full resolution, and the purpose of dialogue is not to drive out agreement or consensus. Howe warns that 'communication that seeks to gain agreement may do violence to the persons who are led to agree' (1963, p. 55). Thus, from the mediator's perspective, the resolution of a conflict is almost a by-product. Of course from the parties' perspective this is most often why they come to mediation. It is of course possible that the parties may not choose to explore their conflict and the potential of mediation may be curtailed. The mediator can only respect the parties' wishes in this eventuality.

Prior to any joint meeting, at the first visits with each party, the mediator would briefly explain that mediation processes may be managed either by the mediator or by the parties. The explorative approach would be offered and explained. In the explorative method, in common with transformative mediation, the parties retain ownership over the process of the mediation meeting. From the outset of the joint meeting, the mediator would concentrate upon listening to the parties. Paraphrasing and amending Howe (1963, p. 37), the mediator would seek to humbly give him/herself to both parties and seek to know each party as the other is (*at that moment*). As the conversation unfolds, the mediator would occasionally intervene to reflect back particular contributions to the parties in an even-handed, compassionate manner. This is so the mediator can try to understand each party in order to be able to hold a mirror to the conflict for the parties to look at. Perhaps the metaphor of a mirror might be substituted by one of a hologram in which the multi-dimensionality of the conflict may be explored and clarified. The mediator would work with moments of emotion, high or otherwise, and may sometimes choose to reflect back moments of disempowerment or recognition, as well as expressions of anxieties and defensiveness or of hurt and confusion. He or she would work with parties if insults were traded, calming the rapid exchange of accusation and helping to surface underlying causes of anger. The mediator would also draw attention to differences of purpose and opinion or of need and concern, impasses, different ways of speaking about things or the use of metaphor[1], and the different ways events, actions or people are related and depicted. Background and contextual aspects of the conflict that the mediator would decide (or *judge* whether) to highlight may appear. The mediator would avoid false mutualising—that is, finding common ground where none really exists—and would similarly resist an impulse to 'reframe', whereby criticism or anger may be translated into softer language. To do this would cover over conflict and invite inauthenticity. The mediator would remain comfortable with moments of silence. Generally the mediator would help to slow exchanges and create space for parties to reflect, would listen for misunderstandings and remain (*politically*) sensitive to the significance of the wider context of the conflict.

Despite the mediator's position of detachment, not being embroiled in the parties' conflict, he or she would sense an attachment through a concern to understand the parties. In doing this, the mediator would strive to reflexively sense his or her own anxieties, prejudices and projections in order to suspend them selflessly and to be better able to 'hear' what the parties are saying.

Thus, explorative mediation differs radically from both the facilitative and narrative schools in humbly following the parties' conversation by yielding the management of the mediation process (control of turn-taking and agenda-setting) to the parties. As in the transformative model, an explorative mediation would travel its course to wherever the parties take it. Also, in keeping with transformative mediation, the explorative style aims to minimise the mediator's influence. But it is a positive engagement with the subject matter and context of the conflict that takes explorative mediation beyond the parameters set for transformative practice. In this territory the mediator may be at risk of exercising unwanted influence over the parties and of becoming biased in favour of one party

---

[1] Reflecting back the use of metaphor has proven to be a powerful means for both helping others reflect and understand themselves and for minimising any interfering influence conveyed via the mediator's intervention. This insight is derived from a counselling intervention developed by the late David Grove that has been called 'clean language' (see Owen 1989).

7 An Instrumental, Ethical and Political Approach

over the other. The mediator would therefore seek to maintain a reflexive awareness of posing questions that border on a critical evaluation of parties' stories. This would be done by summarising or reflecting back, even-handedly, the mediator's understanding of the conflict and posing questions inquiringly in a search for clarity. Moreover, to avoid bringing one's own prejudice to bear upon such moments of reflecting back, the mediator would at times keep to a fairly literal re-presentation (without parroting) of a party's words. Also, in appreciating the perspective of the other, the mediator would try to reflect back her/his understanding in a fashion that seeks to clarify and reveal meaning and is absent of judgement of the parties.[2] Nevertheless, subliminally-conscious triggers to interventions that arise from mediators' culturally and politically inspired apperception of the parties' stories may lead mediators to introduce their own ideas. Even though these ideas emerge unconsciously, they may be consciously noted and felt as judgemental, and so they can then be verbally acknowledged, thereby rendering such moments of mediator influence more transparent.

The mediator may encounter differences between parties in which meanings of the world are not shared. It may be possible for parties to discover an emotional distance between their sense of identity, on the one hand, and a given discourse or lived expression of a social 'reality' to which they would tend to adhere, on the other. At points of 'dislocation', hidden ideological premises may be revealed. The explorative mediator would humbly assist in the co-creation of alternatives to conflict in an unobtrusive manner whilst remaining open to diverse interpretations and inviting the parties to explore the conflict for themselves. Mediation could therefore amount to a form of encounter potentially open to the 'political', with the mediator acting as a promoter of the exploration of conflict. As such, mediation may hold potential to enable development by the parties of a new sense of identity rather than serve to shore up old identities. Such a notion of possible change is held to varying degrees within all types of mediation examined above, yet in execution, much

---

[2] The mediator assesses or, we might say 'judges', the parties' stories to understand them without, metaphorically, sitting in a mental position of judgement about the parties' behaviour. When the mediator feels her/himself to be reacting judgementally, she/he can only try to work reflexively to suspend this disposition and extend a compassionate concern to understand.

mediation practice may serve to contain conflict and close it down (as evidenced in Chap. 5) rather than open up an encounter to exploration in which sentience (albeit transient) of the undecidable nature of alternatives comes to the fore. Thus, the explorative mediator would wish to occupy a subject position of concerned helper of open-minded co-discoverer, not leader or interpreter or assessor but someone who supportively looks to understand both parties simultaneously. (By rendering the mediator subject position more humble and transparent, any role in the co-creation of shared meanings may be more easily restricted to a minor one.)

In summary, the mediator would attempt to model dialogical interaction in the hope that we may all sometimes find an 'ability to go around back and come up inside other people's heads to look out … and say: oh, so that's how you see it?' (Bradbury 2008, p. 15.) In such moments we may experience the laughter of surprise. From the perspective of the other, one may be better able to 'see' oneself. In the clash of perspectives, new contingent ways of understanding ourselves in the world may also emerge. It must be recognised that this ambition may be rarely fully achieved, but any small progress towards it can generate decisions and forms of resolution. As Bohm (1999) and Howe (1963) remind us, the principal of dialogue is to suspend a desire to impose ourselves or persuade, and thus to remain open to the other and to respond to them. But there will always be a resistance to the full achievement of this ambition. De Hennezel observes that 'it is impossible to separate the hard kernel of self-interest from the breath of love for others' (2011, pp. 115–116). Whether this 'kernel' of the person is regarded as an essence or, as argued above, as a provisionally fixed element of an interpellated identity, such resistances, psychological or psychoanalytic, resonate with lived experience. Sometimes we fall a long way short of openness to dialogue. Therefore in keeping with other approaches, when a mediation proves largely unsuccessful, the explorative mediator, in a duty to the parties, would describe the impasse and invite them to consider what alternative decisions may be made in the absence of any form of partial agreement. Although differing somewhat, evidence of such necessary flexibility in responses can be found in Kressel and Gadlin's (2009) study of mediators in a specialist scientific community. They were seen to revert to dealing with issues in a tactical way if a more in-depth approach, seeking underlying causes of a relational or organisational system's nature, did not prove practical.

This short description of an explorative approach sets out an ideal of behaviour that is beset by paradox and poses many obstacles and challenges for the mediator, who must respond uniquely in the moment to the parties. To return to a central theme of this book we must further consider the conundrum of how an explorative mediator attempts to act unobtrusively and in selfless absorption in their work whilst simultaneously assessing and understanding the parties' perspectives. Such an attempt at understanding and verbal recounting will entail bringing influence to bear, and so the mediator must reflexively recognise their inevitable influence and seek to make it as transparent as possible in the very invitation to explore conflict.

Constraints and Challenges for Explorative Mediation

Fear of Failure

A significant containing power of mediation lies in the initial staging of the mediation encounter. That is, the parties have actually come to the meeting and given authority to one or two strangers, in the guise of mediators, to set some parameters for the ensuing conversation. Additionally, parties often curtail extremes of behaviour that might otherwise unfold and may self-censor to varying degrees in the presence of third parties. The material formality in a workplace setting reinforces this defensive tendency. The situation may yet be volatile but there is a degree of voluntariness and some security of confidentiality. Nevertheless, all conflict is at least unsettling and induces anxiety and even fear. Therefore, mediators are concerned to help the parties feel as safe as possible. But anxiety levels may be increased and possibly exacerbated in the course of a genuine exploration of the conflict. Indeed Cloke (2001), for example, advocates a 'dangerous approach to mediation' in which people are helped to 'surrender illusions and fantasies' and hence to 'recognize a diversity of truths' (p. 12).

Mediation processes that are deliberately open-ended and invite uncertainty, whether dangerous or not, may be regarded with unease by commissioners in corporate and public sector institutions, where cost-effectiveness and productivity are paramount. For this reason there is a possibility that, under the gaze of the organisation, the understanding of mediation as a political encounter between persons within a pattern or web of wider causation may be glossed over. Hence there is also much for the mediator to be anxious about, be it that the parties themselves may be anxious and fearful or that the mediation may prove volatile, difficult and intractable if it is not tightly managed. They may feel an overwhelming external pressure to ensure the encounter is controlled. Even though mediation is constructed from the outset as a containing and controlling experience, the mediator may compromise an explorative approach and become more interventionist and controlling, for fear that the mediation may 'fail' to deliver a good resolution for parties and commissioners alike. As was seen with the quasi-transformative role-play mediator, the paid mediator will always feel a sense of obligation to the commissioner.

Therefore, against many contrary pressures and impulses, it is incumbent on mediators to remain as comfortable as possible with the radically contingent and uncertain potential of the mediation encounter. This at least requires that, whilst the mediator may bring a compassionate desire to see parties resolve conflict and do all possible to support them, she or he should resist a temptation to feel responsibility for making this happen. The mediator should divest her/himself of the ownership of resolution. This in turn entails self-reflection upon his or her own fantasies about their role as saviour or heroic peacemaker. Complementing a fear of failing in the role of mediator, on the other side of the same coin, is a desire for success. The logic of such motivating fears and desires, which may subvert an ideal of explorative mediator behaviour, will now be considered further.

Fantasy and Desire to be a Peacemaker and Hero

Mediators are susceptible to a fantasy that they have the skill, wisdom and power to resolve conflict, and the achievement of resolution is what they may knowingly or unknowingly desire. '[I]nsofar as ... fantasy designates the subject's "impossible" relation ... to the object-cause of its desire' ... 'through fantasy we learn how to desire', (Zizek 1992, p. 6). This is a desire, as stated, that it is impossible to fulfil. This model of fantasy, as encapsulated by the Lacanian concept of the 'objet petit a', or the object-cause of desire, is helpful and insightful in considering the role of the mediator. Benvenuto and Kennedy offer a basic introduction to this concept thus:

> [I]t is a property of language to slide around its own incapacity to signify an object, and this object exists then only as a *lacking object* (desire follows this movement). This is what he [Lacan] called the "objet a". (1986, p. 176)

An 'objet petit a' represents an imagined fullness or plenitude once enjoyed (giving a sense of jouissance) and now lacking, and therefore forever desired. Zizek refers to it as 'the object of desire that eludes our grasp no matter what we do to attain it' (Zizek 1992, p. 4). Fantasy and the 'enjoyment' of fantasy compensates for this absent fullness and so becomes a motor for desire. Thus, enjoyment is now felt in fantasmatic[3] anticipation of recovery of this imagined plenitude. Glynos and Stavrakakis (2008) further explain that this

> logic peculiar to fantasy ... entails the staging of a relation between a subject (as lack) and the object [petit a] (as that which escapes socio-symbolic capture), thereby organizing the affective dimension of the subject, the way it desires and enjoys. (2008, p. 263)

The mediator operates within a working space, within the wider workplace, in which she/he may come to feel responsible for a particular intervention and conclusion. The mediator desires success but the conclusion of a mediation can be measured as either a 'failure' (no resolution or partial resolution of conflict) or a 'success' (complete resolution). Thus, the mediator in general may fantasise, with an expectation of enjoyment, that she/he is responsible for and able to bring about a reconciliation of the parties. If she/he succeeds in totality (an impossibility) she/he would

---

[3] This indicates a belief that we all make sense of the world through narrative frames of reference employing varying degrees of fantasy.

have achieved what Glynos terms a 'beatific' fantasy of fulfilment (2008, p. 283). Complete failure (either through the mediator's fault or the parties' fault) would represent a 'horrific' consequence (2008, p. 283). A notion of 'total' success, if virtually approached, may trigger a sense of bodily jouissance or a limit-experience (Benvenuto and Kennedy 1986, p. 179; Glynos and Stavrakakis 2008, p. 261). Yet the jouissance obtained never matches that which is expected, and 'unable to fully satisfy desire, [it] fuels dissatisfaction' (Glynos and Stavrakakis 2008, p. 262).

In this affective and practical movement through the play of mediation, the mediator may have made a conscious or unconscious decision to take control of the meeting and therefore to be responsible for the resulting outcome of the meeting (whilst also holding to the contradictory belief that it is the parties who make any decisions). To do otherwise would be to deny him or herself the enjoyments inherent in the 'role' and identity of mediator. Were the parties really to make their own resolution, the role of the mediator would seem diminished. (At the end of a successful mediation the mediator may say, 'you did it all yourselves', but does the mediator really mean this or does he/she like to imagine their input was of significance?) What is being pursued is an impossible 'objet petit a' in the form of a successful mediation. Here it is the mediator's relationship to the 'conflict' that defines conflict as an 'objet petit a'. A 'successful' closing down of conflict may be represented by the harmonious communication between the parties and a collaborative communion amongst all the members of the mediation meeting. This desire for an impossibly perfect form of dialogical communication and mutual understanding can be what drives mediators' self-identification in the workplace, as they believe/fantasise about the promise of the elimination of their own 'lack'. That is, by believing she/he has succeeded in leading a satisfactory resolution of conflict, the mediator may hide from her/himself an existential sense of lack or incompleteness. The mediator's sense of self is made nearly whole or fulfilled in the execution of a successful mediation. Enjoyment in the task of mediating may be threatened by the parties, who are thereby cast as the volatile and unmanageable obstacle to this 'elimination' of the mediator's lack. The parties must therefore be controlled.

It would seem that potentially any style of mediation could be caught up in this logic of subjectivity. Hence the '*mode* of the subject's [mediator's] engagement' (Glynos and Stavrakakis 2008, p. 265) in mediation practice may be wrapped/rapt in a form of enjoyment rendering the subject 'insensitive to the contingency of social reality' (Glynos and Stavrakakis 2008, p. 265). This is termed, after Lacan, 'phallic enjoyment'. We can argue after Laclau (1990) that practitioners of workplace mediation may become complicit in a 'myth' that social dislocations which inhabit the workplace are aberrations that can be covered over. The mediator's contribution to this overarching 'myth' is enacted by their pursuit of an idealised and imaginary working reconciliation. Mediators desire the achievement of reconciliation and take enjoyment from their expectation of bringing about the end of conflict. Like an 'objet petit a,' this object cause of desire, the aimed-for creation by skilled mediation of a working reconciliation, is 'simultaneously the most *intimate* kernel of the subject and yet also external to this same subject' (Glynos and Stavrakakis 2008, p. 263). The internal fantasy is entwined with prevailing discursive beliefs about dispelling the deviant eruptions of conflict in the workplace that obscure the contingency and inevitability of conflict.[4] So even while the mediator, of course, faces the parties to listen to them as they recount their conflict stories, it is as if the mediator almost looks past the parties towards the idea, on the periphery of their imagination, of 'the conflict'. The parties and the conflict become objectified. As such the mediator experiences a sense of the attraction to the telos of reconciliation at the 'edge' of his or her 'vision.'

To attain some distance from this logic of fantasy (since escape is defined as impossible), the explorative mediator must wholeheartedly release him/herself from the need to control the parties and from the overriding desire to bring about a peaceful reconciliation. Through this movement the hegemonic shackles of organisational discourse may be loosened and a non-phallic enjoyment that is more open to the contingency of social relations may be felt. A second necessary practical and politically significant step to achieve a detachment from fantasy is to pur-

---

[4] This view may be held simultaneously with the contradictory acceptance of conflict as something that is natural to our species.

sue dialogue by only seeking to support the parties in their exploration of their own understanding of the conflict. The mediator thereby searches for an understanding of each party, of their conflict and of the parties *in* their conflicts. This brings a subtle clarification of the central idea of explorative mediation, this being that mediation should explore not just the 'conflict' but also the parties' *understandings* of their conflict. After all, during the mediation, the conflict is only represented by the parties' understandings of it. The mediator's attempts to help the parties explore their 'understandings' should not become solipsistic, nor should the conflict be objectified as the problem. Explorative mediation that is not a form of negotiation nor a translation to a new non-conflict narrative recognises that it is not so much a question of 'separating the party from the problem' (Fisher et al. 1992) or from the narrative (Winslade and Monk 2001) but of finding a new understanding of the self in relation to both the other and to the conflict. The mediator models a non-judgemental or non-critical attitude to the parties and to their representation of their conflictual circumstance precisely so that the parties may be helped to inhabit a political field of respectful, discursive contestation about the conflict. The mediator may thereby strive after 'dialogue' but, importantly, with an awareness of the fantasmatic nature of this ambition, recognise both the empty signification of this word (see Chap. 4) and the false promise of a recovery of an absent fullness.

Striving after an ideal of dialogue requires an explorative mediator to attempt to behave selflessly in an absorbed embrace and with discernment of conflict stories without judgment of the parties. By losing the self in this work, the mediator is better able to attempt to become 'attentive to the radical contingency of their [mediator's and parties'] political practice' (Glynos and Howarth 2007, p. 123). Such a disposition helps the mediator avoid any premature closing down of the exploration of the conflict. This rational and emotional movement towards a model of dialogue demands a level of selfless engagement, but paradoxically this more selfless disposition is combined with a compassionate curiosity to understand each party, an act of understanding that demands an apperceptive assessment, or we might say 'judgement', of the parties' stories.

If mediators seek to 'understand' by listening and following the parties, asking questions of clarification along the way, and selflessly letting

7 An Instrumental, Ethical and Political Approach

go of a managerial responsibility to secure resolution, they may attain an openness to the contingency of the conflict and of their own practice. This openness will help mediators to sustain reflection upon their fantasmatic enjoyment of their chosen role. Such a reflective practice would be deemed 'ethical' by Glynos and Howarth (2007). Their usage of the term goes beyond issues of right conduct and virtue to questions of the subjective embodiment of identity and related modes of enjoyment. It is this subjectivity that may close off awareness of the contingency of social relations otherwise revealed in dislocations of the social caused by conflict. To be captured by fantasy places the subject (mediator or party) in an unchanged relation to prevailing social and political norms and thus in the grip of ideology. Conversely, a 'detachment from (rather than abandonment of) fantasy' (Glynos 2008, p. 291) corresponds to an '*ethical* mode of being' (Glynos 2008, p. 291) in which the subject's relation to social and political norms is changed. Glynos and Howarth thus draw an ideological-ethical axis (2007, p. 112) across which the subject's relation to norms governing practice is transformed through the 'intermediaries of fantasy and mode of enjoyment' (Glynos 2008, p. 289). A mediator may be caught up in a twofold fantasy. In the first she/he identifies her/himself as a skilful leader of conflict resolution. In the second she/he accepts social norms and practices as largely natural and universal. Such an effective dismissal or misrecognition of the contingency of social and political relations will ensure a resultant entrapment within a dominant ideology. To move across the axis from the ideological towards the ethical requires a puncturing of fantasy, thus articulating

> the contours of a political project based upon the ethics of the real, of the "going through the fantasy (*la traversee du fantasme*)," an ethics of confrontation with an impossible, traumatic kernel not covered by any *ideal* (of the unbroken communication, of the invention of the self). (Zizek 2006, p. 259)

Thus, we may resign ourselves to the impossibility of the achievement of an ideal dialogue between mythical sovereign individuals but retain a political project in which the impossible is knowingly attempted, recognising that the subject's 'lack' cannot be 'filled out with subjectivization'

(Zizek 2006. p. 254). In such an attempt we may discern a radical choice in how radically contingent social relations may be interpreted. That is, radical contingency proffers a domain of radical choices. The mediator's role might be to invite parties to 'attempt to show[/see] the essential contingency of all universality' (Laclau 1990, p. 190). Perhaps, in a more mundane sense, this is where we arrive if, suspending our own prejudice and desire to persuade, we can glimpse the world through the eyes of the other, whether or not we find any sympathy with this other perception. It may be that in the act of choosing from an altered set of choices (Bateson 2000) there is an automatic collapse back into a fixed but revised 'subjectivity', but this thought of collapse is mitigated if the act of choosing is carried out collectively and subsequently expressed in practical action.

It is also possible that mediators' conception of their normative sense of responsibility to the 'other' and to 'justice' may curtail their escape from the grip of ideology and draw them back to an over-investment in fantasy. This may involve a resumption of control of the meeting process at the behest of one or both parties. Within the group it is highly probable that parties and mediators may enact basic assumption behaviours (Bion 1961; Hirschhorn 1990). For example, parties often look to the mediator for solutions and a mediator, if flattered, may be apt to respond. Or, the mediator and one party may sub-consciously form a covert coalition against the other party. If a compassionate concern to understand is replaced by judgmental feelings of dislike or annoyance, practices similar to those attributed by Noll to Carnevale in Chap. 2 may emerge.

Whether we accept the negative ontology of the subject's 'lack' and consequent impossible desire for plenitude, the above considerations of psychological and affective motivation underscore the infinite complexity and ultimate impenetrability of the mediator's task. We can deduce that all types of mediation practice, and workplace mediation in particular, operate within extremely challenging conditions of the external environment interwoven with our internal subjectivities. We can develop styles of mediation to address (if never fully overcome) these challenges by careful reflective consideration of the interventions we make and the questions we pose, so as to trace the motivation for them. We can examine the mediation 'situation type' we effectively construct by the subject position we choose, or come to inhabit, in a mediation session. For example, do we choose to function as a directing, expert manager, at one end of the spectrum of influence, or as a humble follower and supporter at the other?

If we accept a Lacanian-inspired ontology, we can interrogate the authenticity of our self-reflection in the following way. Glynos and Howarth describe the authentic as

> a *generalized sensitivity* or *attentiveness* to the always-already dislocated character of existing social relations, wherein creativity and surprise are accorded prominent roles. (2007, p. 110)

This clearly pertains to a psychoanalytic project to puncture the fantasy discussed above. But they warn that modes of subjectivity and enjoyment, being embodied in material practices, are 'not completely reducible to conscious apprehension' (2007, p. 120). From a second, not dissimilar psychological perspective, a *relative* authenticity may be imagined as arising from deeper understandings of motives discovered by reflective/reflexive attention to emotions, assumptions or projections when in dialogue with trusted others. The mediators, who are present because they are not embroiled in the parties' conflict, must surely examine their own authenticity if they are to hold out a hope for the parties to work through conflict towards some mutual understanding. After all, mediation is an invitation to the parties to reflect deeply upon their positions, interests and needs with respect to those of their antagonist. It is therefore also important for mediators to have some sense of the generic barriers to dialogue that confront the parties. These may be expected to surpass anything blocking the mediator's attempts to model dialogic behaviours on the parties' behalf.

Barriers to Dialogue

When we, as individuals, are in conflict with one another, we often find ourselves defending our own view and resisting, rejecting and attacking the other's view, probably attributing blame for the conflict to the other person. As indicated in Chap. 4, we tend to experience stressful feelings of fear, anxiety, frustration, injury, envy, humiliation, confusion, anger and aggression and so on; as a result, our sense of self is disturbed. When we look back at ourselves experiencing these emotional states, we may criticise ourselves for having regressed to a child-like state. We may experience a loss of face if others witness our behaviour. However, the causes of conflict are manifold and there are many structural and environmental conditions conducive to the emergence of conflict between people, both individually and in groups. Even so, there are likely to be elements of these individual characterisations of conflict in all conflict situations. When raw emotional responses have calmed and extremes of emotion are more subdued, feelings of resentment towards the other are still likely to persist. They will be present at the time people come together in a mediation meeting. On arrival at a mediation session in the workplace, antagonists may have worked out justifications and rationalisations for their perspectives and may well be intending to dig in to defend their own views, judgements and opinions, which are interwoven with their sense of identity and worldview.

Hence, the mediator meets with people whose emotional states are already at a heightened sensitivity and they may be very concerned to stick largely to their own understanding of events in a justification of their behaviour hitherto. Nevertheless, many people decide to come to mediation in good faith in search of a resolution. Therefore, we may assume there is an incipient recognition of the possibility (however small) of other perspectives. Getting past the emotional upheaval towards more measured discussion is the first general barrier for the parties and the mediator to overcome (and this upheaval is likely to subside and resurface periodically during a mediation meeting). But there are barriers to human communication that will persist throughout and indeed these barriers might be said to be present in all communication, whether in the midst of conflict or more generally. Howe (1963) provides an elegantly simple and recognisable summarisation of five main barriers to communication, all of them interwoven with each other.

The first to be mentioned is the language barrier. It has already been indicated above that people impute different meanings to the same language. This can occur between people who share many of the same discursive understandings of the world. The words we use arise from our lives up to that point and may carry many associations, emotionally and intellectually. Equally these words are received and interpreted by the other according to their own experience, which, of course, differs from the speaker's. Therefore, the mediator attempts to listen to different meanings and metaphorical differences, and to reflect back words cautiously to clarify and confirm understanding. Beyond different specific meanings, the mediator will also be attuned to more major differences in understanding aspects of the world—that is, to different discourses. However, to this observation of the opacity of the medium of language we can add a further barrier to the collective effort at communication. From the assumption that there is no 'free, intellectual agent [whose] thinking processes are not coerced by historical or cultural circumstances' (Sarup 1993, p. 1), it may be deduced that parties and the mediator alike may not be able to move their intercommunication beyond the confines of a naturalised, organisational hegemony. For example, it might not be possible, despite the disturbing effects of conflict, for either the mediator or the parties to think outside of the discourse of the organisation and its rules of behaviour. In this case it is the ideology conveyed within language and social practices that forms the barrier to communication, as illustrated in Chap. 5. Such entrapment by a pervasive hegemony may prevent discussion that reveals contingent aspects of the specific conflict.

The second potential barrier that is also very significant for the work of mediating is the preconceived image one brings of the other person, of oneself and of the subject matter in hand. Mistaken preconceptions block us from opening ourselves to the other to be able to listen. Being unable to listen to the other also prevents us from reflecting upon our own deepest motivations and identifications. Thus, our preconceptions damage us as much as they do harm to the other. The power of mediation is in the face-to-face encounter, in which preconceptions at best can fall away so that the other can be seen anew and the self can also be listened to and possibly seen anew as well. The mediator works to understand and 'see' each party, as it were, in front of each party. There are infinite possibilities in what we might discover in each other and ourselves.

Re-ordering Howe's list slightly, the next barrier is when people are at cross-purposes and perhaps do not understand their own purpose. Again, the hope of an explorative mediator is that the parties are able to surface and understand what is motivating them. The fourth and fifth barriers, very closely interrelated, already touched upon above and perhaps the most widely recognised, are anxiety and defensiveness. People's internal anxieties and their anxieties about the subject being considered obstruct an open exchange in which the person may risk giving him/herself to the other. There is a world of meaning in this small word 'anxiety' that we cannot do justice to here, but there are glimpses in the model of Lacanian affect and 'lack' already indicated above. In summary, anxiety may block us from behaving 'authentically', in the senses just referred to, so that shared meaning-making cannot occur. If mediators can demonstrate that they desire to understand the emotions, interests and stories of each party, both parties may come to feel validated. Thus, anxiety may be reduced, in turn loosening the grip of preconceptions about the other and the conflict. Thereafter, each may start to view the other person with renewed respect from which dialogue may grow. All approaches to mediation hold out such an ambition for their interventions.

A state of anxiety promotes defensiveness, the fifth common barrier to communication and dialogue. This is most commonly found in resistance to the potential loss of self-identity entailed in being seen to back down. A positive outcome of mediation is the ability of the parties to be flexible about their assessment of the conflict and their role within it, and, we might say, to simply change their mind. But changing one's mind can have identity-shattering consequences and so it is not at all a simple matter. Under conditions of conflict, a sense of self-identity or self-image can become fragile and vulnerable and thus needs to be defended. But ironically, because identity is fragile, it is most open to possibilities of uncertainty, fluidity and change.

If the mediator recognises these barriers to dialogue in her/himself and in the parties, she/he may be able to support the parties in surmounting them in the course of the mediation. This notion of support again comes down to the continued attempt to explore and understand the parties' expressions of the facets of their conflict—that is, within the language, images, purposes, anxieties and defences revealed. This is not to find solutions but understanding. Howe reminds us again that to enter into dialogue does not mean agreeing with the other person or achieving consensus but it does require that we open ourselves to the other and experience their viewpoint 'to bring [ourselves] into responsible relation to the world of persons and things' (1963, p. 56). Similarly to Glynos in his observation that we are unable to escape or abandon fantasy but may only try to attain some detachment from it, Howe recognises, indeed warns us, that barriers to dialogue and resistance to communication cannot be swept away but must 'be accepted as a part of dialogue' (1963, p. 48). Changes to 'minds' and to identities may appear limited and transitory, but in opening the self to the other, subtle lasting change would seem bound to occur, and if the contingency of social and political relations is only glimpsed, preconceptions are likely to be broken down and an (impossible) dialogue may be said to have occurred. Mediation can be a crucible that holds the potential for this to happen.

References

Bateson, G. (2000). *Steps to an ecology of mind.* London: University of Chicago Press.
Benvenuto, B., & Kennedy, R. (1986). *The works of Jacques Lacan: An introduction.* London: Free Association Books Ltd.
Bion, W. (1961). *Experiences in groups.* London: Tavistock Publications.
Bohm, D. (1999). *On dialogue.* London: Routledge.
Bradbury, R. (2008[1957]). *Dandelion wine.* London: Harper Voyager.
Cloke, K. (2001). *Mediating dangerously: The frontiers of conflict resolution.* San Francisco: Jossey Bass Inc.
de Hennezel, M. (2011). *The warmth of the heart prevents your body from rusting: Ageing without growing old.* London: Rodale, Pan Macmillan.
Fisher, R., Ury, W., & Patton, B. (1992). *Getting to yes: Negotiating an agreement without giving in* (2nd ed.). London: Random House.
Glynos, J. (2008). Ideological fantasy at work. *Journal of Political Ideologies, 13*(3), 275–296.
Glynos, J., & Howarth, D. (2007). *Logics of critical explanation in social and political theory.* Abingdon, England: Routledge.
Glynos, J., & Stavrakakis, Y. (2008). Lacan and political subjectivity: Fantasy and enjoyment in psychoanalysis and political theory. *Subjectivity, 24*, 256–274.

Hirschhorn, L. (1990). *The workplace within: The psychodynamics of organizational life*. London: The MIT Press.
Howe, R. L. (1963). *The miracle of dialogue*. New York: The Seabury Press.
Kressel, K., & Gadlin, H. (2009). Mediating among scientists: A mental model for expert practice. *Negotiation and Conflict Management Journal, 2*(4), 308–343.
Laclau, E. (1990). *New reflections on the revolution of our time*. London: Verso.
Owen, I. R. (1989). Beyond Carl Rogers: The work of David Grove. *Journal of Professional Care, 4*(4), 186–196.
Sarup, M. (1993). *An introductory guide to post-structuralism and postmodernism* (2nd ed.). London: Harvester Wheatsheaf.
Winslade, J., & Monk, G. (2001). *Narrative mediation: A new approach to conflict resolution*. San Francisco: Jossey-Bass Inc.
Zizek, S. (1992). *Looking awry: An introduction to Jacques Lacan through popular culture*. London: The MIT Press.
Zizek, S. (2006). *Interrogating the real*. London: Continuum.

8

Conclusion

A Final Characterisation to Contrast Mediation Styles

Mediation styles that eschew control of the meeting process may be criticised for risking a return to destructive 'fighting' in the mediation meeting. Crawley and Graham (as noted in Chap. 2) rely on control of the meeting 'structure' to mitigate any possibility of a resurrection of the conflict's argumentative and recriminatory dynamic. Indeed, when we are steeped in conflict, at worst, we may regress to a less-than-mature frame of mind, as indicated by Noll's theory of mediation (also see Chap. 2). This being so, it might be argued that the facilitative style takes a maternal approach. The parties are in some sense treated as infants. For example, statements of blame and expressions of anger may be reframed and softened (and 'you' accusations turned into expressions of how 'I' feel). Whilst not neutral, the influence exercised may be accepted as of benign intent. More directive styles may then be deemed to represent, at times, paternalistic interventions. Very differently, transformative mediation is far more trusting of the parties' innate human capacity for reconciliation. These mediators thus approach the parties as mature equals

© The Editor(s) (if applicable) and The Author(s) 2016
R. Seaman, *Explorative Mediation at Work*,
DOI 10.1057/978-1-137-51674-9_8

(who are equal in their fallibility also). This, along with a certain detachment, brings transformative practice much nearer to a notion of minimal influence. The explorative style is also more trusting of the parties and seeks to support them by 'following', not 'leading', but unlike transformative practice, it is prepared to risk a greater involvement, increasing the possibility for inadvertent influence. Explorative mediation is thus more overtly collaborative and not neutral. Not to take this risk, it is argued, may result in conflictual identities becoming more entrenched and significant substance of the conflict being left unexplored.

The Myth of Neutrality

This book constitutes an appeal to all mediators to openly recognise the myth of mediator neutrality. Many already do, but the quoted definitions in the Introduction are testament to the continued currency of this concept. Having accepted that they are not 'neutrals', mediators must consider how they intervene and how their actions convey influence and power. Could they be categorised as maternal or paternal interveners, or as neither? Mediators surely need to consciously consider what type of 'face'[1] (Goffman 1972) they present to the parties and to referrers in organisations, and what type of 'subject position' they choose to occupy (and for which the workplace mediator is remunerated). Such consideration in turn leads to reflections upon the operation of power, in society and between individuals, and prompts questions about the role and identity of the mediator in particular, as she/he operates in the workplace.

The present mainstream approach to workplace mediation has been critiqued here for its tendency to manage, engineer or lead a

---

[1] 'Face' is defined by Goffman as the positive social value we attempt to maintain during social interaction. The significance of 'face' for a mediator may be indicated in the following small example. In explaining mediation process and the mediator's role to parties in first visits, it is probable that the words chosen will vary from party to party as the mediator's sense of self and awareness of 'face' changes subtly to accommodate perceived expectations of the specific person sitting opposite them. A part of this movement entails automatic, tiny adjustments when in conversation to maintain 'face', though we imagine we are presenting a consistent self-image. More generally mediators should not fear some loss of 'face' should a mediation be relatively unsuccessful, though this is clearly extremely difficult to achieve.

problem-solving process. The purportedly neutral mediator thereby 'helps' individuals, who are regarded as responsible, autonomous agents with powers of self-determination, to find a path to resolution. The terms 'manage', 'engineer' and 'lead' are replete with connotations of power, yet a critical reflection upon mediator influence seems largely absent from mainstream practice. It has been argued that this lack of self-awareness regarding influence can result in a narrowing and even closing-down of the parties' opportunity to work through the conflict. Consequent disempowerment of the parties can occur in subtle ways, merely as a result of the mediator's direction of the discussion via control of the process (Irvine 2007). Such a closing-down may ultimately result in a colonisation of mediation by organisations, tarnishing the perception of mediation amongst employees. At worst, mediation may be seen cynically as a process for the containment of troublesome (sovereign) individuals rather than one that affords an opportunity for more democratic means to resolve and learn from inevitable conflict.

A Democratic and Dialogic Intervention in the Workplace

In contrast, the post-structuralist worldview of political discourse theorists such as Glynos, Howarth and Torfing, drawn upon in this study, offers a description of individual 'identity' and 'subjectivity' constructed through interaction with the surrounding social, political and cultural environment. This ontology resonates well with a study of mediation as both the identities of individuals and the ideological beliefs they hold about the 'social' and the 'political' are understood, by this philosophy, to be firstly precarious and secondly subject to disruption by immanent antagonism and conflict. The mediator enters the stage at a juncture of a larger personal history of antagonistic relationships. Inside the workplace the mediator now has a choice of styles to select from. This book has advocated a humble, compassionate[2] stance for the mediator, one that

---

[2] A compassionate response depends upon recognition of suffering as non-trivial, identifying with a deserving subject, and, importantly for explorative mediation, an ability to make sense of this

follows the parties' conversation with a view to supporting the exploration of their understandings of conflict before decisions are made about how it may be resolved. This presumes a potential fluidity of identity and of forms of responsibility, which are interwoven with the social context from which confrontational relationships emerge. The huge benefit for organisations of such an explorative mediation method is that resolutions of conflict will be more robust and lasting and allow good working relationships to be rebuilt.

The explorative method also assumes there exists the possibility for a partial escape from the discursive context of dominant organisational and social ideologies permeating the lives of both parties and mediators. It has been argued that the explorative approach to mediation, informed by transformative and narrative mediation developments, may be able to realise such an escape by means of setting a primary objective of the pursuit of dialogue. This has been construed as entailing an explicitly political and ethical purpose for mediation, in addition to its pragmatic and instrumental function. Three types of dialogue have emerged in this book. The one principally used to theorise mediation practice is by definition impossible to fully achieve but operates as a beacon to guide action. Another, believed attainable, is founded in essential, spiritual beliefs (Howe 1963; Buber 2002). A third, secular and non-essentialist, is founded upon the idea of escape from an egoistic autonomy in a post-dualistic merging of thought, mind and body. Whichever is chosen, it is argued that it is necessary to attempt to search for dialogue to better create the potential for meaning-making to occur. When it does, the burden of conflict lifts and smiles abound.

The Paradox of Selfless Engagement

It is bizarre that mediation should not be overtly recognised as 'political' given it is an intervention into conflict, and indeed parties will sometimes bring almost Machiavellian tactics into the mediation space.

---

suffering. Hence, the need to explore the conflict in order to make sense of it is a necessary part of being able to respond compassionately.

In this book it has been argued that the mediator should bring a political awareness and sensitivity to the stories of conflict presented by the parties. Herein lies a paradox, in that the mediator attempts to float above the politics of the conflict somewhat like a pond lily, and yet the mediator's feet are nevertheless rooted in the murky politics of conflict. By virtue of the mediator's relative detachment, she/he may endeavour to adopt a selfless disposition through an intense concentration upon the task of listening, from which understanding of both parties' perceptions may be attained. Thus, in keeping with the metaphor of floating, the mediator attempts to suspend a judgemental disposition. The mediator attempts to strip away some of the artifice of 'face' by not retaining an egoistic concern with how she/he is apprehended, although Zizek would warn us that behind fantasies of 'face' we may discover a void. In contradiction to an attempted selflessness, in order to reflect back understandings of the conflict to the parties, the mediator assimilates their stories with his/her own preconceptions of social, political and organisational life. Thus, this attempt to support dialogue demands a reflexive attention to the mediator's own prejudices and motivations (as considered in the previous chapter).

Here it is important to note again the great significance of the transformative mediation technique. Despite the above critique of transformative mediation, its practice enables mediators to sense their own evaluative assumptions or persuasive expressions that may infiltrate their interventions if they go far beyond a strict adherence to underscoring moments of 'dis/empowerment' and 'recognition'. Training in transformative mediation may greatly benefit mediators who then may or may not go on to develop their practice in different directions, subject to their philosophical and temperamental preferences and their practical experiences of mediating.

An Evolving Practice

Explorative mediation is a practice that combines elements of other styles. It is inspired by both narrative and transformative approaches and yet it retains some aspects of problem solving mediation in that the mediator engages collaboratively with the 'issues'. Mediation methods and principles must surely develop through cycles of theory and practice, although it is unlikely that there can be any comprehensive overarching theory (Irvine 2007) given the infinite complexity of human interaction. All mediation styles have merit and value. Different approaches may be required in different circumstances. Forms of knowing directiveness may be justifiably required in familial, commercial and international mediation settings. But it has been argued above that the aspirations of dialogue should always hold a central place in any attempt at mediation, rather than the happy outcome of a managed negotiation, even though, as a mediation unfolds, it may not always be feasible to continue to pursue this ambition. Dialogue may be held as a guiding beacon that informs the work of the mediator. Explorative mediation has been developed on this premise. Listening deeply to others (a practice central to all mediation styles) is a prerequisite for pursuing dialogue. The overt exercise of power is a barrier to dialogue and shores up fixed identities. We often come into conflict because we perceive that someone or something is blocking the expression of our preferred identity. Here power may be understood as threading through moments of persuasion and denial in which opinion and identity are defended. Mediation can be an invitation to temporarily suspend our desire to persuade others that we are right, and to listen to our enemy instead. As Shakespeare's Clown says to the Duke,

> Marry sir, they [my friends] praise me and make an ass of me. Now my foes tell me plainly I am an ass; so that by my foes, sir, I profit in the knowledge of myself, and by my friends I am abused. (Twelfth Night, Act 5, Scene 1)

Mostly we are not asses but the Clown indicates well how we might come to see our enemies as 'legitimate opponents' (Mouffe 2000, p. 15) to whom we should listen. Seeing another's point of view, especially one that is critical of oneself, is difficult and requires a form of learning in which beliefs about self-identity may need to be adjusted. People usually seek an escape from conflict but sometimes identity is so intertwined with a point of view that alteration of identity and viewpoint may not be possible. Nevertheless, the mediator's job is to demonstrate a profound form of listening (and exploring) so that the parties may themselves have an opportunity to put aside preconceptions and listen and explore. After tragically blinding himself, Oedipus found that 'seeing' was a possessing sense whereas 'listening' allowed him to take things in more deeply and process them internally. Cloke (2001) describes this as 'uncovering hidden choices' (p. 13) that yield transformational opportunities for learning and change, thus freeing the self from the trap of a fixed identity.[3] The behaviour of the mediator may make a silent appeal to the parties through the demonstration of an intense concern to listen, explore and understand, to put aside preconceptions and join in this process of listening and exploring. Therefore the job of the mediator may be summarised as twofold: firstly to help parties listen to each other, to see the world through the other's eyes and to see themselves from the other's perspective, and secondly to listen to the mediator's own prejudices, to be sensitive to the radical contingency of the social and thus to keep open the possibility for dialogue to emerge.

References

Buber, M. (2002[1947]). *Between man and man*. London: Routledge.
Cloke, K. (2001). *Mediating dangerously: The frontiers of conflict resolution*. San Francisco: Jossey Bass Inc.
Goffman, E. (1972 [1961]). *Encounters: Two studies in the sociology of interaction*. London: Penguin Books.
Howe, R. L. (1963). *The miracle of dialogue*. New York: The Seabury Press.
Irvine, C. (2007). *Transformative mediation—A critique*. Retrieved from http://ssrn.com/abstract=1691847
Mouffe, C. (2000). *Deliberative democracy or agonistic pluralism*. Political Science Series No. 72. Vienna: Institute for Advanced Studies.

---

[3] Although Cloke's concept of learning and authenticity, somewhat in contradistinction with that proposed in this book, relates to a more essentialist concept of selfhood.

Index

A

Advisory, Conciliation and Arbitration Service (Acas), 2, 4, 39, 40, 43, 44, 61
Alvesson, M., 74
antagonism, 59, 64, 83, 150, 151, 185
  daily realities of, 82
  diffusion of, 215
  immanent, 245
  interpersonal, 62
  political act dealing with, 84
  political analysis of, 150
  social, 64, 162
Antes, J. R., 172, 207
apolitical humanism, 217
Aristotelianism, 47
Aristotle, 47

B

Barratt, E., 45
Bateson, G., 50
Beer, J. E., 26, 75, 172
Bennett, A., 70, 71, 73
Benvenuto, B., 231
Billig, M., 64
BIS. *See* Department for Business, Innovation and Skills (BIS)
Bohm, D., 75, 77, 78, 82, 83, 228
Boserup, H., 21, 25–8, 34
  mediation styles categorisation, 25–8
Buber, Whilst, 81, 82n5
Burson, M. C., 82
Bush, R. A. B., 15, 23–4, 75, 102, 160, 165–72, 172n1, 173–6, 184, 185, 215–17, 223, 224

Note: Page number followed by 'n' refers to footnotes.

© The Editor(s) (if applicable) and The Author(s) 2016
R. Seaman, *Explorative Mediation at Work*,
DOI 10.1057/978-1-137-51674-9

C

Camden Mediation, 4n3
Carnevale, 22, 23, 215, 236
Carroll, M., 45
Centre for Effective Dispute Resolution (CEDR), 2
Chartered Institute of Personnel and Development (CIPD), 2, 37, 41, 45
Chris
  facilitative mediators with, 113–25
  joint meeting between Paul and, 125–54, 180–213
  quasi transformative mediator with, 177–9
CIPD. *See* Chartered Institute of Personnel and Development (CIPD)
clans, 1, 3
Cloke, K., 3, 5, 66, 67, 72, 74, 75, 92, 170, 229, 249
Clown, 248
Cobb, S., 158, 159, 164
Code of Practice for Disciplinary and Grievance Procedures, 40, 41
Collins, P., 75
Community Advice Centre, 99
  community mediation, 79n4, 214
  organisations, UK, 4
  practice, facilitative, 19
  process in UK, 16–17
conflict
  broadening responsibility for, 61–7
  eruptions of, 89
  management skills, 89
  multi-dimensionality of, 225
  peers in, 90
  psychological mode, 62
  scenario, 94
  transformation, 65
conflict resolution, 1, 2, 10, 63, 66, 70–1, 93, 107, 205, 235
contemporary mediation, 3, 21, 28, 39, 176n4, 217
contextual intervention, 20
contingent approach, 10
contrast mediation styles, 243–4
Crawley, J., 18, 243
Critchley, S., 52, 85
critical discourse analysis, 51, 95
critical theory, 173
Critical Theory of the Frankfurt School, 72
criticism, 22, 25, 60, 72, 76, 135, 226

D

Darwin, 62
De Hennezel, M., 228
democracy, 12, 60, 67
  organisational justice and, 67–72
  in workplace, 71
Department for Business, Innovation and Skills (BIS), 41, 42
  Resolving Workplace Disputes: A Consultation, 42
  Resolving Workplace Disputes: Government Responses to the Consultation, 41
Department of Trade and Industry (DTI), 39, 40
depoliticising mediation, 163
Deutsch, M., 62–4

Index

Diamond, Jared, 1, 3
Dingwall, R., 30–3
directive mediation, 19–20
discourse analysis
   critical, 51, 95
   political, 95
discourse, definition, 51
discourse theory, 52, 97, 163, 164, 209
   post-Marxist, 65
distributive justice, 68
Dolder, C., 89
Dugan, 11

E
Eisenberg, E. M., 78
emancipation, 70, 71
   micro, 12, 74
   in workplace mediation, 72–4
employee individualisation, 44–5
Employment Act 2008, 40
employment legislation, 40
employment relationship, 44, 46
empowerment and recognition, 23, 27, 167–9, 185, 199, 204
English divorce mediation, 30
Eskew, D. E., 94
evaluative mediation, 24, 45
explorative approach, 131, 147n6, 153, 176, 199, 225, 229, 230, 246
   to mediation, 13, 246
explorative mediation
   constraints and challenges for, 229–37
   description of, 224–9

style, 85, 154, 157, 199n5, 208, 214, 226, 244
explorative mediator, 108, 153, 192, 199n5, 208, 210, 227–30, 233–4, 239–40
explorative method, 225, 246

F
face, defined, 244n1
facilitative mediation, 4, 5, 8, 10–12, 17–19, 24, 29, 75, 90, 93, 95, 154, 157 8, 208, 223
facilitative mediation role-play, 95, 149–54
   vs. transformative mediation role-play, 213–15
facilitative mediator, 94
facilitative mediator, joint meeting between Paul and Chris, 125–54
   closing down issues and compromise agreement, 142
   commentary and analysis, 127–31, 134–5, 137–8, 140
   joint meeting exchange stage, 136–7
   joint meeting uninterrupted time, 131–4
   opening up an issue, 138–40
   opening welcome to joint meeting, 125–7
facilitative mediator with Chris, 113–25
   commentary and analysis, 115–22, 124–5
   sequence of extracts, 119–20

facilitative mediator with Paul, 100–13
  commentary and analysis, 101–5, 107–13
  sequence of extracts, 105–7
facilitative model of mediation, 90
facilitative workplace mediation, 29, 157, 165
facilitative workplace mediators, 93
Fairclough, N., 6, 52, 96, 97
  theory, 98
Fairhurst, G. T., 77
family mediation, 31, 32, 91
Folger, J. P., 8, 15, 24, 75, 102, 161, 165–72, 172n1, 173–6, 184, 185, 215–17, 223
Folger's theory, 166, 174
Foucaultian prism, 224
Foucault, M., 81, 163

G
Gadlin, H., 228
Gaynier, L. P., 171, 175
Gergen, K. J., 77–9, 83, 173, 217
Gergen, M. M., 77–9, 83
Ghoshal, S., 44
Gibbons, Michael, 40, 43, 44
  Better Dispute Resolution: A review of employment dispute resolution in Great Britain, 40
Glover, J., 97n3
Glynos, J., 84, 95, 96n2, 231, 232, 235, 237, 241, 245
Goffman, E., 244n1
Goodall, H. L., 78
Graeber, D., 72
Graham, K., 18, 243

Gramscian concepts of hegemonic control, 71
Gratton, L., 44
Greenberg, J., 9, 67, 70, 94
Grove, David, 226n1

H
Harvey, D., 172n1
Hawes, L. C., 78
Haynes, J. M., 26
hegemony, definition, 52
high commitment management (HCM), 46–8
Howarth, D., 51, 52, 64, 65, 84, 95, 96, 96n2, 235, 237, 245
Howe, R. L., 225, 228, 238, 239, 241
HRMism, definition, 46
humanism, 48, 64, 81–2, 151, 172n1, 173, 174
  apolitical, 217
  enlightenment, 64
  idealistic, 152
  individualistic, 34, 81
  liberal, 172n1, 214
  optimistic, 174
  revolutionary, 172n1
Human Resource (HR) department, 44
Human Resource Management (HRM), 35, 45
  policies, workplace mediation, 46–9

I
idealistic humanism, 152
ideo-culture, 46

ideology, 9–10, 42, 51–3, 63, 97, 140, 235,. 236, 239
immanent antagonism, 245
impartiality, 34, 79n4, 92
independent English divorce mediation service, 30
informational justice, 68
Inside the Workplace: First Findings from the 2004 Workplace Employment Relations Survey, 39
inter-clan relationships, 1–2
interest based negotiation, 24
interpersonal antagonism, 62
interpersonal justice, 68
intra-group relationships, 2
Irvine, C., 31

K

Kallinikos, J., 48
Kant, 48
Keenoy, T., 46, 53
Kennedy, R., 231
Kressel, K., 4, 5, 28, 29, 63, 157, 228
    problem-solving style, 28, 63
    relational style, 28, 63
    typology, mediation practice, 20–1

L

Lacanian-inspired ontology, 97
Lacan, Jacques, 95, 96
Laclau, Ernesto, 52, 64, 95, 163, 164, 233
Lederach, J. P., 65–6, 71, 74
    justice issues, 65–6

Legge, K., 46–8
liberal humanism, 172n1, 214
Lukesian concepts of hegemonic control, 71

M

MacAllister, B., 66
Marx, 62
Mayer, B. S., 167
McNamee, S., 173, 217
mediation. *See also* community mediation; contemporary mediation; explorative mediation; facilitative mediation; problem-solving mediation; transformative mediation; workplace mediation
    age-old practice, 1–2
    context, 99
    definitions of, 2–3
    depoliticising, 163
    directive, 19–20
    as emancipatory, 69
    explorative approach to, 13, 246
    explorative style of, 85, 154, 157, 199n5, 208, 226, 244
    facilitative model of, 90
    fascination with, 77
    HR tool, 55
    interaction, observed, 30
    intervention, 7, 32, 35, 61, 69, 70, 73, 76, 98, 167, 186
    mainstream style of, 4
    management, 8, 32
    model, 80

mediation (*cont.*)
  narrative, 10, 24, 28, 75, 115, 158–65, 168, 216, 223, 246
  Noll's theory of, 21–5, 243
  objective, 9–11
  potential of, 59–61
  problem-solving approach to, 157
  programs in USA, 32
  role-play, 94
  transformative approach to, 11, 158, 166, 169–70, 176, 247
  victim offender, 28
mediation encounter, 19, 30, 75, 83, 121, 124, 130, 131, 137, 151, 161, 218, 229, 230
mediation in workplace
  adoption of, 37–9
  government policies, 39–44
  HRM policies, 46–9
  individualisation of employee, 44–5
mediation meeting, 4, 8, 54, 60, 85, 98–9, 104, 128, 130, 135, 149, 151, 163, 164, 225, 232, 238
mediation power, 12
  contradictory currents of, 53–5
mediation practice, 11, 20–8, 59, 92
  aligns with organisational needs, 49–51
  consideration of, 7
  development of, 65
  diversity of, 25
  ensuing critique of, 7
  generic model, 26
  integrity of, 7
  Kressel's typology, 20–1
  place of dialogue within, 74–6

storytelling, 26
styles of, 6–7
types of, 25–6
Waldman typology of, 31
mediation services
  deployment of, 60
  English divorce, 30
  by HRM function, 53
  management of, 47
  providers, 37
  use of, 7
  workplace, 41, 47, 66
mediation space, 60, 69, 74, 116, 159, 171, 246
mediation styles, 10, 33, 99, 248
  Boserup's categorisation, 25–8
  characterisation to contrast, 243–4
  choice and application of, 39
  cognitive, systemic style, 26
  complementary models of, 22
  contrast, 243–4
  counterfactual, 142
  evolution of, 29
  explorative, 214
  facilitative, 4
  generic style, 25, 26
  humanistic style, 27
  narrative style, 27
  non-directive, 78
  problem-solving style, 28
  relational style, 28
  settlement driven style, 25, 26
  strategies determine, 33
  transformative style, 27
mediator. *See also* workplace mediator, facilitative mediator
  ambition, 186

Index 257

authority and role, 34
behaviours and strategies, 34
commentary, analysis and interpretation of facilitative role-play, 99–125
conundrum, 31
encounter frame creation, 30
humility, 97
imagines dialogue, 7–9
intervenes, 60–1, 63
interventions, 19–20, 59–60
joint meeting, 18–19
least-directive style, 28
non-directive, 76
non-neutrality, 32, 54, 183
position of detachment, 226
professional workplace, 93
quasi transformative, with Chris, 177–9
reflectiveness, 92
skill, 19
strategies, 20
therapeutic, 32, 33
transformative, 94, 166, 168, 174, 175, 185, 215
mediator influence, 8, 15, 69, 90
   Dingwall's evidence and counter claim, 30–2
   evidence, 30–5
   opportunities for exercising, 21
   and power, 19
   styles and varieties of, 28–30
mediator neutrality, 15, 34, 35, 54, 90, 147, 158, 166, 174, 217, 244
   evidenced-based critiques of, 33–4
   myth of, 3–7, 244–5

mediator power, 15, 49
   aspects of, 98
   levels of awareness of, 89–93
   and subjectivity, 91
mediator role, 5, 8, 18, 92
   execution of, 5
   perspective of, 68
mediator, role-play material interpretation
   note on mediation context, 99
   subject positions, 95–9
Merry, S. E. (settlement problem identification), 32–5
micro-emancipation, 12, 74
micro-emancipatory intervention, 54
Miller, D., 48
Milner, N., 217
moderately social constructivist position, 96
Monk, G., 27, 158–65, 168, 171, 174
Moore, Christopher, 3, 4, 79n4
Mouffe, C., 52, 59, 64, 163, 164

N

Nabatchi, T., 68
narrative mediation, 10, 24, 28, 75, 115, 158–65, 168, 216, 223, 246
neutral mediation intervention, 35
Noll, D. E., 21–5, 28, 34, 215
Noll's theory of mediation, 21–5, 243
   conclusion, 24–5
   conflict escalation levels, 22
   conflict goals, 21
   outcomes, 23–4
   style and process models, 22–3
non-directive mediator, 76, 83

norm-advocating model, 31
norm-educating model, 31
norm-educating practitioner, 31
norm-generating model, 31

O
Oberman, S., 31
observed mediation interaction, 30
optimistic humanism, 174
organisational justice
　and democracy, 67–72
　factors for measurement of, 68
　models of, 68

P
Paul
　facilitative mediator with, 100–13
　first visit of the mediator with, 179–80
　joint meeting between Chris and, 125–54, 180–213
Pecheux, 96
Plato, 76
political discourse analysis, 95
political theory, 64
post-Marxist discourse theory, 65
poststructuralist theory, 158
potential of mediation, 59–61
problem-solving approach, 115, 119, 130, 147, 154, 165, 193
　to mediation, 157
problem-solving mediation, 4, 11, 29, 63, 75, 76, 93, 112, 115, 121, 125, 151, 157–9, 169, 214, 217, 247
　practice, 11, 93–5

problem-solving process, 103, 129, 245
problem-solving thinking, 19
procedural justice type 1, 68
procedural justice type 2, 68
professional workplace mediators, 93, 175, 213
Promise of Mediation, 165
Pruitt, D. G., 10, 11, 27
Putnam, L. L., 77

Q
quasi-legal officers, 19
quasi transformative mediator with Chris, 177–9
quasi-transformative role-play, interpretation of, 175–213
　commentary and analysis, 178–9, 183–7, 191–213
　first visit of the mediator with Paul, 179–80
　joint meeting between Paul and Chris, 180–213
quasi transformative mediator with Chris, 177–9

R
radicalism, 54, 55, 71
Rahnema, M., 81
REDRESS, 68n2
　transformative mediation scheme, 68
reflexive intervention, 20
relational responsibility, 217
relational styles, 11, 28, 29, 63, 93, 223
resolution of conflict, 1, 2, 7, 53, 214, 232

Resolving Workplace Disputes: A Consultation, 42
Resolving Workplace Disputes: Government Responses to the Consultation, 41
revolutionary humanism, 172n1
Reyes, O., 84
Ridley-Duff, R. J., 71, 73
Rifkin, J., 158–9, 164
Riskin, Leonard, 3–4, 22, 24
 model, 22, 24
Roberts, M., 30, 31
Rogers, Carl, 168, 170
role-play mediations, 94
Rouse, W.H.D., 76
Russell, B., 48n5

S

Sarup, M., 95, 96, 127
Saul, J. A., 172, 207
Saundry, R., 43, 54
schizophrenia, 50
schizophrenic practices, 50–1
Schneider, S. C., 50
self-awareness, 92, 245
self-determination, 15, 29, 31, 35, 90, 93, 130, 165, 166, 171, 174, 183, 217, 218, 245
selfless engagement, 80, 82, 83, 234
 paradox of, 246–7
sense of self-determination, 174
settlement problem, Silbey and Merry's Identification of, 32–5
Silbey, S. S. (settlement problem identification), 32–5
Simmel, 30
social antagonism, 64, 162
social-political-economic mode, 62, 63

social-political-economic relationships, 63
social-political-economic sphere, 63
speech acts, 6
Stavrakakis, Y., 231
Stief, E., 26, 75, 172
stylistic eclecticism, 10
subliminally-conscious triggers, 227

T

therapeutic mediation, 32
therapeutic mediator, 32, 33
Torfing, J., 6, 65, 84, 95, 245
Touval, S., 5n4
transformative approach to mediation, 11, 158, 166, 169–70, 176, 247
transformative dialogue, 78
transformative mediation, 10, 12, 24, 28–9, 33, 68, 71, 108, 115, 119, 130, 147, 151, 154, 158, 165, 176, 178, 184, 186, 191, 199, 205, 207–8, 224, 226
 critique of, 169–75
 purpose of, 184
 role-play *vs.* facilitative mediation role play, 213–15
 scheme, REDRESS, 68
 theory and practice, 165–9
transformative mediator, 94, 108, 166–8, 171, 172, 174, 175, 185, 187, 199, 199n5, 204, 205, 213, 215
 with Chris, 177–9
transformative model, 24, 198, 208, 226

transformative workplace mediation, 209, 215
Tribunals Service, 42

U
UK
  Advisory, Conciliation and Arbitration Service (Acas), 2, 4, 39, 40, 43, 44, 61
  Chartered Institute of Personnel and Development (CIPD), 37
  community mediation organisations, 4
  community mediation process in, 16–17
United States Postal Service (USPS) REDRESS transformative mediation scheme, 68

V
victim offender mediation, 28

W
Waldman, E., 31
Watson, T., 46
Weber, Renee, 8
WERS, 38, 38n1, 43, 44
Wibberley, G., 43, 54
Willmott, H., 74, 81, 163, 164, 173
  paradoxical freedom of modernity, 173–4
Winslade, J., 27, 158–65, 168, 171, 174
workplace
  conflict, 3, 39, 47, 49, 61–2
  counselling, 45
  democracy in, 71
  democratic and dialogic intervention in, 245–6
workplace disputes, 61
  and mediation, 73–4
The Workplace Employment Relations Study: First Findings 2011, 37–8
workplace mediation, 2, 3, 7, 9, 11, 25, 29, 32, 37–9, 41, 45, 47, 51, 54, 55, 60, 66–8, 70–1, 80, 85, 90, 95, 97, 100, 102, 112, 130, 147, 149, 157, 165, 168, 186, 199, 203, 205, 209, 215, 233, 236, 244
  adoption of, 37–9
  emancipation in, 72–4
  facilitative, 157
  government policies, 39–44
  HRM policies, 46–9
  individualisation of employee, 44–5
  organisation, 90
  process, 17–19
  transformative, 215
workplace mediator, 2, 7, 32, 73, 79n4, 98, 99, 148, 151, 175, 176, 183, 186
  facilitative, 93
  professional, 93, 175, 213

Z
Zizek, S., 9–10, 54, 64n1, 70, 80, 231, 247